Advance Praise for *Automatic Influence*

"*Automatic Influence* is the leader's new killer app."

— TODD OSTRANDER, CEO, TECTONIC AUDIO LABS

"*Automatic Influence* reveals the intrinsic motivation in all of us, waiting to be unleashed for the greater good. It offers practical tools to *serve* a team, showing how to use influence for the good of others on the basis of relationship instead of surface tactics. You and your team need this book."

— JEFF ROGERS, CHAIRMAN & CEO, ONEACCORD

"Erik Van Alstine is ahead of his time. The essence of this book is success and how to obtain it, and his approach is brilliant. This is a must-read for the nations of the world."

— DR. CLYDE RIVERS, HONORARY AMBASSADOR AT LARGE FOR THE REPUBLIC OF BURUNDI, REPRESENTATIVE TO THE UN – NEW YORK, FOR THE INTERFAITH PEACE-BUILDING INITIATIVE

"Throughout my life, I've had to face my fears to reach the next level. In *Automatic Influence*, Erik offers a plan to eliminate every useless fear, showing readers where fear comes from and how to beat it. These principles are rock solid and will definitely help you win in life."

— TIM BROWN, HEISMAN TROPHY WINNER, PRO FOOTBALL HALL OF FAME INDUCTEE AND AUTHOR, *THE MAKING OF A MAN*

"In *Automatic Influence*, Erik Van Alstine explores the importance of perception and the power it has to unlock our potential, to change ourselves, and influence others. True to the principles expressed here, Erik has done a great service in opening up the possibilities for positive change, spiritual growth, and social development."

— ROBERT A. SIRICO, PRESIDENT, ACTON INSTITUTE

"My friend Erik Van Alstine has unearthed something special: the root of power and love. *Automatic Influence* offers a revolutionary way to build bridges between people and nations, something I'm extremely passionate about. Thank you, Erik, for this insightful book."

— JAMES ROBISON, PRESIDENT, LIFE OUTREACH INTERNATIONAL, PUBLISHER OF THE GLOBAL NEWS PROGRAM, THE STREAM, AND AUTHOR, *INDIVISIBLE*

"Erik Van Alstine's *Automatic Influence* is both thought-provoking and brilliant. As a professional corporate trainer, I've had the opportunity to work with some of the industry's most respected experts on leadership, and Erik's book has more inspired and *practical* advice on being an effective yet compassionate leader than I've read anywhere else."

— KEVIN HOPKINS, FORMER WHITE HOUSE SENIOR POLICY ANALYST AND AUTHOR, *OPPORTUNITY 2000: TRAINING WORKERS AND LEADERS FOR A NEW CENTURY*

AUTOMATIC INFLUENCE

New Power for Change in Work and Life

Erik Van Alstine

STONE
LOUNGE

New York

Automatic Influence
Copyright © 2016 Erik Van Alstine

Published by Stone Lounge Press, New York

ISBN 978-1-945556-00-5

Book Design: Carla Green
Editing: Bruce Nygren

Special discounts are available on quantity purchases by corporations, associations, and others. For details, and to order additional copies of this book, please visit www.ErikVanAlstine.com or www.StoneLoungePress.com.

Publisher's Cataloging-in-Publication data

Van Alstine, Erik, 1968- author.
    Automatic influence : new power for change in work and life / Erik Van Alstine.
    pages cm
    Includes bibliographical references and index.
    ISBN 978-1-945556-00-5 (hardcover)

    1. Influence (Psychology) 2. Motivation (Psychology)
3. Leadership–Psychological aspects.
4. Self-realization. 5. Change (Psychology)   I. Title.

BF774.V36 2016   158
                    QBI16-1216

First Edition
Printed in the United States of America
2 4 6 8 10 9 7 5 3 1

For Sandra

*"For every thousand hacking at
the branches of evil,
there is one striking the root."*
— Henry David Thoreau

Contents

PART 4 **THE ROOTS OF SUCCESS**

PART 5 **FREE AND FULL**

Acknowledgments

It takes a village to publish a book, and I want to thank all my fellow villagers for helping make *Automatic Influence* a reality.

First and foremost, my wife Sandra. Without you and your help, I'd be a fraction of myself, and this book wouldn't exist.

To my large and growing family, which now includes nine children: James, Savannah, Madison, Derek, Grant, Megan, Ross, Jessica, and Elizabeth. You bring so much life and happiness to me. It's a privilege to be part of your lives.

To my editor, Bruce Nygren. This book was an impassable thicket before you came along. Thank you for the machete work and, of course, the careful clipping that followed. You turned a jungle into a manicured garden. I appreciate you, and every reader should too.

To Cory Emberson, whose keen editorial eye found a thousand errors I could never see. All remaining errors are, of course, mine alone.

To all my friends who took on the early reading of this book and provided a wealth of insights that enabled it to evolve—I thank Jeff Audas, Addison Bevere (extensive help), Eric Boles, Gerald Boyd, Jim Brown, Reggie Brown, Lynn Carlson, Samuel Deuth, Duncan Dodds, Chris Dunayski, Josh Dunn, Tyler Erickson (extensive help), Rick Klaasen (who lugged the early bloated manuscript all through China), Steve Murray, Skyler and Paula Norris, Todd Ostrander, Steve Pappajohn, Jeff Rogers, Robert Rosenthal, Larry Ward, and Jaylynn Widmark.

Finally, to you, the reader, for investing your time in this garden of ideas. I hope you pick the flowers and pass them along.

INTRODUCTION

Remember the Water

"There are these two young fish swimming along, and they happen to meet an older fish swimming the other way, who nods at them and says, 'Morning boys, how's the water?' And the two young fish swim on for a bit, and then eventually one of them looks over at the other and goes, 'What the hell is water?'" [1]

— DAVID FOSTER WALLACE, AMERICAN AUTHOR

There's a profound source of power inside us. I imagine it like a red button in the basement of our minds. This power energizes every emotion, drives every decision, and activates every action.

When we try to change our attitudes or our behaviors without triggering this power, change is hard. We grit our teeth, gut it out, lose steam and, usually, give up. But when we trigger the power, change is easier.

Profoundly easier.

Problem is, this power source is invisible. Even though the red button affects everything we want, everything we feel, and everything we do, we're oblivious to it. We're like the young fish, surrounded by water, asking, "What the hell is water?"

This book is a look at the liquid in which we live, the invisible and pervasive power that *automatically influences* every aspect of our lives. Once we understand the source of this power,

- We discover the secret of happiness and why the pursuit of happiness often misleads us.
- We find ways to fight depression, recover our love for life, and boost our energy.
- We learn how to get along with everyone and build psychological immunity to relationship problems.
- We discover the secret of influence and why one boss inspires loyalty while another boss, doing the exact same things, incites resistance.
- We also discover the root of evil—why some prostitutes are happy in their lives, why Hitler murdered six million Jews, and why every "senseless crime" is more sensible than we think.

TOTAL FREEDOM, COMPLETE FULFILLMENT

What is this power? How does it work? How do we direct it to obtain our highest goals and best life? I'll get to that in short order but, first, think of what this power might mean to you. What would your life look like if you were totally free? Free from fear? Free from unnecessary limitation? If all the things holding you back were gone, who might you be? What might you do?

There's no question, things would be different, because most people aren't free. They struggle with useless fears, imagined inabilities, and blindness to the danger in the status quo.

And what would your life look like if you were completely fulfilled? If you were full of wisdom, purpose, optimism, and love?

No question, things would be different, because people aren't fulfilled. They struggle with boredom, futility, and despair. They're a fraction of their best selves.

Then there's a third challenge—the reality that the world is full of people who are not free or full. We must live and work with them—and they with us. Life isn't a Tibetan monastery with a gurgling stream, Zen garden, and peace-lovers in saffron robes. Every day we deal with people brimming with hurts, hang-ups, ignorance, and ill will.

But what if you could live immune to these negative influences? What if you could solve people problems with ease?

It would change everything.

EXPERIENCING THE POWER

You've heard the saying, "Ignorance is bliss." Parents might be happier not knowing all the stupid stuff their teenagers do. Leaders do better ignoring hate mail and water cooler gossip. Everyone is better skipping the nightly news. But ignorance of our power isn't bliss at all, because this power works against us by default. If we're not aware of what it is and how to control it, we're in trouble.

But when we're aware of it, we can make sense of things and make changes. We can knock the lid off our perceived limitations and reach bigger and better goals.

Over the past decades, I've had the privilege to advise and collaborate with some of the world's great influencers, from *New York Times* bestselling authors to CEOs of some of the world's greatest companies to professors at Ivy League schools. No matter how influential we are, we all struggle. These successful people are much like any of us: We're all under-living our lives. We all need more wisdom.

This is where *Automatic Influence* can help, offering deep insights into the workings of human nature. When we understand how change happens and why, we can take control of the process. For both individuals and organizations, *Automatic Influence* offers revolutionary ways to lead change that works, no matter the goal.

It begins by understanding the power button and how it works.

Then we learn to how to put the power to work. We discover how to take the controls instead of living by default. We learn a better and easier way to change.

Finally, we direct the power toward total freedom, complete fulfillment, and radically better ways to work with people.

SIMPLE VERSUS EASY

The mission is simple. But that doesn't mean it's easy. Imagine we tell the head of NASA, "Listen, just fly to the moon, plant a flag, and come back. Don't make it harder than it is."

First off, NASA lady would give us *that* look. Then she'd say, "Don't be an idiot. There's more to it." She'd talk about perseverance and teamwork and problem-solving and a thousand other things that make the simple idea of getting to the moon difficult. She'd tell us how simple it is to say, "be happier," or "make more money," or "increase sales by ten percent," but how hard it is to actually be happier, make the money, and increase the sales.

Simple isn't easy.

Sometimes, even simple things aren't as simple as they seem. They get complex as we put them to work.

Back in the 1980s, I earned an engineering degree at the University of Washington, and I'll never forget a course called *Statics*. The university had hired a researcher and asked him to teach on the side. So we had a great researcher and a lousy teacher. Or a great teacher, depending on how you look at it. He had only two things to say: *The sum of forces is zero and the sum of moments is zero* (in engineering, "moment" means rotational force).

"That's it," he told the class. "That's all I can tell you."

"Well, can you elaborate for us?" asked a student.

"Not really. It's just what I said. The sum of forces is zero and the sum of moments is zero. That's all you need to know to build bridges and buildings and roads."

Well.

In one sense, his lecture was brilliant. It's been over a quarter of a century since that class, and while I can't remember any other lectures in any other classes, I remember his.

Still, it fell short. We needed to see *how* bridges and buildings and roads get built from this key principle. If he had *elaborated* and *applied* the principle as he went, my memory of him would have been better.

This book is an attempt at an effective combination. It offers a simple idea, ample illustration, and practical application.

HANDLE WITH CARE

Adolf Hitler was a master of influence…for the worst reasons. Mahatma Gandhi was a master of influence…for better reasons. Both used the same tools of influence. So before we pop the clutch and screech down the road, let's remember the first road rule: Power is for *serving* people, not *using* people. Exerting influence without a heart of service is manipulation. "The purpose of human life is to serve," wrote the German philosopher and physician, Albert Schweitzer.

We've also got to start by changing ourselves before we set our sights on changing others. Gandhi said, "You must be the change you wish to see in the world." The most important person we influence is the person in the mirror. The place we need power most is right there in the reflection.

Automatic Influence works. It isn't hype or speculation. It's solid science from cutting-edge studies in cognitive therapy, behavioral economics, and beyond.[2] It works for top coaches and peak performers. It also helps normal people like you and me create more happiness in everyday life. These ideas aren't just theory. I've used them to help some of the most effective leaders in the world.

And these ideas help *me* every day.

REMEMBER THE WATER

"The most obvious and important realities," said David Foster Wallace, explaining his fish story, "are often the ones that are hardest to see and talk about." The last thing the fish sees is water, and the last thing we see is this power that automatically runs our lives.

That can make it tough to explain.

This book offers lessons in the obvious. *But only after the fact.* If your journey becomes anything like mine, the lights will go on and you'll be changed. Then you'll think, *Of course. That's obvious.* By the end, you might wonder if you learned anything at all because the truth is, you already know this stuff. You swim in it every day. It's hyper-practical and super-prevalent.

It's also easy to forget. Back in 2004, I moved to a home near the train tracks on Puget Sound. Trains went by twenty times a day, and I loved the sights and sounds. Over time, however, the sounds faded, and I'd go for days without noticing the trains. I'd lost sight of the obvious.

As with trains, so with the idea of this book. "The real value of a real education," said Wallace at the close of his commencement speech, "has almost nothing to do with knowledge and everything to do with simple awareness, awareness of what is so real and essential, so hidden in plain sight all around us, all the time, that we have to keep reminding ourselves over and over: 'This is water. This is water.'"

Once we've discovered the power, the challenge is to keep it in view.

PART 1
NEW POWER

PART 2
NEW POWER

CHAPTER 1

The Power Button

"Men are not moved by things, but the views which they take of things."

— Epictetus, Greek philosopher

I was in trouble. But I didn't have a clue.

As I walked alone on the third fairway of the Mauna Lani golf course in Hawaii, I thought I was just watching a tournament. What I didn't know is that, for the past forty-five minutes, men were watching *me*. They were skittish and angry, conspiring to force me off the course and put me in jail.

And they would have been right to do it.

Like I said, I was in trouble. All because of the main idea of this book.

A WISER APPROACH

Before I share why I was in trouble, let's get some backstory and understand a few important ideas.

First is wisdom, of which I'm a raving fan. If wisdom were a football team, I'd be the shirtless guy in body paint. I want wisdom for myself, my kids, my friends, and my coworkers. I want you to have it too. Why?

So we all can think better, work better, and live better. Wisdom is power to change the world.

Unfortunately, wisdom is scarce. When I see how we think, work, and live, I see a lot of unnecessary struggle. There are better ways to solve problems and get things done.

Recently I heard about a problem with students at a local junior high school. The girls would go into the bathroom, put on lipstick, then press their lips to the mirrors. Every night the maintenance team spent extra time scrubbing off the kiss marks.

The maintenance workers put up signs, but the girls kept kissing the mirrors.

The principal asked the girls to stop. But the girls ignored her.

She demanded.

The girls ignored her.

She pleaded.

The girls ignored her. No matter what the principal tried, she couldn't stop them.

Finally, she had an idea. She called a few girls into the bathroom and brought in a custodian. "These lipstick marks are causing trouble for us every night," the principal said. "Look how hard it is to clean the mirrors." She motioned to the custodian, who took out a squeegee, dipped it in a toilet, and wiped the mirror.

No more lipstick marks. Ever.

Think about how much the staff struggled before the demonstration. They tried and tried but nothing worked. Then think how little they struggled after. The principal never said a word from that day forward, yet the girls were perfectly compliant.

Wisdom made all the difference.

On a more serious note, consider a problem in nineteenth-century London solved by a physician named John Snow. Dr. Snow lived near Broad Street in London, 1854, where a child died after having the symptoms of blue skin, vomiting, and diarrhea. Within days, dozens of other people living nearby showed the same symptoms.

Then in just one day, a hundred turned blue, and more than a hundred and forty the day after.

The symptoms resembled the "Blue Death," a mystery disease in Russia that had killed over a million people a few years before. No one knew what caused it, how it spread, or how to cure it. Some family members got it. Others didn't. It skipped one household and infected the next.

Snow visited hundreds of the sick and questioned them one by one: *What did you do in the last three days? Where did you go? Who were you with?* He recorded their behaviors, looking for a common denominator.

Suddenly, it clicked. All patients had one thing in common—the Broad Street public water pump. Everyone who was sick drank from it.

Against city opposition, Snow convinced officials to shut the well down and remove the pump handle. In just days, the death toll dropped to zero. Snow saved London and, ultimately, millions around the world, with a single flash of insight: *The source of cholera was sewage-contaminated water.*[3]

FINDING THE ROOT

Henry David Thoreau described wisdom this way: "For every thousand hacking at the branches of evil, there is one striking at the root."[4]

Hacking at branches is hard and futile work, because there are many branches and they all grow back. Striking the root is easier and more effective. One solid whack takes out all the branches for good.

If branch-hacking is harder and doesn't work, while root-striking is easier and works better, why is branch-hacking so common and root-striking so rare? Why did Thoreau depict a thousand people hacking the branches for every one striking the root? Why don't we all choose the easier and better way?

Because roots are invisible.

We can't strike roots we don't see, which means our biggest problem isn't the problem itself. Our biggest problem is *finding the root of our problem.*

Think about Snow in London: The cure was as simple as it gets. All he did was remove a pump handle. But finding the handle—that wasn't so simple. Or think about the principal at the junior high school. The janitor's demonstration took minutes and permanently solved the problem. But coming up with the idea to dip the squeegee in the toilet? That's the stuff of wisdom.

Now think about the focus of this book: *influence.* We struggle to influence ourselves and others. There's got to be an easier way to change, but what is it?

The answer is at the root of influence itself. As I wrote in the introduction, there's a power button in the basement of our minds. When we push it, influence is virtually automatic and change is easier. But when we fail to find and push the button, influence is nearly impossible.

Let me tell a story to explain.

FIVE WORKERS, FIVE VIEWS

Imagine an office setting—a typical workday at the StickRite Label Company. The manager comes to Danny's desk and says, "I've got great news, Danny. You got the promotion."

All the other employees working with Danny overhear the conversation and react. Henry is happy, Susan is sad, Anna is angry, Frank is afraid, and Nick feels nothing at all.[5]

How can five people in the same situation, hearing the exact same information, have five completely different reactions?

Whenever I tell this story to a group, I ask them to discuss it with people around them. So let's imagine we're at a seminar talking about this: "We know the workers have the same experience watching Danny and his boss," I say, starting the conversation. "We also know they don't feel the same. Only one person feels positive. Three others feel negative, and one guy is indifferent. What's going on here?"

"Maybe Henry is happy because Danny is his best friend," says someone in our group. Then another person says, "Susan might be sad because she didn't get the promotion herself." Most of my group discussions describe examples like these, because it takes a while to get to the common cause in all these responses.

The common cause?

It's the way the workers "see."

THE WAY WE SEE

The five workers feel different, because they "see" the situation in five different ways. When I say *see*, I'm not just talking about physical sight, but the way we *characterize and evaluate something as good or bad*. It's what we mean when we say, "I call it the way I see it."

- Henry is happy because he sees something good: an opportunity to get Danny's old job.

- Susan is sad because she sees something bad: Her close friend Danny leaving her.
- Anna is angry because she sees something bad as well: an unfair boss. She was up for the promotion and is more qualified than Danny.
- Frank is afraid because he sees something bad: his job in jeopardy. Danny is the only one who goes to bat for him.
- Nick feels nothing because he sees neither good nor bad. He's new and all the coworkers are strangers.

Everyone sees something different, which means the situation itself isn't what influences them. The real influencer is *the way they see* the situation.

"Men are not moved by things," wrote the Greek philosopher Epictetus, "but the views which they take of things." The *thing* isn't the key. The *view* is the key.

Whenever we see something, either with our physical senses or in our imagination, we instantly *characterize* it. We tell ourselves what is happening. While Danny is getting a promotion, Henry is getting a chance at Danny's job, Sally is losing a friend, Anna is getting betrayed, and Frank is losing a job. Four different things happen to four different people because of the way each of the four *characterize* the situation.

Then we *evaluate*. We *put a value* on the good or bad in the situation. *Is what is happening going to hurt me, help me, or neither? Do I like what I see, or do I dislike it, or am I neutral?*

We do these two things—characterize and evaluate—in a blink. The graphic below illustrates this idea.

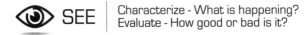

SEE | Characterize - What is happening?
Evaluate - How good or bad is it?

*We **See** when we characterize and evaluate. To "characterize" is to ask, **What is happening?** To "evaluate" is to ask, **How good or bad is it?***

SEE AUTOMATICALLY INFLUENCES *FEEL*

The different ways the workers see the situation *automatically influences* the way they feel. Henry sees something good, so he automatically feels good. Susan, Anna, and Frank see something bad, so they automatically feel bad. The graphic below shows the automatic influence between *See* and *Feel*.

The way we see automatically influences the way we feel.

When I use the word "feel," I don't mean "to touch," like what I'd mean by saying "this feels like velvet." I'm referring to the varying strengths of positive and negative emotion. It's what I mean when I say, "It feels good to get a new job," or, "I don't feel good about this new plan."

I'll use a heart icon and this standard definition to describe the term, *feel*.

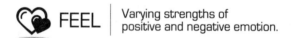

The way we feel refers to the varying strengths of positive and negative emotion.

Most of us believe our feelings are the deepest part of us. But this story of Danny's promotion shows how appraisals run deeper than feelings. The way we see a situation comes before our feelings and creates our feelings. It may only be a millisecond before, but the *seeing* precedes the *feeling* and in fact *causes* the feeling.

Imagine a truck pulling a trailer. The seeing is the truck; the feeling is the trailer. Feelings follow seeing just like trailers follow trucks. We see things a certain way and pull along a trailer filled with emotions.[6]

Most of us assume it's the other way around, because we know how emotions influence our motivations and behaviors. We'll get to that later, because emotions have a *follow-on influence*. But at this point we need to be clear that the *initial factor* is the way we characterize and evaluate.

Feelings don't just come out of thin air. If we're feeling stressed or depressed or angry, these feelings are the result of the way we see our circumstances, just like Henry, Sally, Anna, Frank, and Nick saw different things in the same situation. Whenever we see a situation, we see more than raw facts. We see meanings and implications as well. Our emotions are a response to everything we see—the situation, along with the meanings and implications we draw from the situation.

Think of the junior high school girls in the bathroom, watching the custodian's demonstration. The instant they saw toilet water on the mirrors, they felt disgust. The principal gave them a new view of the condition of the mirrors, and this automatically influenced the way they felt.

Here's another way to say it: *feelings follow focus*.[7] Our "focus" is just another way of describing the way we "see" things. Focus is first, feelings are second.

REASON AND EMOTION

Most people believe emotion and reason are at odds with each other. Emotion is the enemy of reason, and reason is the enemy of emotion. *Some people are reasonable*, they believe, *while others are emotional*.

But experts say there's a deep rationality to our emotions. The deeper we look into human nature, the more we see reason and emotion working hand in hand. We use our reasoning to appraise what is happening, and how good or bad it is. This, in turn, automatically triggers emotions.

"There is no emotion without thought or reason," writes one of the world's foremost authorities on emotion, Richard Lazarus. "Our emotions are really products of the way we construe what is happening in our lives…without appraisal, there is no emotion."[8]

Of course, it is possible for our emotions to get the best of us. But we must always remember that our appraisal, driven by reasoning, triggers emotion. Reason and emotion go hand in hand, because the way we *See* automatically influences the way we *Feel*.

FEEL AUTOMATICALLY INFLUENCES *ACT*

Just like the way we *See* automatically influences the way we *Feel*, the way we *Feel* automatically influences the way we *Act*.

The way we feel automatically influences the way we act.

Emotions create motivations, which lead to decisions and behaviors. The girls in the bathroom didn't just feel disgust. They acted on their feelings. Or think of the five people around Danny. They didn't just *see* something. They didn't just *feel* something. They *did* something too.

- Happy Henry went to HR for a job application.
- Sad Susan invited Danny to lunch for consolation.
- Angry Anna went to HR to file a complaint.
- Fearful Frank started putting in applications for a new job.
- Nothing Nick had no motivation to act.

Our feelings automatically influence our behaviors.

Since we're clarifying terms, let's get clear on what I mean by the term *Act*. It's not just behaviors. It's words, too…and decisions. And expressions of emotion. It's one thing to feel angry. It's another thing to fly off the handle and throw chairs.

 Words, decisions, behaviors, and expressed emotions.

The way we act refers to words, decisions, behaviors, and expressed emotions.

Putting it all together, we find that the way we *See* automatically influences the way we *Feel*, which automatically influences the way we *Act*. There's an automatic progression from perception to emotion to behavior.

THE SEE-FEEL-ACT PROGRESSION

Throughout the book, I'll describe this as the *See-Feel-Act progression.*

The See-Feel-Act progression. The way we see automatically influences the way we feel, which automatically influences the way we act.

It all starts with the way we see. Perception is the power button that triggers emotion and behavior.[9]

SEEING THAT WE SEE

Not only do we see, but we also can *see that we see.* We can step back and look *at* the lens that we normally only look *through.* We can ask, *Am I seeing this right? Are there better ways to see this?*

Here's how I describe these categories of perception and meta-perception.

- See. We "see" when we instantly and unconsciously characterize and evaluate. We decide what is happening, and how good or bad it is.
- See that we See. This is when we step back and look at our view. We're aware that we're perceiving something in a certain way. We're no longer unconsciously immersed in the flow of perception. We're above the flow, observing the flow.

Animals don't have the ability to see that they see. They can't self-reflect. They're always immersed in their perceptions. But human beings have a special endowment to get above the flow, and this is the essence of our power. Because of our ability to question the way we see, we can choose a different way of seeing things. We can change our point of view.

Someone might say, "But I can't choose the way I see things. I just see the way I see." If we were chimpanzees, I'd agree. But we are human beings with the advantage of self-awareness and choice. Unlike geese who must fly south for the winter, we can choose to stay north instead.

We can help others see differently as well. Think of how the teacher changed the way the girls saw the bathroom mirror. The teacher helped them change their view, and it automatically influenced the way they felt and the things they did.

Think again of Thoreau's observation: "For every thousand hacking at the branches of evil, there is one striking at the root." Perception is the root. Emotion and behavior are the branches and leaves.

When we try to change emotion and behavior without first changing our perception, we hack at the branches. Change is hard. But when we change the way we see, we strike at the root, automatically influencing emotion and behavior.

Change is not so hard anymore.

INVISIBLE ROOTS

We can observe the way people feel, in facial expressions, body language, tone, and so on. We also can observe what people do.

But we can't observe the way people see.

When Danny's coworkers reacted to his promotion, we could see their facial expressions and body language. We could hear their comments. But we could not see how they were actually *seeing*. That's under the surface. Unless each person was deeply self-aware and told us how they were seeing, all we are doing is guessing.

Social life involves a lot of guessing about how people see things, because we only see above the surface. We can't observe the way people characterize things. We can only observe the *effects* of their characterizations.

The same is true for ourselves. Many times, we feel angry or afraid but aren't sure where the feelings came from. We are guessing about our own characterizations too, because we see things quickly and unconsciously. We don't know what triggered the emotion—it's just there.

This is why I represent the way we see as a root-level idea. It's not only the prime source of our emotions and our behaviors, but it is invisible.

BACK TO MAUNA LANI

Now that we understand the See-Feel-Act progression, and the power button of perception, let's go back to my experience at Mauna Lani.

As I wrote earlier, there I was, walking along the third hole, in a heap of trouble—but I didn't know it.

What was going on?

It was December 2014, the third day of a golf tournament called the Hawaii State Open. I wasn't just a spectator but also a competitor in the three-day tournament.

I had played well on the first day but poorly the second day, so I missed the cut and wasn't eligible to play the third day. Derek Barron, my son-in-law, had played well, though, and made the cut. So I had decided to watch him play his final round.

I walked to the first hole to watch Derek hit his opening shot. Wes Wailehua, the tournament director, was there announcing the players before seeing them off. I walked by Wes and nodded hello, but he looked angry and suspicious.

"What are your intentions?" Wes asked me.

That's strange, I thought. *Why is he asking me that?*

"I'm here to watch Derek and track his shots," I said.

My explanation didn't seem to calm Wes's suspicions, but I couldn't understand what was going on, so I went on my way.

I wondered why he was upset. I was dressed in golf clothes, so I looked like a player. *Was that the problem? Impersonating a player? No, there were others in the crowd dressed that way too.* Also, I had a backpack full of food and water for the five-hour walk. *Was he upset I brought this pack with me? No, others had packs too.* I figured Wes must be dealing with other trouble that was spilling over on me, so I shrugged it off.

About forty-five minutes into the round, Derek and his group had just finished the third hole and walked down the path to the next hole. I was walking about fifty yards behind, looking down to write Derek's score. When I looked up, there was Wes again, sitting in a cart blocking the path. He wasn't facing toward the next hole, like normal. He was facing toward me. With that same glare.

I went to walk around his cart and he stopped me. "Mr. Lawrence, what are your intentions?" he asked. "This is a serious matter, and we can't have you out here."[10]

I thought, *Mr. Lawrence? What in the world?*

Then it clicked. I knew why Wes was upset. I almost laughed out loud, but held it together as I replayed the events of the previous night in my mind.

The night before, Derek had talked on the phone with Wes, because one of the competitors in Derek's group, a guy named Lawrence, had written down the wrong score on one hole. Since the scorecard wasn't corrected, Lawrence had been disqualified from the tournament. Derek and I stayed in the same hotel room, so I overheard his side of the conversation and talked about it after.

At the first hole that morning, Wes assumed I was *Mr. Lawrence, stalking Derek for revenge.* He was concerned for Derek's safety and had asked me, "What are your intentions?" The way Wes saw it, I was following Derek, scorecard in hand, to intimidate him for disqualifying me the day before. Or maybe I was going to pull a gun out of my backpack.

For forty-five minutes, the security team saw me as an angry competitor, possibly carrying weapons, walking beside the guy who got him disqualified.

Standing there with Wes glaring at me, I finally understood what was going on. The suspicious stare, the hostile treatment, it all made sense.

"I'm not Mr. Lawrence," I told him with a smile. "I'm Derek's father-in-law, Erik Van Alstine."

"Oh my God," Wes said, as he slumped down in his seat and put his hand on his forehead. "I am so sorry." Everything changed. His facial expressions. His mannerisms. The suspicious glare instantly morphed into smiling relief. "This whole time we thought you were going to do something terrible," he said. "We've all been on edge. I can't believe I treated you like that. Is there anything I can do?"

"Yes," I said as we laughed together. "You can drive me up to the next hole to watch my son-in-law."

"I'll do better than that," he said. "I'll drive you anywhere you want!"

I jumped in and off we went. "We almost had you arrested," he confided as we drove along. "If you didn't cooperate with us, we were planning to have the police escort you off the course."

"Man, that would have been fantastic," I laughed. "Getting arrested under false pretense…that's on my bucket list!"

What was powering Wes before that confrontation on the third hole? His *perception.* The way he saw me. That's the power button of human nature.

Which is why everything shifted when the perception shifted. When Wes had seen me as Mr. Lawrence, he automatically felt alarmed and suspicious and acted by alerting security. But when Wes saw me as Mr. Van Alstine, his feelings and behaviors changed automatically. Here's a graphic showing the progression:

SEE	FEEL	ACT
Mr. Lawrence.	Suspicion and alarm.	Alert security team.
Mr. VanAlstine.	Relief.	Call off security.

Everything shifts with perception. When we change the way we see, our feelings and our actions follow naturally.

GETTING SMART ABOUT CHANGE

When we try to change attitudes and behaviors without first changing the way we see, change is hard.

Imagine what might have happened if I stood defiant on the first tee and said to Wes, "Hey, don't talk to me that way! I can do whatever I want." If I had tried to change Wes's attitude without changing the way he saw me, I might have gotten that ride in the police car. That day the circumstances didn't change. The situation didn't change. What changed was *the way Wes saw the circumstances.*

The secret of automatic influence is to *start with perception.* Perception is the power button. One click changes emotions, behaviors and, ultimately, the outcome of our lives.

CHAPTER 2

The Challenge of Change

"To improve is to change; to be perfect is to change often."
— WINSTON CHURCHILL, BRITISH STATESMAN

"There's no way we'll make it," Mark said to me. "We can't survive this."

It was early 1999. For over seven years, I had built a company from a desk beside the bed in my Seattle apartment into a firm with multimillions in sales and almost eighty employees.

Mark, my business partner, confirmed what we both knew: "We lost our largest client three months ago and now they're suing us," he said. "And now our second-largest client is moving their business. We've tried everything. What else can we do?"

I sat there in my arched-window office overlooking Broad Street, trying to grasp the implications. For months, we'd been working eighteen-hour days to get through the crisis. The well-being of all the employees and a hundred investors hung in the balance. My family would be impacted, too. My wife Sandra was pregnant with our sixth child.

There had to be a way to fix things.

But the problem was insurmountable. Mark slumped in his chair across from my desk. I was nauseated and numb. It felt like the final drop of hope had finally drained out of me, and all that was left was the gut-kick of grief. *How could this happen? Why is everything falling to pieces?*

Up to this point, I had been a rising star in business. Local news reported my success. Employees celebrated my leadership. I had seemed unstoppable.

But this looming failure changed everything. Sitting with Mark, I realized there was nothing I could do. It was over.

I felt helpless, worthless, and terrified.

I put my head in my hands and cried.

AS THE WORLD TURNS

Anyone who thinks life is easy hasn't been around too long. We all struggle to succeed in a challenging world. No one starts a business expecting failure. We don't marry planning on a divorce. We don't expect life to push us over the edge.

It's like riding a city bus when an eight-hundred-pound gorilla boards. *Will we live through the ride?*

This is the challenge of change itself. The world turns, overturning our lives. Business failure, divorce, layoffs, and setbacks—they're all the stuff of life, the unfortunate pages in every story of every person who's ever lived. The moment we feel like we've regained our balance, the world wobbles, and we're off balance again. Life pushes us into fearful and difficult situations, and there's no getting around them.

It's not just about disaster stories but about small things too, the challenges lurking in every cranny of our lives. There's that issue with our child we don't want to confront. Or someone at work dropped the ball. Or we want to ask someone out or ask for a raise or ask for the sale, but we fear rejection.

As long as we have relationships, we're bound to have relationship challenges. As long as we have jobs, we're bound to have job challenges. As long as we have goals and dreams, we're going to have challenges reaching them.

PADDLING OR DRIFTING?

People often think, *I don't have to accept change.* But all we need is a look in the mirror to see that things are changing whether we like it or not. Change can be like a parent helping a toddler into the car for preschool.

He's either going to go nicely or go kicking and screaming. But no question about it, he's going.

I like to picture change as a river, with us in canoes. If we stop paddling, we'll drift. There's no status quo on this river, no staying in place. We can't be passive. We must be alert and aggressive. Paddling is progress. Everything else is drift.

"We've long believed," wrote General Electric CEO Jack Welch, "that when the rate of change inside an institution becomes slower than the rate of change outside, the end is in sight. The only question is when."[11] Jack was referring to organizations, but the same goes for people. If our paddle-pace isn't stronger than the river-pace, we're drifting.

Will we rise to the challenges of change? Will we paddle the river? Or will we drift into despair and defeat?

This is why we need power. We can't sit back and expect progress. Or success. Or happiness.

THINGS WE CAN CHANGE, THINGS WE CAN'T

When we think about life, we should separate changeable from unchangeable things. The Serenity Prayer reads,

> God, grant me the serenity to accept the things I cannot change, the courage to change the things I can, and the wisdom to know the difference.[12]

The first part of the prayer is about *things we cannot change*. We can't change the schedule of the sun or the laws of nature. We can't change the place we were born or our biological parents. We can't change the pace of modernization and the pressure of global competition. We should accept these things.

The second part of the prayer is about *things we can change*. We can change the way we see things, which automatically changes our attitudes and behaviors. We can change our skills with effort over time. We can even change our intelligence (see the *Penny Thick* chapter). The Serenity Prayer asks for the courage to make these changes.

Then there's the third part of the prayer—*the wisdom to know the difference*. Sometimes we think we can change things, but we really can't:

- We think traffic might move faster if we honk and yell.
- We think we can get peace of mind by getting even.
- We think we can shortcut our skill development and still succeed.

These are exercises in futility, like straining to push a cement wall.

Then sometimes we make the opposite error—thinking we can't change things when actually we can.

- We think we're trapped in anxiety and depression, but we're not.
- We think a bad circumstance means unhappiness, but it doesn't.
- We think our habits are set in stone, but they're pliable.

While we separate changeable from unchangeable, we should also separate *harmful change* from *helpful change*. We thought the promotion would help us, but it makes work worse. Or we thought we'd be happier with the divorce, but our children are distant and we're lonely. Or we thought the new workflow would help, but it was a disaster. Some changes help us, some changes harm us, and some changes waste our time. It takes wisdom to know the difference.

CHOOSING HOW WE SEE

"Do not let what you cannot do," said basketball coach John Wooden, "interfere with what you can do." Right here, right now, you and I can eliminate every shred of worry about unchangeable things. For every situation we cannot change in the world around us, there are many great things we *can* change. We can learn to focus on changeable things.

We can also recognize that *we choose our response to things by choosing how we see things.*

In October 1986, President Ronald Reagan took the podium at a White House piano recital to thank the pianist, Vladimir Horowitz, for his outstanding performance. As Reagan began to speak, his wife Nancy edged the leg of her chair off the platform and fell into a row of potted yellow chrysanthemums. Getting to her feet, she said, "I'm all right. I just wanted to liven things up."

President Reagan then said, "Honey, I told you to do that only if I didn't get any applause."[13]

An incident that might have humiliated one presidential couple validated the humor and strength of another…because of the way they chose to see it.

THE ONE THING WE CONTROL

Things that happen to us are often beyond our control. But the way we see them is *always in our control.*

To "control" something is to "exercise restraint or direction" over it, which is another level of power than simply changing something one time. We don't just pull the reins once and redirect the horse. We keep the reins in hand and maintain our guidance all through the ride. When we control the way we see, we have a lasting and more powerful effect on our emotions and behaviors than when we only change the way we see things one time.

Throughout the book, I'll describe perception change along with the more powerful idea of perception control. Both take practice.

We often think, *I see it the way I see it, and that's the way it is.* But it isn't. We can step back, see how we see, change how we see, and control the way we see.

Perception-control is self-control. We control the way we *Feel* and *Act* when we control the way we *See.*

| Controlling the way we see… | …controls the way we feel… | …which controls the things we do. |

Notice the remote control icon next to the See, Feel, and Act icons. I'll use this to show how controlling the way we see controls the way we feel, which controls the things we do.

There's a scene in the film *Bruce Almighty* when Bruce realizes he has all of God's powers for the week. It triggers a song by the German music group Snap! titled, *The Power,* as Bruce points his fingers and blows up a fire hydrant.

This is how I feel about the power of perception. There's tremendous power in controlling the way we see things. Power over depression and despair. Power to be bigger than our circumstances. Power to forgive and always do the right thing, no matter who tries to incite us.

To *be different*, we've got to *see different*.

Remember Epictetus, who said, "Men are not moved by things, but the views which they take of things." The view moves us. Not the thing. The view. We can change the way we respond by changing our view.

LIFE IS TOUGH. TOUGH IS GOOD.

Now let's consider the way we view change itself. When we look at the changing world around us, what do we see? Do we see ourselves falling behind? Do we despise change? Or do we embrace it? When we look at ourselves grappling with change, do we see ourselves paddling or drifting? What would happen if we learned to see change in powerful new ways, and learned to *love* paddling the river?

It would change everything.

It's common to believe people are optimistic because their lives are easier. *If they had my problems, they wouldn't be so cheery.*

This is a myth. Researchers in optimism and pessimism say most people experience equal proportions of good and bad circumstances. The only difference is *the way they see their circumstances.*[14]

One way to thrive is to see things happening *to* us as things happening *for* us. Take my business bust, for example. I survived it. Today, I can take a punch. Fighters are formed by punches.

I didn't just get stronger from my business crash. I got wiser. Just last month as I write this, I collected a check for double the average family's annual income on a side business deal, all because of a lesson learned in the crash about the importance of contract law. If I hadn't learned the lesson years ago, I wouldn't have cashed that check last month.

Thank God for the crash.

On top of getting tougher and wiser, my mind is clearer. Back when I expected life to be easier, I made life harder. How? By believing, *this should not be happening to me.* I doubled every trouble, because every problem became two: the actual problem plus this belief. Think about how we do this.

- The report is due in a week and we can't get people to cooperate. *This should not be happening.*
- Our teenage son is disrespectful and making trouble at home. *This should not be happening.*
- Nick and John are at each other's throats, and since we're the leader, we need to patch it up. *This should not be happening.*

In this way, we climb every hill of difficulty with a self-packed sack of rocks. We make life harder by expecting it to be easier.

In the low moment of my life when my business went bust, I struggled in this trap. Despite the fact that most businesses eventually fail, I expected to be the exception to the rule. I didn't think circumstances could blow me off course. So when I failed, I struggled with the philosophical problem piggybacking my real problem. I wasn't just asking what was wrong in my immediate situation: I was asking what was wrong with life itself.

I made things harder because I expected things to be easier.

When we see life as something that's unfair, that's harder than it should be, we're discouraged and resentful. We do everything we can to avoid the challenge of change.

But when we see how difficulty makes us stronger and wiser, we feel grateful and hopeful. We're inspired to face the challenge.

👁 SEE ➤ 💗 FEEL ➤ 📣 ACT

SEE	FEEL	ACT
Life is harder than it should be.	Discouragement and resentment.	Avoid the challenge of change.
Difficulty makes me stronger and wiser.	Gratitude and hope.	Face the challenge of change.

Two ways to see difficult circumstances, and the way these two visions automatically influence our emotions and behaviors.

I used to dream of the easy life, but today I'm happy to say that dream is in the trash where it belongs. Now I dream of a great life, not an easy life, and I look for the strength and wisdom to paddle the river full force.

Life is tough.
Tough is good.
So, life is good.
I love it that way.

Sure, easy times are good times, too. It's great when things go our way. We like vacations and we're happy when we all get along.

But it's the hard times that really help us. They prove our resolve. They show us what really matters. Believe it or not, they even create happiness. Theodore Rubin wrote, "Happiness does not come from doing easy work, but from the afterglow of satisfaction that comes after the achievement of a difficult task that demands our best."[15]

What might happen to our attitudes if we always saw hard times helping us?

It would change our approach to every trouble. We'd paddle with intensity instead of drifting with our head in our hands. We'd face trouble instead of avoiding it.

So let's say, *bring on the tough stuff.* The thing that discourages most people encourages us. Nothing can keep us down.

This book is about hope. But not some sort of everything-will-be-easy kind of hope. We're talking about battle-tested hope, hope that's been forged in the heat of fear, failure, and frustration. Hope that's made of tempered steel, because it's been fired and pounded and quenched and pounded again. We're talking about embracing the things that forge us into men and women of steel. We're talking about absorbing blow after blow, always living to fight another day, and always getting up more times than we fall.

Life is a proving ground, an arena of adventure. We're fighters in that arena who take a punch, and another, and another, then slap our chests and shout, *Is that all you got?!*

All the while, we're *smiling.*

That's what I mean by *hope.*

THE HARD WAY AND THE EASY WAY

While we embrace this new view of hardship, we should also embrace wisdom. Why? Because some hardship is avoidable, and we should do our best to avoid unnecessary hardship.

"There are three kinds of men," said American humorist Will Rogers. "The ones that learn by readin'. The few who learn by observation. The rest of them have to pee on the electric fence for themselves."[16]

We can learn the hard way or the easy way. The easy way is to learn from the experiences of others by observing, listening, and seeking wisdom. Let's call this *vicarious experience*. We watch what others do and take a lesson from it.

The hard way is *direct experience*, meaning that we learn from the things that happen directly to us.

Let's say Chris walks too close to the edge of a cliff, falls, breaks his leg, and spends three months in a cast. That's a direct experience for Chris, and the lesson is *steer clear of the edge*. This is an expensive lesson. It costs a lot of pain, a lot of money in the form of lost wages and hospital bills, and a lot of lost time.

But say we hear about Chris's situation or even see Chris fall. We get the same lesson as Chris. We get a *vicarious experience* that doesn't cost us anything but our attention. We learn the easy way.

The strange thing is that we tend to neglect easy learning and opt by default for hard learning. The easy way requires small, immediate payments of attention. But paying attention is still paying, and most of us skip the bill. We refuse to pay the small price right now, so we pay big later on.

This is painful to watch. The longer I live, the more I see how Will Rogers was right. A few learn the easy way, and everyone else learns the hard way.

A while back, someone posted this on the Internet:

A popular Internet meme, telling the hard truth.

Ouch. When we neglect wisdom, there's a *stupidity tax* to pay.

Imagine Stupid Stan sees a sign in a field: DANGER: MINEFIELD. Stupid Stan ignores the sign, walks in, steps on a mine, and loses a leg.

That's stupid.

Then three months later, Stupid Stan crutches into another field with a similar sign, steps on another mine, and loses the other leg.

That's another level of stupid.

How much lost time, money, and opportunity will it take to convince us to love wisdom?

Where can we get wisdom from the experiences of others? Good books offer them, especially biographies. Observation is good, too. We watch people make choices and reap the consequences, both good and bad. Every choice and consequence is an opportunity to learn. Wise people share their hard lessons from experience, when we ask them and listen. Consider the wisdom literature of Solomon and Aesop as well. The key is a constant watch for wisdom.

RIGHT LESSONS, WRONG LESSONS

While we're watching, let's also be careful to *learn from wise people.* Not just *older* people. *Wise* people. Wisdom doesn't always come with age, so the world is filled with old fools. Even though they have a lifetime of experience, they draw the wrong lessons.

Consider how James "Whitey" Bulger, the Boston mobster played by Johnny Depp in the film *Black Mass*, teaches a lesson to his young son Douglas. Douglas had punched a classmate in the face. Now, at the dinner table, it's time for the father-son talk.

"Hey buddy, I need you to listen very carefully to what I'm saying because there are lessons again and again throughout your whole life," said Bulger to his son. "You gotta learn from these things, right?"

He pauses to make sure Douglas is listening. "It's not what you do," he says, slowly, "It's *when* and *where* you do it."

He pauses again. "And *who* you do it to…or with."

Whitey pauses again to let it sink in. Then he delivers the most important part. "*If nobody sees it,*" he says, "*it didn't happen.*"

Douglas's mom is horrified. "Jimmy, he's six. You really think that's the best thing to be telling your kid?"

"Yeah," says Bulger.

That may be the worst advice. Ever. But notice that it's a "lesson" drawn from experience. There's a big difference between our life experiences and the "lessons" we draw from them. And while no one draws them out quite as badly as Bulger, there are all sorts of terrible draws. We need to be careful whom we listen to.

REASONS WE RESIST

There are all sorts of reasons we resist change, but let's look at three of them: *complacency, useless fear,* and *imagined inability.*

Let's start with the crafty lure of *complacency.* We don't see the need for change. We don't see the dangers of floating downstream, and we don't see the opportunities up the river. We're *blind to danger* or we're *blind to opportunity.*

When we're *blind to danger* we say, "Things are fine as they are," but things aren't fine at all.

Imagine a chain-smoker who says, "Smoking calms my nerves and helps me stay trim." She ignores the warnings and runs the risk of lung cancer. Or imagine a manager who says, "We don't need to worry about our competition; our customers are loyal." He fails to improve and runs the risk of losing customers to the competition. In both cases, there's a false feeling that things are okay.

Complacency also happens when we're *blind to opportunity.* Imagine there's a job opening near where a woman named Abbey works. Same schools, same commute, same benefits, but it pays $20,000 more.

Abbey doesn't know about the job opening, so she can't make the most of this opportunity.

Economists call this *opportunity cost,* which is the price we pay for failing to take advantage of the best opportunities available to us.

The danger of complacency is its subtlety. One month at a time, one year at a time, we miss opportunities even though it seems nothing bad is happening. By the time we finally figure out what's going on, we've missed out. Then we get even more discouraged, which means more drifting.

When I competed in the golf tournament at Mauna Lani, I remember driving through Kona for the first time. I was surprised by the number of drifters. Leathery panhandlers and dreadlocked derelicts lined the streets. It felt like an even split of tourists and down-and-outers.

It wasn't just the *number* of drifters that struck me. It was the *type* of drifters. They weren't old, infirm, or insane. They looked like people who had the ability to choose a better life but *didn't want to.* They had dropped their paddles some time ago, and this is where the current of life had brought them.

They didn't look happy. They seemed like empty shells. In the drift, they'd lost their vitality. Something had hollowed out their souls.

I see this same drift-despair in normal people, not just in tropical transients. The beach bums of Kona are just a stark picture of the same hollowing that happens when any of us get complacent.

I see the escape mindset in companies as well. Organizations that don't paddle will drift, because what was considered *exceeding expectations* a year ago is now simply *meeting expectations.* Client expectations evolve, which means meeting yesterday's expectations is drifting back.

So I help leaders look upstream, look downstream, see clearly, and spark motivation to paddle. I remind them that paddling makes us fully alive. We tackle challenges instead of trying to escape them, because any other life is a trap. The best stuff is upriver, and we're going after it.

The second reason we resist change is *useless fear.*[17] We're afraid that something bad might happen, so we avoid opportunity.

I say *useless fear* because some fear is *useful,* like the fear of heights. Years ago, I walked with my wife Sandra to see the Nakalele Blowhole on the north side of Maui. We took a path that went just inches from a hundred-foot drop, and it freaked me out. As it should.

Whenever a threat is real, it's useful to fear. We *should* fear driving ninety when the speed limit says thirty-five. We *should* fear walking near a mother grizzly with cubs. It's useful to fear the sudden sharp pain in our chest. Useful fear moves us to escape real threats.

But when there's no real threat, or the chance of threat is slim, that's *useless fear*. Useless fear is like a rubber snake boys use to scare their mothers. It looks harmful, but it isn't.

If useless fear is a rubber snake, useful fear is a rattlesnake. It looks harmful because it *is* harmful. The key is to identify rubber snakes and rattlesnakes, avoid the rattlesnakes, and not be rattled by the rubber snakes.

Here's the See-Feel-Act progression for useful and useless fear.

👁 SEE ➡ 💚 FEEL ➡ 📣 ACT

Real danger.	Useful fear.	Avoiding is healthy.
Danger that isn't real.	Useless fear.	Avoid things that should be faced.

The See-Feel-Act progression for useful and useless fear.

I remember presenting in front of a camera for the first time back in 2004. Even though I've been speaking since 1987 and had been on-camera many times, I'd never had a camera directly in my face. I was anxious because all the other recordings were back-of-the-room sort of things.

The day of the shoot, I wanted to cancel and almost did. But I went and discovered that it wasn't nearly as bad as I had imagined. It was a rubber snake, a useless fear. That day opened up a whole new set of opportunities for me, and it enabled me to create video programs that are now being used around the world. I had to overcome *useless fear* to get to the next level.

A third reason we resist change is *imagined inability*. We tell ourselves, *I can't learn math. I can't get over this habit. I can't handle the workload.* We see ourselves as unable, even though we have the ability.

Imagined inability is like a plastic chain, the kind they use in movie props and with Halloween costumes. They look real, but they'll break easily when we pull on them.

In the same way we separate useful and useless fears, we also must separate *actual inability* and *imagined inability*. No matter how much we shout at a football game on television, the players can't hear us. We can't affect the outcome. This is actual inability. (We're still going to shout, though!) Likewise, we don't have the ability to change the weather, or change the past, or change the day of the week. These are ironclad facts of life.

But *imagined inability* is different. We believe we can't learn to lead others better, but we can. We think we can't control our temper, but we can. We imagine we're unable to finish the work project by the deadline, but we can.

Sometimes the problem is a lack of know-how. We might say, "I don't know how to change, therefore I can't change."

A constructive counter-response could be, "I can figure it out. I can develop my skills. I can get good advice."

Or we might have tried to do something in the past but failed. *This is impossible*, we think. We clamp on plastic chains and never try again.

SEEING WRONG, FEELING WRONG, ACTING WRONG

Notice how all of these three forces—complacency, useless fear, and imagined inability—all spring from the wrong way of seeing.

SEE	FEEL	ACT
Blind to danger or opportunity.	Complacency.	Do nothing.
Danger that isn't real.	Useless fear.	Avoid things that should be faced.
See self as unable.	Helplessness.	Do nothing.

The three reasons we resist change and how all of them spring from seeing things wrong.

- We feel complacency because we can't see the dangers and missed opportunities involved in the status quo.
- We feel useless fear because we imagine danger that isn't real.
- We feel hopeless and inadequate because we inaccurately see ourselves as unable.

These three reasons we resist change all trace to wrong ways of seeing, which points us to our escape: We can get totally free by changing the way we see.

MOVING AGAIN

Thankfully, low points aren't the whole story. When my business failed, I started seeing life as a river and myself as the paddler. The business was lost, but I chose to get back into my canoe. I took the hard lessons I learned in 1998 to heart, so when the great recession of 2008 hit, I was ready and actually flourished.

"If you falter in times of trouble," wrote an ancient philosopher, "how small is your strength."[18] Troubled times are strength tests. As the years go on, I pass more tests than I fail. I'm getting tougher and wiser over time. Every day I'm getting better at paddling the river.

CHAPTER 3

Two Ways We Phrase

"Picture yourself vividly as defeated and that alone will make victory impossible. Picture yourself vividly as winning and that alone will contribute immeasurably to success. Great living starts with a picture, held in your imagination, of what you would like to do or be."

— HARRY EMERSON FOSDICK, AMERICAN PASTOR

It's 1986. I'm about to compete in my first competitive round of golf, a junior tournament in the Seattle area. I'm eighteen. I have only played golf for a year, and this is my first time to play in front of people who will judge my performance.

I'm stressed—what an understatement! My head is a three-ring circus, filled with freak shows and mayhem. It feels like a troupe of chimpanzees is skipping around in my skull to the rapid drumbeat of my heart.

The announcer calls my name to the spectators. "Now on the first tee, Erik Van Alstine." The audience claps, and then waits for me to hit the ball.

I can hear a pin drop. The head-circus reaches a peak, because the first shot is what most spectators see. It sets the momentum for the rest of the round. The game, and my dignity, hang in the balance.

I step up to the box, almost too shaky to balance the ball on the tee. I tell myself, *Don't miss the ball, Erik—don't miss the ball.*

SAME IDEA, DIFFERENT EFFECT

Experts in language tell us ideas can be phrased with equal meaning but in opposite ways. *Don't miss the ball* is the same idea as *hit the ball*. *The number three is not even* is equal to the phrase *the number three is odd*. *The spider is not dead* is similar to the phrase *the spider is alive*. The first set of phrases is negatively phrased and the second set, positively phrased.

The phrasing is opposite, but the idea is the same.

Experts tell us our minds process these equal-opposite phrases in different ways. Positive phrases are processed in one step, negative phrases in two. The mind pictures the phrase *the spider is alive*, for example, in one step. It pictures a live spider and that's it. The mind has a harder time, on the other hand, with the phrase *the spider is not dead,* because it has to take two steps. First, the mind accepts and pictures a dead spider. Then it takes a second step and un-accepts the picture, as if rubber stamping it, NOT TRUE.

"Before denying the contents of a [negatively phrased] sentence," writes the French linguist Lucien Tesnière, "the mind must first affirm it."[19] Cognitive scientist Steven Pinker writes, "To hear or read a statement is to believe it, at least for a moment."[20] Comprehension creates "a temporary context in which the sentence is true," writes cognitive scientist Lance Rips.[21]

The phrase *the spider is alive* creates a picture of a spider twitching its legs, poised to scurry across the floor. But the phrase *the spider is not dead* pictures a dead spider, legs all curled up around the body, with a rubber stamp, NOT TRUE, framing the picture.

The positive phrase, **the spider is alive**, has the same meaning as the negative phrase, **the spider is not dead**. The left picture usually creates fear, and the right picture, disgust.

This phrasing factor has implications for the way we use words. The first implication is that negatively phrased ideas might get us to believe, then feel, then react the opposite of our intentions.

Think of how I saw my first shot that day at the golf tournament. *Don't miss the ball, Erik—don't miss the ball.* What was the picture in my mind? Missing the ball. I saw a vivid picture of a shot so terrible that I'd be embarrassed. It was marked with a rubber stamp that said, "DON'T."

The problem is, the rubber stamp only *frames* the picture. It doesn't erase the picture. It's like going the Louvre Museum in Paris to see Leonardo da Vinci's famous painting, the *Mona Lisa*. We remember Mona. But we don't remember the frame that holds her on the wall.

Pictures stick in the mind. Frames, not as much.

So when we phrase ideas in the negative, we see the opposite of what we want. Studies show that when jurors are asked to disregard a statement, they do the opposite.[22] Once the statement is planted in the juror's mind, they accept it.

CONCEIVING IS BELIEVING

Why are we so quick to believe? Because we're wired to instantly believe what we see in the physical world, and we take that same faith into the conceptual world.

Think about how quickly we believe things we see in real life. If we see a bald eagle flying overhead, we instantly believe we see it, and try to snap a photo, or point it out to a friend. We don't question our perception. We believe. Immediately. There's no gap between perception and belief.

This might be why we also immediately accept ideas from the conceptual world. When we conceive of an idea, we "see" it in our imagination and instantly believe it. "We believe *life is a bowl of cherries* just as immediately and thoroughly as we believe *this is a bowl of cherries*," writes Harvard psychologist Daniel Gilbert.[23]

The instant response is to believe an idea as if we saw it with physical eyes.

VIVID IMAGINATION AND REALITY

Not only do we see pictures with the mind's eye, and instantly believe what we see, we also *react* to the pictures as if they were real. The mind interprets vivid imagination almost the same as reality.

I attended a seminar years ago where the speaker asked us to close our eyes and imagine a fresh lemon in our hands. "Smell the light fragrance of lemon as you bring it to your nose," he said slowly. "Feel the cool, dimpled texture as you hold it. Turn it with your fingers. Now place it on a wooden cutting board." He paused again. "Pick up a knife and cut it in half. Listen as you cut. Smell the rush of fragrance as juice sprays in the air." He paused once more, letting the experience sink in. "Now bring half the lemon to your lips," he said. "Bite into it. Bite deep. Feel the juice filling your mouth." My face puckered. My mouth watered. From the sound in the room, everyone else's did too.

Why did we pucker? The lemon wasn't real. It was just a game.

Or why do our hearts leap when watching a scary movie? It isn't real. They're all actors. That blood is fake.

We know. But we still leap in our seats.

Brain anatomy offers a clue. "If I were to ask you whether a penguin's flippers are longer or shorter than its feet," writes Gilbert, "you would probably have the sense of conjuring up a mental image from airy nothing and then 'looking' at it to determine the answer. You would feel as though a picture of a penguin just popped into your head because you wanted it to, and you would have the sense of staring at the flippers for a moment, looking down and checking out the feet, glancing back up at the flippers, and then giving me an answer.

"What you were doing would feel a lot like seeing because, in fact, it is. The region of your brain that is normally activated when you see objects with your eyes, a sensory area called the visual cortex, is also acti-vated when you inspect mental images with your mind's eye."[24]

This explains my reaction to the imaginary lemon. Imagination feeds signals to the same part of the brain as perception does—so if the imagi-nary picture is compelling enough, it feels real.

Again, the idea is that *the mind interprets vivid imagination and real-ity almost equally.* Which means we can create imaginary experiences and react to them as if they were real.

Back to my first golf tournament. I stood there telling myself, *Don't miss the ball, Erik—don't miss the ball.* My phrasing created vivid pictures of missing the ball. I pictured failure even as I tried to encourage myself to succeed, then reacted to the failure. Every time I imagined the miss, for thirty minutes leading up to that opening shot, I created a virtual experience of failure—and all the anxiety and embarrassment that go with it.

Is it any wonder what happened next?

REALIZING MY FEAR

I swung and hit the ball, but just barely. The ball shot forward just a foot off the ground, went about thirty yards, and embedded in a plastic flow-erpot next to the ladies' tee.

Everyone was silent.

"Where did it go?" I asked.

"It's up there," someone said, pointing to the left. "I think it hit that flowerpot."

Ugh. This is horrible. I grabbed my golf bag and walked up to the ladies' tee. Sure enough, there was a ball-sized hole in the black plastic wall of the flowerpot. I had to wait an eternity for a rules official to come sort it all out.

I stood there while everybody watched.

I was hot with embarrassment.

Finally, an official arrived and made the call: I had to take a one-shot penalty, drop a ball, and hit again. I swung, and this time it went further forward, but again, a bad shot. I picked up my bag and sluffed toward the ball, thinking, *stupid, stupid, stupid!*

This reminds me of a man named Job from an ancient story who said, "What I feared has come upon me."[25] I played terrible for the rest of the round. I don't know if I placed dead last, but it sure felt like it.

Think about the domino effect from seeing to feeling to acting. I saw repeated failure in the situation, even as I told myself not to.

This terrible picture of failure automatically influenced me to feel fear and shame. Then these emotions automatically influenced the way I acted, creating the poor performance I had feared.

👁 SEE	➡	❤ FEEL	➡	📣 ACT
Repeated failure.		Fear and shame.		Poor performance.

"Seeing" repeated failure can trigger fear and shame, which then influences performance.

Neuroscientists who study choking under pressure have found that fear disrupts our "implicit memory," the place that stores skills that have become automatic through practice. Any overthinking, not just negative thinking, can disrupt free-flowing performance. But fear has special power to do this, because fear triggers overthinking more than any other emotion.

Whenever we picture failure, we create anxiety and intense focus on the problem, disrupting our ability to interview well, or talk in front of a group, or finish a project near a deadline. We're so caught up in fear that we can't perform.[26]

TURNING IT AROUND

How do we turn things around? One way is to use positive phrasing to change the way we see, which of course automatically influences the way we feel and act.

Effective performers use words to image success, triggering constructive emotions and behaviors, while ineffective performers image failure, triggering destructive emotions and behaviors.

Before we go on—some caveats. First, there's more to success than changing the way we see. It's naïve to think that I would have become a top-flight golfer that day by telling myself to *hit the ball* instead of *don't miss the ball.*

Second, sometimes it's good to picture failure and feel fear. Failure-picturing is only wrong when it triggers *useless fear,* a fear that's either unfounded or, in this case, a fear that disrupts our performance. There are *many situations where useful fear improves performance.* When we see danger and feel useful fear, we break complacency. We plan better. We're more alert and motivated. We avoid unnecessary risk. Useful fear is healthy and productive.

But useless fear is another story. Whenever we face useless fears, the way we phrase matters. When we make pictures that trigger confidence instead of fear, we improve our performance.

In hockey, scoring fifty goals in a season is a spectacular achievement. Only a few top players do it, and hockey great Wayne Gretzky did it nine times. A reporter once asked Gretzky about the difference between a player who scores fifty goals per year and a player who scores only five goals per year. "It's a way of thinking," said Gretzky. "It's not really about talent. A fifty-goal scorer is focused on the back of the net. That's what they see. But the five-goal scorer can tell you the name brand of every pad of every goalie in the league. They see the goalie. I see the back of the net." Certainly, there is more to Gretzky's greatness than the way he saw things, but there's no question it contributed to his performance.

Ever since I learned about the two ways we phrase, I've built a habit of phrasing constructively. Instead of seeing myself miss a shot, I see myself making a shot. This subtle switch is making a difference in my performance in every area of life—as a leader, a father, a husband and, of course, a golfer.

Almost thirty years after that miserable shot into the flowerpot, I stood on the first tee at the opening round of the 2014 Hawaii State Open (just two days before my near-arrest). Years earlier, it had been just a local junior tournament, but this was a regional tournament with top amateurs and pros from all over the Pacific Northwest. The competitive pressure was higher. The course was tougher too.

The announcer said, "We'd like to welcome to the first tee of the Hawaii State Open, Erik Van Alstine." I stepped up to the tee as a different player with a different picture in my head, laser-focused on what I wanted, with no thought of anything else. I pictured a solid strike into the middle of the fairway. *Smash it down the middle*, I said to myself.

I hit a perfect shot.

"Nice drive," said a spectator.

That whole day I saw the shots I wanted to hit and hit to the pictures. I never thought, *don't miss*. I thought, *make the shot*. I finished the round with a score in the mid-seventies, good enough to pair me with three pros the next day.

PICTURE-POWERED

The See-Feel-Act progression shows how we are *picture-powered*. The pictures we hold in our mind, the way we "see" things, has an automatic influence on the way we feel and act. So if we want to change things, we need to change how we see things.

Effective influencers know that *the deepest source of influence is the way we see*, so they use words to change perceptions instead of working on attitudes and behaviors. Amazon CEO Jeff Bezos, for example, leads by including an empty chair at every meeting and talking about it. "That's the customer's chair," he says to his team. "Remember that as we make decisions." Whenever leaders see that chair, and remember Bezos's description of it, they see the situation in a different way, which in turn automatically influences attitudes, motivations, and behaviors.

Effective influencers also *manage themselves* by managing the way they see. The week before Christmas a couple years ago, I went to Michaels, an arts-and-crafts retailer, on an errand for my wife, Sandra. The place was packed. It took an eternity to get the stuff, get in line, and finally get to the register.

When I got there, I looked in my wallet. The credit card I planned to use was missing. My first reaction was, *I can't believe Sandra took my card. Now I'm going to have to do all this again because she didn't remember to give it back. And why did she take it in the first place? She has her own card.*

I thought this because I have a place for everything, so it was unusual for the card to be missing. But I decided to keep my Christmas joy, hold off on premature judgment, and find out what had happened. I called Sandra and she said, "Yes, I have it. I rescued it for you."

Hmm. She "rescued" it. That's a weird way of admitting she took it and is making me drive all the way home to get it and come back again. But over the years, I've been burned making snap judgments about stuff like this, so I decided to stay positive and wait for more detail. I simply said, "Okay, I'm just a couple minutes away. I'll come home and get it, then come back."

I drove straight home and asked, "What did you mean when you said, 'I rescued it'?"

"You left it at the movie theater last night," she replied.

"What?"

"Yeah, remember when you paid for too many tickets and talked to the manager about getting a refund for one of them? Well, you gave him your credit card, got distracted while waiting, and left the lobby to go to the theater. Fortunately, I was getting popcorn and he remembered that I was your wife and gave it to me. Otherwise your card would still be there."

Wow. That changed the way I saw the situation.

Hearing her explanation, I was relieved. "I'm so glad you did that for me."

"Yes, I am glad too. Now could you go back over to Michaels and finish the errand?"

CHAPTER 4

Word after Word after Word

"A word after a word after a word is power."
— Margaret Atwood, Canadian poet

I'm driving alone when a thought hits me: *He's ignoring you.*

"No, that's not how it is," I say out loud. "I can't be sure Roger is ignoring me. He didn't return my text, but sometimes texts don't go through, and it's easy to forget things in all the busyness. I believe the best about Roger."

Who am I talking to? Myself. I'll do this while driving or out on a walk—it's better to have these conversations in private than in shopping malls or coffee shops.

Strange as it may seem, I talk to myself this way all the time. Ask my wife Sandra and she'll tell you. She walks into the kitchen and there I am at the sink, saying, "Erik, you can figure this out," or "Come on, man, get a grip on yourself."

Since I was in college, I've learned to use my spoken words to dispute my thoughts and take control of the way I see things. Why? Because words are powerful. Just as Superman had power to stop a train, words have power to stop trains of thought.

Some have a hard time with the idea of talking to ourselves. *That's what crazy people do*, they think. But didn't they just *say* those words to themselves in their minds? Of course! In seminars I ask, "How many of you in this room talk to yourself?" Most raise their hands, but there are a few who don't.

"Okay, that's interesting," I say. "The people who didn't raise their hands are saying, 'Oh, no, I don't talk to myself.'"

THE WORD-STREAM

Despite what we believe, we talk to ourselves *a lot*. In fact, we're more verbose than the most annoying talkers we've ever known. We rattle and prattle and jabber and rant. We chatter and babble and gabble and blab. The mind never shuts up. The words go on and on and on.

Don't believe me? Here's a sample word-stream:

I'm hungry. Chinese food sounds good. Orange chicken. But the calories. I'm getting fat. Look at my stomach. Disgusting blubber. Counting calories is a drag. Maybe fresh-Mex instead. No, I've been eating great; it's time for a break. Pizza. But it will make me tired. That's okay, I'm done with work.

Ugh, work. Ron's been talking behind my back. The boss and Ron are close. This is trouble. There's a file folder on the passenger seat. Boss wants me to work it over the weekend. I should throw it out the window, watch it flutter in the mirror. No, that won't help. Todd from sales needs to shave his goatee. It's all calico. Gross.

Oh, there's my song on the radio! TLC. Baby-Baby-Baby. 1992 seems like only yesterday. I wonder how Jaime looks now? We were seventeen then. How long till the next reunion? 2016 minus 1992, that's sixteen plus eight, what's the number? Man, I hate math. Okay, twenty-four years. Twenty-fifth reunion is only a year away. Sheesh, I'm old. There's no way Jaime would be interested in me. Look in the mirror. Lines in my face getting clearer. Aerosmith. I wonder what's on the oldies station? The more I'm in the sun, the older my face looks. But I don't want to look pale. Ahh, Cabo in six weeks. That's going to be good. I wonder what the temperature is down there right now? Let's look. Eighty-six, with an overnight low of seventy. That's perfect.

That's just sixty seconds or less of a conversation that runs *sixteen hours a day*—or however long we are awake. We talk to ourselves with more intensity and speed than the most annoying fast-talker we can imagine.

We usually don't think of this as "talk," but a quick look at the difference between *inner words, spoken words*, and *written words* makes this all more apparent.

Inner words are things we say in our mind, but they don't come out of our mouths. When I stood at the first tee in that junior golf tournament, the spectators didn't see my mouth moving as I told myself, *Don't miss the ball, Erik, don't miss the ball.* I said it in my mind—inner words.

Then there are *spoken words*. Spoken words make pictures just like inner words do, but they have more power because they control attention and create more action. The mouth is moving. The sounds are coming out. It seems like more is happening than when we're just saying things in our minds, and this lip-moving and air-moving tends to create more commitment and belief.

"Deep within us, directing our actions with quiet power," writes psychology professor Robert Cialdini, "is our nearly obsessive desire to be (and to appear) consistent with what we have already done. Once we have made a choice or taken a stand, we will encounter personal and interpersonal pressures to behave consistently with that commitment."[27]

Spoken words "take a stand." When we say something out loud, we hear what we say and believe it more. Spoken words make pictures more pervasive and permanent in the mind than inner words, and they're a form of action, which means they create commitment.

Then there are *written words*. Written words last longer than spoken and inner words. They have better reminding power. They also tend to commit us more, because they can go public any time in the future.

Two thousand years ago, on a hillside in Palestine, a small group of people heard Jesus say, "Blessed are the peacemakers." At the time, his words were *spoken words*. But soon after, a follower named Matthew wrote them down. They became *written words*. In the centuries since, billions of people have read these words.

My point is, more people are likely to see written words than to hear spoken words. Also, written words are remembered longer. This is why Cialdini emphasizes the power of written words. He says, "We want to live up to the things we've written down."[28]

THE PICTURE-STREAM

Words often represent pictures in the mind, which means word-streams create picture-streams. Look again at the one-minute dialogue and see the pictures (in bold type):

> I'm **hungry. Chinese food** sounds good. **Orange chicken**. But the **calories**. I'm getting **fat**. Look at **my stomach. Disgusting blubber. Counting calories** is a drag. Maybe **fresh-Mex** instead. No, I've been **eating** great, it's time for a **break. Pizza**. But it will make **me tired**. That's okay, I'm done with **work**.

> Ugh, **work. Ron's been talking behind my back**. The **boss and Ron** are close. This is trouble. There's a **file folder** on the **passenger seat**. Boss wants me to work it over the **weekend**. I should **throw it out the window**, watch it **flutter in the mirror**. No, that won't help. **Todd from sales needs to shave his goatee. It's all calico. Gross.**

> Oh, there's my song on the **radio**! TLC. **Baby-Baby-Baby. 1992** seems like only yesterday. I wonder how **Jaime** looks now? **We were seventeen** then. How long till the next **reunion**? **2016** minus **1992**, that's **sixteen plus eight**, what's the number? Man, I hate **math**. Okay, **twenty-four years. Twenty-fifth reunion** is only **a year away**. Sheesh, I'm **old**. There's no way **Jaime** would be interested in me. **Look in the mirror. Lines in my face** getting clearer. **Aerosmith**. I wonder what's on the **oldies station**? The more I'm **in the sun**, the older **my face** looks. But I don't want to look **pale**. Ahh, **Cabo** in six weeks. That's going to be good. I wonder what the **temperature is down there** right now? Let's look. **Eighty-six, with an overnight low of seventy**. That's perfect.

That's over forty pictures in just one minute of inner words.

The question isn't *whether* we talk to ourselves. That's a given. The real question is *how* we talk to ourselves and the effect it has. Do we build up or tear down? Do our words create or destroy? Do our words solve problems or create problems? "Word after word after word is power," wrote the Canadian poet Margaret Atwood. As one word surfaces after another, things happen. Words affect the way we see things. The way we see ripples into emotions and behaviors, which create outcomes that affect the direction of our lives.

Sigmund Freud wrote, "Words have magical power. By words one person can make another blissfully happy or drive him to despair, by words the teacher conveys his knowledge to his pupils, by words the orator carries the audience with him and determines their judgments and decisions. Words provoke effects and are in general the means of mutual influence among men."[29]

Words can instantly change what we see. Imagine someone yells, *Look out!* We were paying attention to something else before, and thanks to words, we switched our view.

Words don't just change the way we see in one instance. They can control the way we see, long term. Words have controlling power, like a remote control switching a channel on a television. The more constructively we talk to ourselves, the better we control the pictures playing on the screen of our minds.

Controlling the way we see...	...controls the way we feel...	...which controls the things we do.

Words have the power to control the way we see, and by extension, control the way we feel and act.

Words are the scene-selector of the mind. They have the power to control the way we see and by extension, control the way we feel and act.

My wife Sandra and I talk about words—both good and bad—spoken to us when we were young that we remember to this day. A cutting remark. A compliment. A criticism or praise. One way or another, word after word after word is power.

REROUTING THE FLOW

Think of how we irrigate land. We redirect the flow of water into canals and create diversion dams. Water that ran randomly before now runs purposefully to make things grow.

That's what I suggest we do with the constant stream of conversation going on in our head. It's time to redirect and dam some of it up. We can speak in ways that divert the flow or even stop some of it. We can cultivate better things for our lives, just like farmers divert water to cultivate crops.

It takes work. Dams don't make themselves. Canals require planning and digging. Same with redirecting the word-flow. We need to start respecting the power of words. Let's monitor conversation to detect cause and effect. Let's observe how words influence our motivations, so we can start changing the way we talk. Let's walk away from imaginary conversations just like we walk away from real ones. Let's put an end to self-abuse. Let's dispute destructive pictures, while we affirm and build and inspire.

No question—this isn't easy and it's awkward at first, like learning a foreign language. But with time and effort, we can become fluent. We can divert the stream of thought.

MAKING PICTURES DISAPPEAR

Words don't just create pictures. They can make pictures disappear. This means that words have even more power than we might have imagined. *Words control what we don't see*, as well as what we see.

Imagine a red Ferrari. These two words, "red Ferrari," just created a picture in our minds. If we tell ourselves, "Don't think about the red Ferrari," what happens? We get the opposite of what we wanted. We see a red Ferrari with a rubber-stamped DON'T across the front of it.

The point is, the negative phrasing creates the picture, even as we try to suppress it. The more we try to suppress pictures by telling ourselves not to think of them, the more we actually think of them. Picture suppression only makes pictures more intense.

Now imagine a yellow Porsche. Can you see it in your mind? Bright yellow, with silver wheels and red caliper brakes. These words make a picture. I'm picturing a GT3 with the tail wing, the fat tires, and the six-speed manual shifter. I'm also thinking of all the fun I'd have driving it.

All the while I was picturing the Porsche, what happened to the red Ferrari? It disappeared. Of course, the Ferrari is back now because I just worded it onto the movie screen. But the second before I mentioned it, it wasn't there. My thoughts about the Porsche had *displaced* the Ferrari. Picture suppression doesn't work, but picture substitution does.

We can only think one conscious thought at a time. This means a choice for one picture is a choice against all other pictures in that moment. We lock on to one picture and block out all other pictures.

Why is this picture-blocking idea so important? Because it affects the way we see, which, in turn, affects everything we feel and do. If a picture is blocked, it can't click the power button. We aren't influenced by things that never get into view.

Consider tobling, for example. In seminars, I ask participants if they've ever been tempted by the alluring smell and unbelievable taste of tobling: "It's irresistible, isn't it?"

Actually, it's quite resistible because no one's ever heard of it, so they've never been tempted by it either. How do I know this? Because tobling doesn't exist. It's just a dessert-word I made up.

How can we be tempted or influenced by something we've never experienced? Likewise, when something is out of sight, it's out of mind—and it can't influence us. That means picture-blocking gives us tremendous power to pull the plug on temptation and distraction.

This is good news!

Think about what might happen if we never saw tempting food—with our physical eyes or with our imagination. Would we be tempted? No. We're tempted because we imagine a bag of Cheetos or see a commercial for the new bacon cheeseburger or look into our pantry and see a sleeve of Oreos.

When the temptation gets into view, whether in reality or our imagination, it starts having power over us, which is why researchers find that a clear candy jar on a receptionist's desk gets forty-six percent more action than an opaque one.[30] When we can't see the candy as well, we aren't influenced as much. And when we can't see it at all, we can't be influenced. This means we can unplug the power by making things invisible—by picture-blocking.

Words can do this. Words make things appear and disappear.

PHRASE FORWARD

Effective influencers use words to create constructive pictures. They *phrase forward.* They say, "Hit the ball," instead of, "Don't miss the ball." They say, "Show up on time," instead of, "Don't be late." They say, "Turn in an excellent report," instead of, "Don't turn in a sloppy report."

Can you feel the difference? One approach phrases back to the problem, while the other phrases forward to the solution.

Think about the phrase, "Don't be late." The picture it creates is of showing up late. That picture then triggers emotions like fear, frustration, and disappointment.

Then think about the phrase, "Show up on time." It creates a picture, too, but of success, not failure. This positively phrased picture triggers emotions like satisfaction, peace, and confidence.

It seems like a trivial technique, but makes a big difference. Great influencers know how to use positive phrasing to move themselves and others forward.

There is a place for negative phrasing, but used with caution. Effective leaders use both positive and negative phrasing in careful combination, because sometimes it's extremely productive to picture problems and feel fear. Fear is the most powerful motivator in human nature.[31] When danger is real, when bad consequences loom, fear is an ally that rallies us to act. It signals an important problem that deserves full attention. But when the danger isn't real, or when fear hampers performance, we've got to out-game it.

So the strategy is, *Use positive and negative phrasing in ways that harness useful fear and eliminate useless fear.*

For example, we can talk about being late and spell out the consequences. "When you show up late," a boss might say to an employee, "it affects team morale and productivity. It sends a signal that you don't care about your work or that you can't manage your time. It says that you don't respect the rules or honor authority."

In this way, the boss points to *principle-centered consequences* of being late. Not capricious consequences. Not the consequences the boss will impose because the boss is the boss. Rather, the consequences that naturally follow our choices.

When a boss or a parent fails to show the principle behind their ideas, they come across as manipulative. But when they point to principles, they come across as fair-minded and trustworthy.

Once consequences are spelled out, the boss should switch over to phrasing forward. "Here's what I want from you," the boss might say in the second half of the conversation. "I want you to show up on time. When you show up on time, it improves team morale and productivity. It tells me and others that you care about your work. It says that you can manage your time. It says you respect the rules and honor authority. Next time, show up on time."

Notice how the boss has converted all the negative phrasing into positive phrasing. Negative phrasing and consequence consideration is a small part of a process that puts bigger emphasis on positive phrasing, in the same way a jeweler uses black velvet to stage a brilliant diamond.

PRACTICE REPHRASING

It takes practice. I know because I've been phrasing forward consistently for two decades now, and it's become second nature. I hear backward phrasing in conversations and autocorrect it in my head. I create simple and positive pictures of what I want, instead of spending unnecessary time dwelling on pictures of what I don't want.

When people hear positive phrasing, they're not quite sure what is happening, but they can feel the effect. The influencer is clearer and more validating. The influencer is better known for what they are for than what they are against. People believe the influencer is for them, not against them.

The effect is profound.

Across the world right now, in executive suites, in conference rooms, in break rooms, in classrooms, and in dining rooms, we're using words to control the way we see. Are we creating views of success? Are we encouraging people forward?

STRONG, POSITIVE INFLUENCE

Too many people think positive phrasing is going soft. They think optimism is warm fuzzies and weakness. *You can't have positivity and be a strong leader*, they think.

I think the opposite. The more positively things are phrased, the stronger a leader can be.

In seminars, I sometimes demonstrate the idea of *push and pushback* by asking a participant to put up his hand. Then I put my hand against his and push. He resists. When I push, he pushes back.

This is a healthy response. We're wired to resist coercion. When someone pushes, we push back. But we need to clarify something here. There's only pushback when the participant perceives us to be pushing *against* them. So the better way to describe this idea is *push-against* and *pushback*. I'm pushing against his hand, and by extension, against him. He resists this.

But when we change the perception of *pushback* to a perception of *push-with*, resistance goes away. I ask the participant to turn his hand over to push a table or a desk, and I put my hand on the back of his to help him push. Since I'm *pushing-with*, the participant doesn't resist. He appreciates my help.

Take a look at the two ways people might see "pushy leadership," and the two different ways they'll respond.

SEE	FEEL	ACT
Leader pushing with and for you.	Affirmed and supported.	Cooperate.
Leader pushing against you.	Abused and manipulated.	Resist.

When people perceive the leader pushing for them, they feel affirmed and supported and they cooperate. When they see the leader pushing against them, they feel abused and manipulated, and they resist.

No question, coaches and leaders need to push. But they need to make sure they're being perceived as *pushing with* people, not *pushing against* them. When I talk to leaders, I say, *Go crazy with intensity*. Just go crazy *with people*, not *against them*.

LINING UP THE WORDS

Perception is power. That's the central point of this book. Everything we feel, every decision we make, everything we do—it all starts with perception.

There's more to the power-story, however, because words can control perception. Words can create perceptions. Words can destroy perceptions. Words have tremendous power.

Remember Margaret Atwood's point about the flow of words: "A word after a word after a word is power." We can't just say something once and have that be it. We've got to get the words lining up, one after another. We've got to take control of the word stream, and the only way I know how to do that is to create a powerful substitute stream, one productive word after another.

PART 2

THE RIGHT USE
OF POWER

CHAPTER 5

Automatic Humility

"You see, but you do not observe."

— SHERLOCK HOLMES, FICTIONAL CHARACTER

I first discovered I had a "perception problem" in a seminar back in 1996. Before that seminar, I thought I was seeing things quite well, *thank you.* But after that experience, I was floored. Insulted, even. I never imagined I could be so blind to things around me.

How about you? Do you see yourself as blind? Or do you imagine yourself a paragon of perception? Most self-identify as highly perceptive.

"I recall an autocratic company president," writes marketing expert Robert Rosenthal, "who, when given details on a collaborative process that brought together the best thinking inside and outside his company, smirked and said *he* was the only one needing to be consulted."[32]

Too many of us are like this president. We're not only blind, but we're blind to our blindness.

Which is why we're mystified by guys like Bob Arno.

PICKING POCKETS FOR FUN AND PROFIT

"Bob Arno is the last man you'd want walking next to you on the street or standing beside you in a crowd," says a television interviewer. "Because believe it or not, he can pick your pocket, or even swipe the tie right off your neck, and you'd never even know it."

In a series of video clips, Bob walks the Vegas strip, slipping wallets out of purses and pockets of unsuspecting victims.

Fortunately, Arno isn't a criminal. Instead, he's the world's leading expert on pickpockets and does these demonstrations to reveal the tricks of the trade.

Arno uses his skills to entertain as well. For the opening of his act, he enters the back of the room, greeting the audience with handshakes and pats on the back and high fives as he makes his way to the stage. In less than a minute, he steals a dozen pens, glasses, and watches. Then he asks the victims to come up on stage and get their stuff, where he continues to rip them off in front of everyone, removing suspenders and belts and ties. The audience rolls. Victims *know* they're getting taken. Eyes wide open, they try to see what he just took, how he took it, and what he's taking next. But they can't!

What is Arno's secret? Why can't his victims see what he's doing? Fast fingers certainly help, but that's just half the story.

THE LIMITS OF PERCEPTION

The rest of the story is about the limits of perception, and all the ways we fail to see our limits.

But there's a silver lining in this dark cloud of limitation, an incredible irony in the insight ahead. The moment we see how blind we truly are, we start seeing better. We listen more. We ask for input. We get *automatic humility*.

"To be wise," writes Cornelius Plantinga, "is to know reality and then accommodate yourself to it." Seeing reality accurately is the key to wisdom.

Think about flying. The pilot constantly watches the gauges, checking altitude, airspeed, direction, location, and so on. Without a clear view of reality, the pilot can't fly. In the same way, we need a clear view to pilot our way through life.

The challenge with reality is there's so much of it. Every waking moment, we're fire-hosed with sensation. There's no way to drink it all in. The optic nerve transmits ten million bits of information from the eye to the brain per second. And that doesn't account for any of the other senses—touch, taste, hearing, and smell. It also doesn't account for the hot-spring of imagination, pumping up thoughts that constantly flood our mind. Information overload is a permanent fact of life.

So, how do we handle this overload? We ignore most of it. We see just a few things and overlook everything else. We watch *those* leaves fall to the ground and miss all the other leaves. We feel *these* raindrops splatter the back of our necks, and ignore the drops falling everywhere else. We think about *that* program on television, ignoring hundreds of other shows.

Sure, we soak in a lot. We do a lot of looking around, but only with one glance at a time. Partial perception is a permanent fact of life. Every day we dip our teaspoons of attention into a mighty flood tide of reality. We can only scoop up tiny doses.

THE SECRETS OF THE STEAL

Back to Bob Arno. Guys like him know we're teaspooners and take advantage of it. The magicians, the pickpockets, the illusionists all understand how perception works, and use that knowledge to work their magic on us in plain sight.

First, consider the concept of *selective attention*. We've got a limited capacity to pay attention, but are shocked to see how limited our attention actually is. "The capacity of [conscious thought] at any single moment is surprisingly limited," writes Bernard Baars, senior fellow at the Neurosciences Institute in San Diego. "We cannot read this sentence and listen to a conversation at the same time. Nor can we pay attention to the s-p-e-l-l-i-n-g of a word without taking a risk that we will miss some of its meaning."[33]

The corollary principle of selective attention is *inattentional blindness*. At any moment in time, we see one thing, making us blind to everything else. When we lock on to one thing (selective attention), we block out everything else (inattentional blindness). Attention creates a constant lock-and-block effect.

Back in the day when more people wore watches, I used to ask seminar participants to think about theirs. "Don't look at your watch," I'd say, "but take out a piece of paper and draw as much detail from memory as you can. What does the band look like? The dial? The numbers on the dial? Just take a minute and draw a detailed picture."

After they drew the picture, they'd compare it to their watch. Most were shocked to see how different the drawing was. One person put numbers instead of tick marks for the hour indicators. Another person assumed the date window was on the right instead of the left. Someone drew twelve of the hour markings instead of six. The more they compared the two, the more they saw glaring differences, regardless of how many years they'd owned their watch.

"How can we look at our watch many times a day every day for so many years and miss so much?" I asked.

The answer is, of course, *selective attention*. When we're looking at our watch, we're looking for the *time*, not the design.

Then I'd say, "You just looked carefully at your watch. Did you see what time it was?" Most participants couldn't answer.

That's *inattentional blindness*. They were blind to the time because they were paying attention to the design.[34]

"Many people believe that merely by opening their eyes, they see everything in their field of view," writes Arien Mack, author of the groundbreaking book *Inattentional Blindness*. "In fact, there is no such thing." Outside our current focus, "there is no conscious perception of the visual world."[35]

That's a pretty bold statement. *No conscious perception? How can they say that? I see what's going on around me quite well, thank you.*

"We think we should see anything in front of us, but in fact we are aware of only a small portion of our visual world at any moment," write Harvard's Chabris and Simons. "The idea that we can look but not see is flatly incompatible with how we understand our own minds, and this mistaken understanding can lead to incautious or overconfident decisions."[36]

Inattentional blindness doesn't just apply to the visual field. It applies to other senses too, like our sense of touch. "We did find clear evidence of *tactile numbness* in situations in which the subjects were attending to some other task," writes Mack. Attention-limits apply to *touch* as well as sight.

This is how Bob Arno works his magic. "The trick to successful pickpocketing," says Arno, "is that if you have to touch the victim, you *mask the illegal contact with benign contact*." Arno runs his own video in slow motion to show just how he uses *tactile inattention* to his advantage. He puts his hand on the victim's shoulder. The victim senses Bob touching them. Once attention is set to the shoulder, the victim is insensitive to touch at other points. Arno is free to unbuckle, unstrap, and reach in. While he touches the left pocket, he slips the wallet out of the right pocket. While he touches the shoulder, he unslips the tie. To take off the watch, he grabs the wrist as if shaking someone's hand with both hands.

The trick is to sequence the touch so that the benign area gets attention first. After the spotlight of attention has been set, the magician has a heyday in the dark areas outside the spotlight.

Most of us refuse to believe we could be so unaware, which is what makes Arno's show so entertaining. People are shocked to see watches and ties disappear, and they laugh hysterically. The concepts of selective attention and inattentional blindness seem so counterintuitive that Arno catches people off-guard time and time again.

Why are we so blind to our blindness? The answer is found in a third principle, *assumption backfill*. "We all have the illusion of seeing far more," Baars continues, "because the brain cleverly takes snapshots of high-information regions in the visual scene and fills in the rest with plausible guesswork."[37] We can't see our blind spots because, to us, they aren't blind spots at all. We fill in empty spaces with assumptions.

In a 2007 *New York Times* feature, journalist George Johnson wrote about a conference where magicians shared their secrets.

> After two days of presentations by scientists and philosophers speculating on how the mind construes, and misconstrues, reality, we were hearing from the pros: James (The Amazing) Randi, Johnny Thompson (The Great Tomsoni), Mac King, and Teller—magicians who had intuitively mastered some of the lessons being learned in the laboratory about the limits of cognition and attention....Secretive as they are about specifics, the magicians were as eager as the scientists when it came to discussing the cognitive illusions that masquerade as magic: disguising one action as another, implying data that isn't there, taking advantage of how the brain fills in gaps—making assumptions, as The Amazing Randi puts it, and mistaking them for facts.[38]

This is assumption backfill in action.

"Humans adapt incredibly quickly to consistent patterns," says Chip Heath, a professor at Stanford University. "Consistent sensory stimulation makes us tune out. Think of the hum of an air conditioner, or traffic noise, or the smell of a candle, or the sight of a bookshelf. We may become consciously aware of these things only when something changes: The air conditioner shuts off. Your spouse rearranges the books."[39]

Without some change to trigger our attention, we pattern everything over. In this way, we ignore most of the things happening around us.

Some time ago, I used this idea to work magic on my kids. I used to store a case of Diet Rockstar energy drinks on a shelf in my garage. "These are off limits," I told them. But they often "forgot" and took them anyway. This happened for about six months. So I tried an experiment. After I drank the last can in the case, I left the empty box on the shelf. I put my new case one shelf over, in plain view.

Wouldn't you know it, they stopped taking the cans because they didn't see them. The kids had been conditioned to look in one place for one case of energy drinks, never two.

About a month after the successful experiment, I decided to give my teenage son Ross an energy drink as a reward for vacuuming. He finished the job, then came up to my office and said, "Dad, there are no energy drinks. The box is empty."

Perfect. My plan was working.

IGNORING OUR IGNORANCE

Even though our perception is extremely limited, it's human nature to believe we're seeing everything we need to see.

"You cannot help dealing with the limited information you have as if it were all there is to know," writes psychologist Daniel Kahneman, author of the book *Thinking, Fast and Slow*. "You build the best possible story from the information available to you, and if it is a good story, you believe it. Paradoxically, it is easier to construct a coherent story when you know little, when there are fewer pieces to fit into the puzzle. Our comforting conviction that the world makes sense rests on a secure foundation: our almost unlimited ability to ignore our ignorance."[40]

Back in 1996, when I first learned about these perceptive limits, I was a CEO of a multimillion-dollar corporation that I had built from scratch. So I imagined myself even more perceptive than the average Joe. I was blind to my blindness, ignorant of my ignorance. I didn't listen near as much as I listen now, because I didn't think I needed to. I rejected advice and thought less of those who disagreed with me. When I did "listen," it was often just waiting for people to stop talking so I could continue to tell them how things *really were*.

That's why I was so floored by the insights of this chapter. It felt like the lights went *off*, not *on*. The more I understood about selective perception, the more I realized how wrong my attitude had been. These insights revolutionized my leadership. They instantly and automatically changed me.

From that point forward, I reminded myself of my limits. I studied perception. I read books on the subject, I did everything I could to counter my know-it-all syndrome, because I knew I could slip back in an instant.

SENSATION AND BRAINSATION

Even when we are seeing things clearly, there's more to seeing than meets the eye. All our senses—sight, sound, taste, touch, and smell—are influenced by the inner working of the brain, which means we can distort reality even when we're looking right at it.

The Pepsi Challenge is a good example of this. Back in the 1980s, marketers ran blind taste tests between Coke and Pepsi in supermarkets and malls across the country. Marketers set out unlabeled cups, one with Coke, the other Pepsi, and asked, "Which tastes better?"

When 57 percent chose Pepsi, and 43 percent chose Coke, the Coke executives flew off the handle. They did their own taste test and results showed the opposite conclusion. People preferred Coke, not Pepsi.

Were the Coke executives cheating? No…Well, sort of. They weren't running a *blind* test. They were running the same test, but with labels clearly marked. Participants knew what they were drinking. And they said Coke tasted better.

How could this be? The puzzle went unsolved until 2004, when neuroscientists from Baylor University ran the challenge again, but with a modern twist: a functional magnetic resonance imaging (fMRI) machine that scanned participants' brains as they tasted. Researchers concluded that the sight of the brands activated a higher-order brain mechanism that, in turn, improved the participant's perception of soda taste.[41]

So, who was right, Pepsi or Coke? The answer is…both. And this gives us the twist in our perception story. Perception is a *combination* of feeds from reality and imagination. In the visible-brand taste test, the inner feed of brand experience sent an overlaying signal, adding to the outer-feed of soda taste. Inner and outer feeds combined, making Coke the winner.

This tells us perception isn't a straight experience of the outside world. It's a combination of inner and outer feeds. When we taste things, we get the outer feed of sensation from our taste buds. But we also get an inner feed to the "taste center" of the brain from another part of the brain. Sensation gets color-corrected, so to speak, by the added inner feed of the mind. Coke tastes better because the mind literally sweetens the taste with brand association.

Wow.

This isn't just true for seeing. It's true for other senses too. "Today we know," writes MIT professor Marvin Minsky, "that visual systems in our brains receive many more signals from the rest of the brain than signals that come from our eyes."[42] Everything we perceive—sight, touch, taste, sound, and smell—is influenced by the mixed signal of sensation and *brainsation.*

A WHIPPING, WHIRLING STROBE LIGHT

Now let's start up the techno dance music to prepare for another mind-blowing principle. Think about how fast our spotlight of attention snaps from one place to another. Like right now as we read these words. If we could see the movement of our eyeballs, we'd think they were danc-ing…to a hardcore techno beat.

This effect is something I'll call *attention snap*. Our attention snaps back and forth quickly from one thing to another as we scan the world around us.

Consider the paragraph below. Even though the letters are jumbled up, most of us have no trouble reading and understanding the meaning.

> Aoccdrnig to rscheearch at Cmabrigde Uinervtisy, it deosn't mttaer in waht oredr the ltteers in a wrod are, the olny iprmoatnt tihng is taht the frist and lsat ltteer be at the rghit pclae. The rset can be a toatl mses and you can sitll raed it wouthit a porbelm. Tihs is bcuseae the huamn mnid deos not raed ervey lteter by istlef, but the wrod as a wlohe.

"In 1879," writes brain expert Nicholas Carr, "a French ophthalmol-ogist named Louis Emile Javal discovered that when people read, their eyes don't sweep across the words in a perfectly fluid way. Their visual focus advances in little jumps, called saccades, pausing briefly at different points along each line."[43] We take snapshots of information, and our brains fill in the rest from previous experience and association (i.e., assumption backfill).

AUTOMATIC HUMILITY

These ideas about the way we see instantly made me more circumspect. I now question my assumptions and really try to look before I leap to conclusions. I listen more carefully and have stopped thinking I know it all.

I heard a story of four people on a plane: the President of the United States, the World's Smartest Man, a Boy Scout, and a priest. The engine failed and they all had to bail out, but there were only three parachutes.

The President of the United States grabbed a chute and jumped, saying, "I'm the President of the United States, the world needs me."

The World's Smartest Man grabbed a chute and jumped, saying, "I'm the world's smartest man. The world needs me."

The priest, with a sad and sober face, turned to the Boy Scout and said, "Son, I've had a long, good life. You go ahead. Take the last parachute."

"No worry, Father," said the Boy Scout. "There are still two parachutes left."

"What do you mean?" replied the priest.

"The world's smartest man jumped out with my backpack."

I think a lot of us are like the World's Smartest Man. We think we're seeing the parachute but grab the backpack by mistake. We don't take enough time to look before we leap, because we think we know everything we need to know.

But when we start seeing how blind we are, it changes things. We take time to listen, to clarify, to understand. We don't just listen to be polite. We listen because we want to. We know that we're making assumptions and mistaking them for facts, and without double-checks and outside help, we'll make critical mistakes.

When we understand how limited our view is, we want other people to help us see. We know that one point of view isn't enough. We want feedback from diverse personality types and roles and ages, because this helps us get more spotlights on the dark landscape of reality. When we see ourselves as blind, it triggers a useful fear of missing out. We start asking, *What else am I missing?* This automatically influences us to listen better and learn more.

In relationships, at home, at work, in all of life, there's nothing more powerful than *automatic humility*. When we realize how blind we are, we're more cooperative, more understanding, more open to feedback. Relationships flourish as we help each other.

But when we fail to realize how blind we are, we don't see as much need for others, we jump to false conclusions, and resist feedback.

In all my years working with companies and relating to people, I've found that this principle is one of the most important. To pull the plug on people problems, we need *automatic humility*.

THWARTING THE PICKPOCKETS OF ERROR

The irony is that knowing that we're easy to fool makes us harder to fool. Several years ago, a friend of mine, Carissa Hayden, took a student trip to Europe. Before she left, her mother gave her the full safety rundown: *Pickpockets and thieves are on the loose everywhere. Pay attention to every bump and brush. That's how they rip you off.*

Off Carissa went. Whenever someone brushed up against her in a subway or on a crowded street, her first reflex was to put her hand over the top of her purse. She made it through the whole summer without an incident. The thieves had to find another unsuspecting tourist, because Carissa was a tough target. By learning the secret of the steal, she kept from getting ripped off.

In the same way, when we see that we don't see, we start seeing better.

CHAPTER 6

Rope Lines in Thule

*"By prevailing over all obstacles and distractions, one may
unfailingly arrive at his chosen goal or destination."*
— Christopher Columbus, Italian explorer

My dad spent some of his early years in the Air Force, stationed at Thule
Air Base near Pituffik, Greenland.

Deep in the Arctic Circle, Thule is one of the coldest and windiest
places on earth. Temperatures can reach forty degrees below zero with
sustained winds near seventy miles an hour, creating wind chills of more
than a hundred below. Just nine years after Dad's stay there, researchers
measured the fastest sea-level wind speed on earth—207 miles per hour.

Then add darkness twenty-four hours a day from November to
February, along with snow flurries and whiteout conditions, and we're
talking killer weather.

Whenever the big storms rolled through, called "Storm Condition
Delta," the men would hunker down in buildings. But sometimes they
had to go from building to building to get more food. "It was 1963," my
dad said. "I remember how we ate canned K-rations dated as far back as
1942."

That's some old food.

But old food was still good food, and the guys had to eat, so they installed rope lines from building to building. Everyone going from one building to another had to grip the rope as they crossed. Forget to grip the rope, and you're a human popsicle in half an hour.

Dad said several men died in the storms that year. For some reason, they didn't keep their grip.

THE FLURRY OF PERCEPTION

In this book, I've been hammering the key point: *perception is power*. The way we see, meaning the way we characterize and evaluate things as good and bad, is the trigger for everything else. All our motivation, emotion, and behavior flow automatically from it.

The problem is, perception is wild, crazy, and prone to error. The weather of the mind is like the windstorms of Thule, filled with flurry and fury. Unless we're intentional, these storms will kill us. The only way to stay alive is to grab the rope, to harness our attention, and keep our bearings in the thought-storm.

The rope line represents techniques to control perception. It's a similar analogy to the remote control I suggested earlier, where I showed how words work as a remote control to switch the way we think. When we talk to ourselves in constructive ways, both in our mind, out loud, and in what we write down and remember, we control the scene on our mental screen. We stay gripped to the rope.

Controlling perception, in turn, controls our emotional responses and our behaviors, as seen in the graphic below. Perception control is self-control.

Controlling the way we see...	...controls the way we feel...	...which controls the things we do.

Controlling the way we see controls the way we feel, which controls the things we do. This chapter is about techniques to control perception.

The Greenland rope line analogy is apt, because our lives truly do hang in the balance. The person we eventually become, and the influence we have on others, is decided by the rope lines.

Here are a few ways to keep our grip.

THOUGHT-LOCKING

The first is *thought-locking*. As soon as a temptation or an unproductive thought surfaces, I work to block it by locking onto a substitute thought. If the red Ferrari was the destructive thought and the yellow Porsche was the constructive one, I block out the red Ferrari by switching my attention to the yellow Porsche.

Take eating as an example. I switch my focus to all the good things I can eat, and describe these things out loud. This automatically locks on to what I want and blocks the rest. Instead of thought suppression (*Don't think about the triple-chocolate-decadent dessert*), which only sets my attention on what I don't want, I substitute a better thought (*Wow, sliced apples with cinnamon will energize me*).

TIME-BLOCKING

Another strategy is *time-blocking*. In the same way we choose our thoughts, we can choose how we spend blocks of time. Time-blocking is setting aside weekly or daily time for a specific purpose, undistracted, so we're free to focus on priorities. It's not enough to *say* something is a priority. We need to *schedule* it.

For example, I block out 8 a.m. to 10 a.m. for writing, six days a week. I put my phone away. I shut down email and Internet. I give my best to the work.

SPACE-BLOCKING

Another strategy is *space-blocking*, removing things from spaces that tempt and distract, like getting bad food out of the pantry and fridge, or leaving the phone at the door of the conference room. When we put things out of sight, we put them out of mind.

CHOOSING RELATIONSHIPS WISELY

Another strategy is *choosing relationships wisely*. When we choose relationships, we time-block and space-block without knowing it.

Think about what happens when we're with people. We hear their words, and those words create pictures in our minds.

The more we hang out with certain types of people, the more we share perceptions as the conversation flows. Relationships are like two streams of consciousness flowing into a single, larger stream. There's a mixing of perception.

Which means the choice of relationships is a choice of perceptions. When we choose to spend the afternoon with one friend over another, our choice affects the mental stream. We pick up unconscious standards and values. We acclimate to certain ideas and ways of thinking. Relationships have watershed effects on the stream of thought, changing the downflow course in one direction or another, for better or worse.

This is why we must choose relationships wisely, investing effort to get around the people who will help us construct the right flows of thought.

SEEKING DIVERSE FEEDBACK

Which reminds me of another strategy: *seek diverse feedback*. When we understand how limited our view is, we want other people to help us see. We know that one point of view isn't enough. We know that points of view similar to ours aren't enough. We want feedback from diverse personality types and roles and ages, because this helps us get more spotlights on the dark landscape of reality.

WRITING AND SPEAKING CONSTRUCTIVELY

Another way to grip the rope line is *writing constructive declarations* about self, purpose, and life, *then reviewing and speaking them regularly*. We can use the power of written, spoken, and inner words to cement what is important, what we believe, and where we're going. The only way to do this is to write these declarations down and speak them daily, meaning, use the time-blocking strategy and schedule them. My current practice is to sandwich my day with them, and read them while listening to inspiring music.

For example, I use Spotify to play the soundtrack to the film *Gladiator*, which puts me in a powerful state of mind while I read a list of constructive statements I keep on an EverNote app in my iPhone. As I read the statements, I picture myself living them out and feel the impact.

Over time, this shapes the way I see myself, my purpose, and the world around me.

Here are a few of the statements that help me:

- I see myself as poised and powerful under pressure.
- I see everyone as they are, as people, having equal value and needs as myself, and it feels great to honor and serve them.
- I communicate powerful and practical wisdom, helping myself and others think better, work better, and live better.

Notice that these phrases help me see in constructive ways. They hit the power button. They automatically influence my motivations, my emotions, and my choices and behaviors. My choices, in turn, create outcomes that change the reality around me.

We can also use words to dispute destructive thoughts and affirm constructive ones. We can use words to make pictures disappear. We can declare what matters most, we can write and state our goals, we can repeat ourselves. We use the remote control to decide what stays and goes on the movie screen of the mind.

BUILDING SITUATIONAL TRIGGERS

Another strategy is *building situational triggers*, which are reminders about how to see, attached to specific circumstances. It's a sort of "if this happens, see it like that" kind of logic.

For example, whenever I'm getting on a stage to talk to people, I remind myself, *I love these people*. It's just a quick phrase in my head, but it sets the tone of my talk. Or say I'm preparing for a pressure situation, like the opening shot in a golf tournament, or an important meeting, or a looming deadline. I use the situation to trigger the reminder: *I am poised and powerful under pressure.*

I have at least a dozen of these triggers, and they help me be my best in each situation. I'm not perfect at it, to be sure, but I'm much better for it. I'm training myself to *see right, every moment of sight.*

ASKING THE CARDINAL COGNITIVE QUESTION

Another rope line strategy involves monitoring our emotions for underlying perceptions, identifying the perceptions, and then changing them.

Whenever we're feeling really good or really bad, we should ask the cardinal cognitive question: *What was just going through my mind?*[44] It's a sentence. Or a picture. It's a way of seeing. We discover it, then adjust.

The idea is to flood our minds with constructive perceptions, and by extension, flush out all the destructive perceptions that trigger the destructive emotions, motivations, and behaviors.

We don't have to go back twenty years and deal with every single thing that's ever happened to us. Instead, we can flood our mind with constructive thinking, and those new ways of thinking will automatically displace the old ways.

PHRASING POSITIVE, NEGATIVE, AND POSITIVE

Another way to stay gripped to the rope line is the technique from Chapter Four, which starts with positive phrasing, then considers negative consequences, then converts consequences into positive opposites.

First, we talk about what we want. We talk up the solution instead of obsessing about the problem. We say, *Hit the ball down the middle*, instead of, *Don't miss the ball*. We say, *Show up on time*, instead of, *Don't be late*.

Then, once we understand how to phrase in the positive, we carefully combine positive and negative phrasing to make the most of useful fear, the most powerful of the motivations.

Let's say my problem is getting motivated to complete a project with a looming deadline. The positive phrasing is, "Finish strong and do it right." The negative phrasing is, "Don't finish weak and screw it up."

I start with the positive, telling myself, *Okay, Erik, you can finish strong and do it right.*

Then I think about the consequences. *If you finish weak on this, you'll feel terrible afterward, and the work will suffer. If you screw this up, you'll miss out on that upcoming pay raise. If you fail, you'll disappoint the whole development team.*

Then I switch all the negative phrasing from these consequences into positives: *Okay, Erik, you can finish strong and do it right. When you finish strong, you'll feel great afterward, and the work will shine. When you do it right, you'll position yourself for that pay raise. You'll make the whole development team proud.*

Negative phrasing forms a backdrop for positive phrasing, like the jeweler uses black velvet to backdrop a diamond.

CLARIFYING GOALS AND VALUES

Another way to keep a grip on the rope is to *clarify goals and values*. When we spend enough time looking at our goals and clarifying why we have them, we start seeing things a different way. This new way of seeing triggers new motivations and decisions.

What does the future hold? A lot of it is up to us. Will we live by default, or by design? If we do nothing, we'll get the default. But if we choose to set goals and review them often, we grip a rope line that will get us to the next building. With determination, we can overcome barriers and get to our destination no matter how many roadblocks and detours we have to get around.

LEARNING TO LOVE WISDOM

Another way to keep our grip on the rope is *learning to love wisdom*. When we discover how valuable wisdom can be, we start looking for it. We start storing it up for the crossroads of life. We watch for it wherever it can be found. We find wise counselors. We don't ask fools how they see, because that just reinforces error. Instead, we ask wise people. Then we listen carefully. We work to see how they see.

We human beings are extremely vulnerable to error because of the subjective ways we see things, and if we understand our vulnerability, we'll instantly get wiser, because we'll start questioning our judgments and listen to counsel.

LOOKING AT THE LENS

A final way to grip the line is making a habit of *looking at the lens*, meaning, seeing how we see and seeing how others see. We step back and look *at* the lens that we normally only look *through*.

Think about the concept of *empathy* for a moment. Empathy is the ability to *feel how people feel*. But it's not necessarily the ability to *see how people see*. Empathy lives at the branch-level, not the root-level. It's a second-stage factor in the See-Feel-Act progression, not the first stage.

Think back to my problem with Wes at Mauna Lani. Empathy wouldn't have solved my problem. On the first hole, I knew how Wes felt, and I felt bad for him. I imagined that something must have been bothering him and was sorry to see him out of sorts. So I had empathy. But I didn't see how Wes saw. So I wasn't able to resolve the conflict.

Empathy isn't enough. We can't solve problems by feeling how people feel. We need to go deeper and see how they see. To solve problems, we must put *perceptual intelligence* before *emotional intelligence*.

Experts in negotiation tell us that people who take time to see how others see create better agreements than people who feel how others feel. They understand why the other party reacts the way they do, and what they truly want. This means they're better at creating mutually beneficial solutions. They work better with others because they understand them better.[45]

JUSTIN SMITH, "FROZEN SOLID"

In February 2015, Don Smith found his son Justin, a 26-year-old Pennsylvania man, "frozen solid" in a foot of snow. Justin had been walking home after a night out with friends, and the sub-zero temperatures caught him off guard. His father went out looking and found him on the side of the road, his eyes frozen open. "I held him and sobbed, 'Justin, don't leave me.' He was frozen, like a block of concrete."

When medics arrived for their "death investigation," they saw a glimmer of hope and worked to revive him. They airlifted him out, thawed out his body, spent two hours performing CPR. They even used a machine to warm up his blood.

Suddenly, his heart started beating again.

Weeks later, Justin woke up from a coma, happy to be alive, and resolved to be more careful in the weather.[46]

There's hope beyond our mind-storm. If killer weather has frozen us, today is a new day of recovery and caution. We can take the lessons of the past to heart and grip the rope lines from here forward.

CHAPTER 7

Automatic Love

"People will forget what you said. People will forget what you did. But people will never forget how you made them feel."

— Maya Angelou, American poet

Recently I watched an episode of *The Crocodile Hunter*, starring the late Steve Irwin.

The show opens with Steve driving his dirty SUV across the Australian outback. As a wildlife expert and host of the show, he's looking for Australia's deadliest snakes.

"I've always wanted a chance to show people what amazing snakes we have in this country," Steve says into the camera. "In the bush, they're not biting anyone or scaring anyone. They're just living peacefully with all this power stored in their venom."

Suddenly he sees a twelve-foot python on the road and stops. He gets out and walks up close. The python snaps at him. Steve stays out of the strike zone, then gently grabs the snake by the tail. Why? To get it to safety.

"He's a beauty," Steve says with a boyish smile, as he lets it go into the grass. "While most drivers see a snake on the road and swerve to run it over, I stop to make sure it gets to safety. I also never grab a snake by the head, because that can harm the snake and make it want to bite." By handling the tail and the body gently, he keeps snakes calm.

Later in the show, Steve climbs down a ravine to find the death adder. "Have a look at this little beauty," he says as he picks it up. Steve smiles like a kid at Christmas, his face full of awe. "Aren't they glorious? This is the death adder. Death adder by name, but not by nature. As you can see the death adder is very placid, very quiet and timid, and not inclined to bite. Just gotta keep my fingers out of the way."

In a later scene, a snake snaps at Steve. "You're a grumpy snake," he says, still smiling. "This snake is particularly aggressive. The reason being is, I've got him cornered. He feels confronted, like I'm going to hurt him, perhaps even eat him. His only defense is aggression."

Steve's final trek in the show is to the far side of the Outback, to see the most venomous snake in the world, the inland taipan, also known as the "fierce snake." "This is my country, and I've grown up around here," says Steve. "The fierce snake, he's an old mate of mine. The fierce snake has enough toxins that in one bite he'd be capable of killing one hundred adult humans. Pretty awesome."

No question about it, Steve's in love with these snakes. They're magnificent creatures with great value. One of them is an *old mate of mine*. Another is *glorious*. Another is a *little beauty*. When snakes snap at him, he stays endearing. They're just *grumpy* and *cranky*. When they hiss at him, he understands and forgives.

LOVING THE SNAKES

What if we saw contentious people like Steve sees snakes? When people hiss, we'd say, "Oh, they're just a little cranky and grumpy, but *glorious.*" When people bare fangs we'd stay gentle, never "grabbing them by the head." When people strike out at us, we'd still say, "They're old mates of mine." If this was our response, how different might things be? If we kept our endearment despite the hissing, what might happen?

It would change things. Big time.

We'd live a life of *automatic love*.

I'm including a chapter on love because love is the greatest motive for influence. Influence without love is manipulation. Power requires responsibility, and our responsibility is to wield power in a way that *serves* people instead of trying to *use* them.

If we succeed greatly but fail to love greatly, have we really succeeded? Britain's expert in language and culture, Friedrich Muller, wrote that "a flower cannot blossom without sunshine, and man cannot live without love."[47] USC professor and love expert Leo Buscaglia said, "Love is life, and if you miss love, you miss life."[48]

WHAT IS LOVE?

Love is a supreme virtue, but what is it? Merriam-Webster describes it as "a feeling of strong affection." Then it defines *affection* as a "feeling of liking and caring." The common word in these definitions is the term *feeling*, which puts *love* in the *Feel* stage of the See-Feel-Act progression. Notice love in the center section of the graphic below.

SEE	FEEL	ACT
What goes here?	Love belongs here.	What goes here?

Love, a feeling, belongs in the center section of the See-Feel-Act progression, which means something else triggers love.

This means there's something else, besides love, that triggers love.

What is it? *Seeing people as people, of equal value and with equal needs as ourselves.* Love is the automatic response to seeing people right. When we see people as they are, we feel love, and are motivated to serve people instead of use people or ignore people.

Here's the progression.

SEE	FEEL	ACT
People as people, with equal value and needs as self.	Love.	Behave in many kinds of loving ways.

Seeing people as "people with equal value and needs as self" triggers ***automatic love.***

Every time we think about people, we see in one of a few basic ways, which I'll describe as *equal value*, *less value*, and *no value*. There are more ways to see people, of course, but these three are important.

- The first is seeing people as people of equal value as self, with equally important needs. Seeing this way automatically triggers love, appreciation, and a desire to serve.
- The second way is to see people in a diminished way, which triggers feelings of superiority and a desire to use people.
- The third way is seeing people with disinterest, or not seeing them at all.

The graphic below shows these basic ways of seeing people, and the emotional and behavioral consequences.

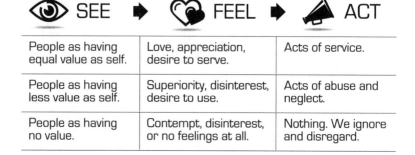

SEE	FEEL	ACT
People as having equal value as self.	Love, appreciation, desire to serve.	Acts of service.
People as having less value as self.	Superiority, disinterest, desire to use.	Acts of abuse and neglect.
People as having no value.	Contempt, disinterest, or no feelings at all.	Nothing. We ignore and disregard.

Three basic ways to see people, and the feelings and actions that automatically result.

We can even diminish people as we place high value on them by seeing them only for what they can do for us. When we see people as tools to achieve our purposes, even when they are highly valued tools, we diminish them. Let's say I'm an entrepreneur looking for an investor and run across a rich guy. I value this guy, but if I only see him as a resource for me, meaning, if I only see him as a walking wallet, I've mischaracterized him as an object.

Or say I'm a lonely stay-at-home mom looking for a friend to talk to and someone agrees to spend the day with me. I might highly value my friend, but if it's only for what she can do for me, I've diminished her. She's a way to meet my emotional needs.

Or say I'm a father pushing my son to achieve in sports, not for his sake, but for my own sense of superiority. I place great value on my son, but not as a person. He's a tool to build my self-esteem.

The idea is, even when we attribute great value to people, we might be devaluing them at the same time, because we're seeing them as objects to manipulate for our benefit. We "objectify" people when we value them to use them, or when we're upset with them because they're in our way.

THE DEHUMANIZING BOSS

Leaders constantly fall prey to objectifying their employees. They often see people only as tools and barriers, because they lead organizations, which means it's their job to use people to reach organizational goals. This mindset often diminishes the humanity of their people.

This is why leaders must constantly correct for this tendency. When leaders have a goal to help humanity, they often use that noble goal as an excuse to run over the humans in their immediate world. They treat people as tools to reach good and selfless goals.

Apple Computer founder Steve Jobs was notorious for this. He served humanity in profound ways, but he also hurt the human beings who worked with him. Co-workers described him as a "giant jerk." He was rude, mean, and a terror to work with.

Walter Isaacson, a Steve Jobs biographer, asked Jobs's best friend, Jony Ive, "Why was Jobs such a rude person?" "When he's frustrated, his way to achieve catharsis is to hurt somebody," said Jony. "He feels he has a liberty and license to do that. The normal rules of social engagement, he feels, don't apply to him. He knows how to efficiently and effectively hurt someone. And he does that."[49]

When we see people as objects, it's easy to treat them as such. People pick up on this and resent it. The cure is to keep *equal emphasis on the goals and the people who help reach those goals.*

SEEING NO VALUE

The third way of seeing people is to fail to see them at all or see them as having no value. It's easy to overlook others in the busyness of life.

A few years ago, I spent a day with a popular leader. Let's call him Joe to protect his identity. Joe and I played a round of golf, talked about our work, our families, and found that we had a lot in common. At the end of the day, Joe and I had become friends.

So I thought.

A year later, we both were at another event and, as luck would have it, we were paired for another round of golf. On the first tee, Joe introduced himself to me as if he'd never seen me before.

"I'm Joe," he said to me. "What's your name?"

He looked straight at my face but didn't recognize me.

"Erik," I said. "We spent the day together in Arizona last year."

"Oh," he said, a little embarrassed. "Sorry, I'm terrible with names."

But it was more than that. He didn't recognize my *face*. We all forget names, but forgetting a face too? After a whole day together? That's not as common.

I thought, *That day last year I was invisible to him.* He looked *at me for a whole day but didn't see me at all.*

I struggled to keep my respect for him. His public persona is caring and charismatic. But after this experience, I was tempted to see him as a man who claimed to care for people but didn't.

Before I go further, let's pull Joe out from under the bus. One in fifty people have *prosopagnosia*, the inability to recognize faces. Joe might have had that or a mild form of it. Also, some people have trouble recognizing some faces just like they have trouble remembering names. When researchers test people's recognition of *celebrity* faces, which are much easier to remember than some stranger we met a year ago, the average recognition is fifty percent. On top of all that, Joe is a popular guy, which means he's spending time with people in all kinds of events. In the whirlwind of Joe's life, it's probably hard for him to remember all the names *and faces*.

TAKING INVENTORY

Instead of getting bitter about Joe, I started taking inventory, because I know *I'm a blind man.* The insights about automatic humility help me see how I overlook most of the reality around me, including people in my airspace. *Now that I know how it feels to be treated this way, am I doing this to others?* I started looking at the way I treated people and sure enough, found the same problems. Not as intense as with Joe, but similar enough to set me on my heels.

Several months after the incident with Joe, I played golf at another event in the Seattle area. As I walked along, I thought about how I came across to my playing partners. Did I remember their names and faces? Was I interested in them enough to get their names and remember? Did I see them as people equally important as me?

Then later I remember seeing one of the three guys I played with at the Seattle event and for just a moment, I didn't recognize him. I didn't go as far as Joe did and reintroduce myself, but I do remember thinking, *I'm just like Joe here.*

The more I looked, the more I saw my oblivion and disregard. I wasn't seeing people right. I was disregarding my wife, my children, my business partners, my co-workers, and my friends in all sorts of ways. I started asking them, "What's it like to relate with me? When I'm with you, do I treat you well?"

They started to tell me. I was shocked to see how bad things were. Everywhere I went, I felt like I needed to apologize for being such a clod. In my oblivion, I diminished them. Not on purpose. But by default. I was treating them as less important than they really were, or treating them as if they were objects floating in my orbit, or treating them as if they didn't exist.

My wife, Sandra, likes to remind me that "it's not what you say but how you say it." Of course, she's absolutely right. Profoundly right. But in the early years of our marriage, when I was steeped in confident ignorance, I sloughed it off as woman-talk. "Listen, I'm not coming across near as bad as you're making it. Stop being so emotional."

But she wasn't being too emotional. She was seeing things for what they really were. I was deluded, because I *didn't* see things for what they really were. She was seeing right. I was seeing wrong. I was blind to the other side of me, you know, the outside of me, the side that other people see.

Everyone already knew about my problem. Even though I didn't see it, they saw it. And it affected them. They struggled just like I struggled after that incident with Joe.

Then I started to realize *how long* my mistreatment had affected people. Years after the fact, they still remember the ways I've treated them, just like I'm still remembering my incident with Joe.

Poet Maya Angelou certainly had it right when she said, "People will forget what you said. People will forget what you did. But people will never forget how you made them feel."

Then I thought about how everyone knew of my problem, but no one wanted to tell me. They just left me in my blindness like I did with Joe.

I've been monitoring myself for some time now, and I see that there's no solving my problem in one whack. It's a process. I can see people right one moment then slip into seeing people wrong the next moment. I'm constantly susceptible.

I also started realizing that everyone has this problem. My wife has this problem. My children have this problem. My business partners have this problem. Some of us have this problem in greater measure than others, to be sure, but *everyone has this problem*. We get so caught up in our own lives, so focused on our own needs, that we discount and disregard those around us. Or we value people only for the things they can do for us, instead of valuing them for who they are.

Think about your boss, your co-workers, or your relatives. Think about the people you check out your groceries or manage the register at the mall. Do you treat them the best you could, all the time?

For most, the answer is no.

We might try working on our attitude, but we slip right back into the bad attitudes we always have. We might try working on our behavior, but we go right back to doing the same things as before. We stress and strain, hacking at the branches.

Why not push the power button? Why not get to the root of the love problem? The root-level strategy is to *change the way we see people*. This automatically influences our feelings and behaviors.

DOG VIBES, CAT VIBES

Whenever I'm a keynote speaker at an event, I see something different in people's eyes. In their mannerisms and behaviors too. Most of them are interested. They're engaged. Afterward, they greet me with enthusiasm. They smile. They want to talk to me. I can tell from the body language, eye contact, and the tone in their voice: *They value me.*

Then when I go to an event where I'm not the main speaker, the vibe is different. I'm not recognized outside my limited sphere of influence, so I don't get the same engagement from people. I become invisible.

I'm okay with this, by the way. We're all busy, and we can't give everyone our full attention. I say this to point out how different these two scenarios *feel*. We can all remember times when we've felt valued. We've also all remembered times when we've felt devalued. The point is there's a major difference, and we can feel it.

Think about dogs. They're happy to see us and make eye contact. They are interested in us. When we call them, they come to us. Their mannerisms show that they see value in people. We instantly detect this and appreciate this. It's one reason we love dogs.

But cats, not as much. Sure, they're fuzzy and cute, so we love them for that. But we don't get the same sense that they value us. They don't come to us when we call, and scientific studies show that it's because they truly don't care.[50] They come when they need something from us like scratches or food. They give and receive on their terms, not ours.

There's a big difference between *dog vibe* and *cat vibe*.

In a way, we're all giving out the dog vibe or the cat vibe in each moment we're with people. We can all feel this vibe from others too.

We can also tell when people try to look like they care, but they don't. People who use tactics of influence without changing the way they see people are like cats in dog masks. We see the cat-eyes showing through the holes.

Consider smiling. The 19th-century French neurologist Guillaume Duchenne identified the difference between a fake smile and a real one based on the way the *orbicularis oculi* flexes around the eye. "The emotion of [authentic] joy," wrote Duchenne, "is expressed on the face by the combined contraction of the *zygomaticus major* muscle and the *orbicularis oculi*. The first obeys the will, but the second is only put in play by the sweet emotions of the soul."[51] The *Duchenne smile*, as it has come to be known, is an authentic smile that moves the eye muscles. But the fake smile only moves the muscles of the mouth.

The following photographs show the difference between the two smiles. Can you see it?

*The photo on the left is not an authentic expression, because it doesn't activate the **orbicularis oculi** muscles around the eyes. The photo on the right is an authentic smile. © 2016 Paul Ekman Group, LLC.*

Of course. We all can tell the difference. Except the guy doing the smiling, who thinks he's pulling it off. The only way to make a smile work is to actually see people as valuable, which automatically triggers actual positive feelings toward them.

Here's another example of how we pick up subtle cues. In one study at the University of Chicago, men were asked to look at two identical photos of the same woman. Keep in mind these were *identical* photos. They weren't the same woman in a different setting, or in different lighting, clothing, or makeup. Everything was identical, except for one touchup that participants couldn't identify when asked.

Without hesitation, the men said the photo on the one side was more attractive. They saw beauty, warmth, and femininity in one photo, but less warmth in the other. They couldn't see a physical difference between the photos, but they felt an emotional difference.

What was it? The size of the woman's *pupils*. In one photo, her pupils were retouched to be slightly larger than normal.

See for yourself. Here's a similar photo, with normal pupils on the left and larger pupils on the right. Can you see the difference?

Identical photos, with one exception: pupil size. Participants find the right photograph more warm and attractive, but cannot tell why. © 2016 Ross Van Alstine Visual Art & Photography.

Whenever we see someone as having value, it shows in our pupils. "Pupil size serves as a signal between individuals, usually at an unconscious level," writes University of Chicago professor Eckhard Hess. "What is really appealing about large pupils in a woman is that they are an indicator of interest which can be interpreted as sexual interest."

The men looked at the photo like the one on the right and thought, *That woman sees value in me.* This made them more interested in return, enlarging their pupils. "When men view a picture of a woman with large pupils, their own pupils dilate," Hess wrote. "In other words, seeing large pupils gives rise to larger pupils."[52]

This could be the physiology behind love at first sight. Say we're on a blind date. We see the other person for the first time. They're attracted to us, and as a result, their pupils are larger. We see the larger pupils, feel the attraction, and become attracted ourselves, which enlarges our pupils.

In this way, pupils have a cupid effect—they hook people up by creating a mutual attraction, and it's all running unconsciously and automatically. We have no clue what's going on in the pupils. All we know is that undeniable *loving feeling.*

WE CAN'T FAKE IT

There's no faking it. We can't choose to enlarge our pupils and contract the muscles around the eye. Which means we can tell when people value us and when they don't. The dog vibe and the cat vibe are unmistakable, because the way we see people automatically comes through in our facial expressions, our pupil size, our attitudes, our body language, and so on.

In 1975, the American rock band the Eagles released a song titled *Lyin' Eyes*, about a city girl leading a double life.

> You can't hide your lyin' eyes
> And your smile is a thin disguise.
> I thought by now you'd realize,
> there ain't no way to hide
> your lyin' eyes.

We've always known the truth of the song, but it's nice to see science back it up.

This means surface tactics of influence will backfire. Let's say we're a manager, and we learn the tactic of managing by walking around. If we fail to correct the way we see people, they'll see through it, and we'll just be the big jerk walking around. If we believe we can get out there and gladhand a few people, while thinking less of them as we do it, our beady pupils and fake smiles will give us away. If there's a cat behind the dog mask, people will see it.

There's terrific justice in this. Manipulators can't really manipulate as well as they believe. They try to lie, but their eyes tell the truth.

We've been talking a lot about the cat vibe, but let's switch over to the dog vibe for a bit. Think about how we feel when we're valued and validated. It automatically inspires us to want to be better people.

Unfortunately, this valuing doesn't happen near as much as it should. If appreciation were water, we'd all be wilted plants. But the upside is that authentic appreciation is more appreciated now than ever. When we pour the water, people come alive.

University of California psychology professor Robert Rosenthal shows how teachers who expect students to perform better actually trigger better performance. When teachers were told that a group of average students were "gifted" students, the teachers treated them like gifted students, and their grades rose.[53]

Another example of this is Alfred Oberlander, district manager of the MetLife Insurance Company, who found that when he put new agents in office groups he described as "outstanding," the agents performed better, regardless of their aptitude.[54]

Or when foremen in a factory were told that a group of female workers tested at greater intelligence and dexterity, even though they were selected at random, their production numbers went up, and the foremen later evaluated them as indeed having superior intelligence and dexterity.[55]

When people expect good things from us, we rise to the occasion. The German writer Johann Wolfgang von Goethe described this effect in his eighteenth-century novel *Wilhelm Meister's Apprenticeship*. "When we take people merely as they are," said one character in the novel, "we make them worse. When we treat them as if they were what they should be, we improve them…"[56]

TURNING THINGS AROUND

The challenge is to see people as people, of equal value and needs as us, whenever we're with them. The path to automatic love is to *see people right, every moment of sight.*

This challenge becomes particularly important in the middle of "people problems." Whenever we run into a "people problem," we run into a love test. Will we see people, even when they're hostile, as people of equal value as ourselves? Will we see problem people like Steve Irwin sees snakes?

PART 3

GOOD, EVIL, HAPPINESS, AND THE ULTIMATE HUMAN GOAL

CHAPTER 8

Maximum Good, As We See It

"We're all the same. We all want the same thing in life. Everybody going around like ants and we all want the same thing."

— ANDREA CORR, IRISH MUSICIAN

My first reaction to this Andrea Corr quote is, *Sounds like something a musician would say. On an acid trip.*

Why? Because we're clearly not all the same. Just look at American politics. Democrats the same as Republicans? The difference is massive. Right now as I write this, we're headed into an election year with Donald Trump on one side and Hillary Clinton on the other. These candidates couldn't be more different. Same is true for their followers. America is a deeply divided nation.

Then look at all the crazy stuff going on in the world, like the senseless crimes we see on the nightly news. There's a big difference between crazy criminals and peaceful citizens. Then consider ISIS. There's a big difference between terrorists and the rest of us.

We're all the same? You've got to be kidding me.

Then head to work and look at all the strange behavior on the job. There's a big difference between boss and line worker, accounting and sales, union and nonunion.

Then head home and look at how differences between people lead to domestic abuse, divorce, and wrecked families.

Country singer Billy Currington sums up the struggle in a song about an old man in a bar talking divorce, war, and politics, capped off in chorus as he says, "God is great. Beer is good. And people are crazy."[57]

But are people as crazy as they seem? The deeper I look, the less I feel that. The deeper I look, the more sense things make. The deeper I look, the more I agree with Andrea Corr.

There's a story about a successful novelist who went to a party for the launch of his book. Everyone praised his work, and he broke down in tears. But not tears of joy. Tears of grief. He felt miserable and walked out.[58]

No one could make any sense of it.

Because they looked at the surface. Once we get below ground, everything made perfect sense. "I know I'm not a good writer," he said. "And at the launch party I realized that not only is my work mediocre at best, but I have no real friends. I thought, *People won't be honest with me. They know I'm mediocre. But they keep giving me phony compliments.*"

Think about the See-Feel-Act progression here. What did the novelist see? He saw his friends as phonies, and his work as inadequate. He saw something terribly bad in his situation. And he felt bad in response. His view of himself, his work, and his "friends" triggered sadness, which in turn moved him to break down and leave the party.

Given the way he saw the situation, what he felt and did makes sense. *If* his friends really were phonies, and *if* his work was mediocre, his emotions and behaviors were sensible.

This doesn't mean he's right to see things that way. He might have been seeing the situation completely wrong that night. His wrong way of seeing automatically influenced wrong ways of feeling. But the key here is that it made perfect sense if we accept his point of view.

Once I understood this, I started to question my assumptions about "senseless crimes" and "crazy people." Every time I got the chance to see from the other person's perspective, what seemed senseless made sense. I couldn't find any senseless crimes. I couldn't find any crazy people. Sure, there are some out there, but nowhere near as many as we think.

Which made me wonder if Andrea Corr wasn't merely right, but profoundly right.

BIPOLAR SEE, FEEL, ACT

"Careful experiments show that you have a like-dislike reaction to everything you are experiencing," writes University of Virginia psychology professor Jonathan Haidt, "even if you're not aware of the experience."[59] We're always evaluating what we see, then triggering an emotional response to like or dislike.

Look again at the way I defined the term, *See*. It is to characterize and evaluate something as good or bad. In every experience, we instantly ask and answer two questions. *What is happening? How good or bad is it?*

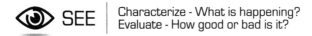

SEE | Characterize - What is happening?
Evaluate - How good or bad is it?

To *See* is to characterize and evaluate something as good or bad. It is to ask and answer the questions, what is happening, and how good or bad is it?

Notice the two directions—good and bad—in the way we evaluate. Experts describe these two directions with the term, *bipolar*. Not bipolar in terms of bipolar disorder, but bipolar in the sense of "two poles" or "two directions." A light switch is bipolar because it works in two directions. A thermometer is bipolar, measuring in two directions. A weathervane isn't bipolar, because it measures wind in more than two directions: north, south, east, west, and so on.

With this in mind, let's look at the bipolar ideas in the other elements of the See-Feel-Act progression. Here's how I defined the term, *Feel*.

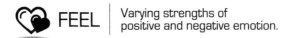

FEEL | Varying strengths of positive and negative emotion.

To *Feel* is to experience varying strengths of positive and negative emotion.

Notice the bipolar terms, *positive* and *negative*, to describe emotion. "Emotion is the process which starts when something is perceived and appraised," writes psychologist Magda Arnold. "We decide that it is good or bad for us."[60] When we see something good, we like it. We react with positive emotion. When we see something bad, we dislike it. We react with negative emotion.

We don't just react emotionally. We react behaviorally as well. We take action to create more good and less bad in our lives.

Here are the elements of the See-Feel-Act progression with their bipolar descriptions.

SEE	FEEL	ACT
Good and bad.	Good, bad, like, dislike, pleasure and pain.	For more good and less bad.

The See-Feel-Act progression works in two basic directions. We see good and bad, then react emotionally, feeling good and bad, liking and disliking, feeling pleasure and pain. Then we act in ways that increase good and decrease bad in our lives.

Bipolar language runs through the entire See-Feel-Act progression, showing that our natural instincts run from our basic ideas about good and bad. We see everything in two basic ways, and we respond to these two basic ways of seeing.

Human nature is bipolar.

All this bipolar discussion reveals a constant human goal: *more good, less bad.* Think back to the opening quote of this chapter, where Andrea Corr said, "We're all the same. We all want the same thing in life. Everybody going around like ants and we all want the same thing." I'm not sure if Andrea was ready to explain what that "same thing" was, but let's answer it for her. We all want *more good and less bad.* This is the universal and constant human goal.

MORE GOOD, LESS BAD

Let's test this idea of *more good and less bad* by thinking of all the things we want in life. We want a fulfilling life. A great job. A rewarding career.

Or maybe we want a cold soda. With pizza. And a trim waist. In a perfect world, we'd have it all.

We want meaningful relationships. We want more money and less hassle. We want a better grip on our emotions. Oh, and we want a soy latte. Then we want directions to the nearest bathroom.

On our job, we want productivity and harmony. We want freedom from fear and office politics. We want a reasonable boss, the right hours, a flexible schedule. And fair pay.

We don't just want the low-level things. We want higher-level things too. We want to make a difference in the world. We want freedom and peace. We want to live, to learn, to love, and leave a legacy.[61] We want our lives to have meaning.

If we boiled this never-ending list down into its common theme, couldn't we say that it is *more good and less bad?* On and on we go. Everything we can think of pursuing sums up nicely under the goal of *more good and less bad.*

MORE GOOD

Now that we're solid on the fundamental drive for *more good and less bad,* let's simplify things.

Isn't *less bad* a good thing?

Hassle is bad. So less hassle is good. Debt is bad. That means less debt is good. Crime is bad. So less crime is good. Whenever we take stuff away from the bad side, we're doing something good.

Let's say we're taking a walk in the woods near our home, and it starts to rain. We're wet, cold, and thirty minutes from the nearest fireplace. Once we get home, we feel relief, because our situation was bad and now it's not. Relief is a good thing.

So we can simplify the idea of *more good and less bad* and just call it *more good.*

- It's good to arrest criminals because it reduces the bad things they'll do in society.
- It's good to buy mints because it takes away something bad—foul breath.
- It's good to get rest because it takes away something bad—fatigue.

Think about how economists describe the stuff we buy as "goods." Every product in the market claims to do good things for people by relieving pain or promoting pleasure. Preparation H and Tylenol relieve pain. Sweet tea and country fairs promote pleasure.

Just to clarify, there are things that seem good now but lead to bad later. People commit adultery and take heroin because it seems good in the moment. But they regret it because of the bad it causes later on. So if we're truly interested in having more good in our lives, we'll avoid adultery and heroin. The only reason people do these things is a lack of foresight. In their moments of indulgence, they see only two seconds into the future, much like a chimp or a boy band might. They live out the song lyric that reads, "All that counts is here and now."[62]

If all that counts is here and now, heroin and adultery are good. Even the heroin user and adulterer want *more good,* which is why they do what they do. They just seek *more good* in the wrong way, and end up with a lot less good than they anticipated.

FROM MORE GOOD TO MAXIMUM GOOD

Now that we've established the idea of *more good* as a universal goal, let's take one last step up from *more good* to *maximum good.* We don't just want to go to any good movie; we want to go to the best movie showing now. We don't just want more good from our work team. We want as much good as they can create. We want the best we can have under the circumstances.

Imagine an apple, an orange, and a banana on a table. We're hungry enough to eat just one, and all three seem good to us, so which do we choose? The answer is, *the one we see as maximum good in the moment.*

Let's say we think the banana is good, but we think the apple is better, and the orange is best. We don't choose the banana or the apple, even though they're good. We're looking to *maximize the good,* so we choose the orange.

Maximum good isn't just about maximum quantity, because there are many situations in life where more is worse, not better. Consider pepper. I think a sprinkle of pepper on macaroni and cheese is pure heaven. But a tablespoon of pepper—yuck. Same with honey. Solomon, the ancient king, wrote, "If you find honey, eat just enough. Too much of it and you will vomit."[63] A teaspoon of honey on toast is good. But if we glug down a full cup, we'll throw up.

As with pepper and honey, so with many other things. Time with loved ones is a good thing. But too much time and we're sick of them. Time on vacation is a good thing. But too much leisure is a fast track to depression.[64] Fulfilling work is a good thing. But an entire life at the office is no life at all.

The lesson is, *too much of a good thing is a bad thing.* Whenever we get beyond a certain point, good isn't as good any more. Much of life follows an *Inverted-U* pattern, like we see below.

The Inverted-U. Our sense of good increases with quantity up to a certain point, then decreases.

This Inverted-U shows how our sense of good maxes out somewhere in the middle of the curve. Past a certain point, some things aren't as good as they were. We hit maximum good in the middle, then the goodness declines.

Just recently, I heard a management slogan, *Pressure makes diamonds.* Managers might hear this and get inspired to turn up the pressure to bring out the best in people. To a point, it will. But past a point, this approach backfires, because people don't respond to intense pressure like carbon does.

There are other pressure metaphors to sloganize, like *pressure busts a pipe* and *pressure makes explosions* and *high blood pressure makes heart attacks*, but I don't see managers sloganizing those. Too much pressure at work is a bad thing. It might be why the turnover is so high and the morale is so low.

The point is to find the sweet spot in the middle of the curve, where there's *maximum good. Maximum good* is the high point on the graph and the high principle for what we all want. It's the summary and finish line of human intention.

WHAT ABOUT EVIL?

But wait, some might think, *what about all the evil in the world? What about Hitler? ISIS? Colombian drug lords?* How can we say that everyone wants maximum good? What about murderers and pedophiles? The world is filled with evil people whose primary goal is clearly not maximum good.

As crazy as it sounds, even evil characters doing a lot of evil things are pursuing this primary goal. They are doing what *seems good* to them. In a 2015 television series on A&E Network titled *8 Minutes*, a Houston pastor and a team of former prostitutes offer working girls an escape. Pastor Kevin Brown poses as a john and invites prostitutes to a hotel room for a trick, then switches things up with an intervention. He and his team offer a new life—with food, shelter, social support, jobs, and rehab. They know they have about eight minutes to convince girls to escape before the pimp shows up.

As I watched this series, I was amazed at how many girls wanted to stay in the life. Yes, they *wanted* to stay in the life. They refused the offer.

Take Jenny, for example. She passed on Kevin's offer, because she saw good in her situation. "I'm happy with my life, because I've got a good pimp now," said Jenny as they recorded her on a hidden camera. "He gave me a bank account and doesn't beat me like the previous pimp."[65]

Most people would believe Jenny's in a bad place, but she sees herself in a good place. There's a lot of evil in her situation, but she doesn't see it that way. She sees good things in prostitution.

Now consider Hitler and the Nazis. There's no greater example of evil in the modern world than in Hitler, the German dictator responsible for the horrific death of almost six million Jews and five million ethnic minorities in the Holocaust, as well as the instigator of World War II, which turned entire nations to rubble and eventually took the lives of over sixty million people. Did Hitler think he was doing evil? Did the Nazis think they were doing wrong?

"The answer appears to be no," according to social scientist Roy Baumeister, one of the world's foremost experts on violence and cruelty:

Perhaps it should be a qualified no, for many of them had serious doubts and misgivings, and some objected strongly to the Nazi regime's actions as morally wrong. But these people, who saw or suspected evil, were not the ones most involved; indeed, many of them ended up withdrawing from active participation in the killings. The people who carried out the worst acts did not believe they were doing evil, or at most they struggled between doubts and conflicting obligations.[66]

The Nazis were utopians who believed they were building a better society. They characterized the Jews as dangerous enemies of the German nation, and therefore felt it was a good thing to move them into isolation, like the United States had done by moving Native Americans to reservations. The Nazis saw themselves getting justice for their unfair treatment in the aftermath of World War I.

The Nazis also saw Jews as sub-human, as *untermensch*. In their view, the Jews were dangerous animals, like wolves that attack ranchers and cattle, like rats that spread disease. The man directly reporting to Hitler and responsible for the concentration camps, Heinrich Himmler, began the "extermination" with what he felt was a "sense of decency." "We will never be cruel when it is unnecessary," he said in a speech to the military officers carrying out the executions. "We Germans are the only nation in the world with a decent attitude toward animals, and we will have a decent attitude toward these human animals….This is a page of glory in our history….We had the moral right, we had the duty to our people, to destroy this people which wanted to destroy us."[67]

There's no question: the Nazis were the epitome of evil. But here's the key point again: *They didn't see themselves doing evil.* In their eyes, they were doing something good—maximum good, given their circumstances.

This is scary. It means people can see wrong and feel wrong and act wrong in response, all the while believing they are seeing right, feeling right, and doing right. If we see things the wrong way, meaning, we see things wrong and think we see right, all our emotions and decisions and behaviors will be wrong yet feel right to us.

In the opening pages of his book *Evil: Inside Human Violence and Cruelty*, Baumeister echoes this fear. "One starts a work like this wondering, 'Why is there evil?' But after reviewing what is known about the causes of aggression, violence, oppression, and other forms of evil, one is led to the opposite question: Why isn't there more evil than there is?"[68]

MAXIMUM GOOD, LIMITED ATTENTION

In the *Automatic Humility* chapter, we learned how our attention is highly selective, like a tight spotlight in the dark theater of reality. When our attention is focused on one thing, we don't see other things. On top of that, Princeton psychologist George Miller demonstrated how we can only hold about seven pieces of information in working memory at one time.[69] So when we go to appraise maximum good in a situation, we do so with limited attention and a short list of relevant factors.

Think back to the heroin users and adulterers. They limited their attention to the moment and didn't make space to think about the future impact of their choices. Heroin and adultery was maximum good in the moment of choice. Not in later moments, of course. But they didn't think about the later moments.

The way out of the trap is to be careful about how we see. We must carefully manage our attention, staying gripped to the rope lines I mentioned in Chapter Six. Remember the analogy? I described the extreme weather in Thule, Greenland, and how the soldiers set up rope lines between buildings so they wouldn't get lost in the flurries. The only way to stay alive was to keep a solid grip. In the same way, the only way we'll make it through the flurry of temptations in life is to manage our attention. Staying focused on the right things is like staying gripped to the rope. It's a matter of life and death.

Another qualifier for *maximum good* is our limited capacity to experience good things. There are over six hundred thousand restaurants in the United States,[70] but we only have enough appetite for one meal a night. If we visited one new restaurant every night, we'd need *seventeen hundred years* to visit them all. And that's just in the United States.

In a world of almost limitless options, we have an extremely limited capacity to experience good. We have to choose what we feel is best from a massive array of alternatives.

Another maximum good qualifier is *chance*. If someone promises good to us, but we believe there's no chance of getting it, we'll discount the promise. If we believe there's no chance we can achieve something, we don't let ourselves even consider it. There's a new job opening in the company, but we don't believe we can beat the other applicants, so we don't even put in for it. Our appraisal of maximum good always accounts for the *chance of good*.

As with chance, so with *time*. Ten thousand dollars today is a good thing, but that same ten thousand dollars ten years from now, or fifty years from now, isn't nearly as good. It diminishes in goodness like distant buildings get smaller on the horizon. Long-term goals aren't nearly as compelling as short-term goals because of the time factor.

Given these and other qualifiers, let's change the wording of our universal human goal to read, *maximum good, as we see it*. We want as much good as we can have, given all our constraints. Our beliefs about what is best differs from person to person, and our brains can only process so much information as we consider our options, and we have to choose, because we can't have it all. So we choose what we think is maximum good in each moment, given the constraints.

We don't wake up every morning reminding ourselves we want maximum good. We just want it. It's instinctive. It's the prime principle, the universal goal that governs all our decisions.

INFLUENCING WITH MAXIMUM GOOD IN MIND

Now that we understand this prime principle, it should help us see people in a different light. Everyone around us, from the sinner to the saint, pursues *maximum good, as they see it*. People are doing what they think is best, for their own reasons, in everything they do.

Influencers who understand this are more effective than those who believe everyone sees the same as they do, or that people are senseless idiots.

- CEOs and managers need to see workers constantly pursuing maximum good as they see it, no matter how it appears on the surface.
- Parents need to see their children as constantly pursuing maximum good as they see it, as misguided as a child's ideas of maximum good might be.
- Peers should see their co-workers and friends as always attempting to maximize good, as they see it, given the circumstances.

Effective influencers see a question floating over everyone's head, and always work to answer it from the other person's perspective: *Why is your request more important than my current priorities?* If we ignore this floating question, or don't see it in the first place, we won't get cooperation.

PAUL, ROBERT, AND THE WISE MANAGER

Effective leaders also know that people change for their own reasons, not the leader's reasons. So they work to discover those reasons and connect them to shared goals.

Let's imagine two co-workers, Paul and Robert, have been fighting for weeks and bringing the whole department down. You're the manager, and your goal is to get Paul and Robert to get along.

First, you sit down with Paul to talk things through. "Paul, I've seen the trouble between you and Robert, and I'd like to help," you say.

"Robert is the cause of it," says Paul. "He's saying bad things about me. He's a backstabbing jerk."

"There's trouble between you two, that's for sure. Why might you want to change things?"

"I'm tired of it," Paul says. "I can't sleep, I hate coming to work, and I can't get things done. Robert is stressing me to the limit."

Notice how you ask Paul to voice *his reasons* for change instead of offering yours. Why? Paul's reasons are different than yours, and more important to him than yours will ever be.

"So it sounds like change here would help you sleep better, make your work better, and help you get more done," you say. "Any other reasons you might want this resolved?"

"I just don't think it's right to always be at each other's throats," Paul says. "I grew up watching my parents fight and I hated it. It was awful."

Now you're getting to more important reasons. Notice that they still aren't your reasons.

"Okay. Imagine you worked things out with Robert, maybe even became friends," you say. "What might the positives be?"

"Man, it would be a relief," says Paul. "I could get back to doing my work instead of feeling so stressed. It would be nice to have an ally in Robert instead of an enemy. I wouldn't have to watch my back all the time. I'm always wondering who he's talking to behind my back."

"Got it," you say. "You'd have an ally at work instead of an enemy. You'd feel relief. And you'd get more work done. Why are these important to you?"

"Because I love my work when it's not so stressful," says Paul. "I want to get along with Robert, because I don't want to live in strife like I see in so many people. My dad and mom divorced when I was ten, and it wrecked my world. I don't want to do that to others."

"Okay, I'm getting the picture," you say. "Getting along with Robert would mean a lot to you. You'd work better, feel better, and sleep better. You'd have the peace of mind that he's for you and not against you. You wouldn't have to keep watching your back. And you'd get back to loving your work like before. These are really good reasons to get things resolved. So, what's the next step, if any?"

"Well, I could go talk to Robert," says Paul. "I could at least deal with things from my side. I've been saying bad things about him too. I could tell him I'm sorry for that and see what happens."

"Yes, that sounds good," you say. "How about I have a quick talk with Robert like I just did with you and see if he'd be interested in a meeting? I won't say anything about what you've said to me, I'll just let you talk it through with him. Let me get back to you."

"That sounds good," says Paul.

What did you do to solve the problem? You helped Paul make his own case for change. You worked with his reasons, not yours. Here are the steps you took:

> First, you asked, "Why might you want to make this change?" You got Paul voicing his own reasons for the change, not your reasons.
>
> You wrote down Paul's reasons as you heard them, and restated them to Paul, in his own words. You helped Paul build his own case for the good in the change.
>
> Then you said, "Imagine you changed. What might the positives be?" You got Paul to talk about the good in the change. You encouraged Paul to use his own words because you know the power of words. You wrote down the outcomes as you heard them, using spoken words and written words to help Paul build a case for change.
>
> Then you asked, "Why are these positives important to you?" This encouraged Paul to think deeper about the good things in the change, and speak them out. Again, you listened and wrote.

Then you summarized everything Paul said, saying it again. You repeated Paul's own spoken words to help him cement the good reasons in his mind.

Then, after building a solid case for the good in the change, you asked, "So what's the next step, if any?" You encouraged Paul to think about the next thing he could do.[71]

This approach helps people build an effective case for maximum good, from their perspective, not yours.

THE HARMING HELPER

Unfortunately, most follow a different tactic than you did with Paul. They see what's wrong and want to make it right. So they *tell people what to do.* They give direction, hit resistance, and turn up the pressure. "Paul, bury the hatchet with Robert," they say. "You're making trouble and it's bringing everyone down."

Instead of taking the approach you took earlier, they rely on a *directing style* that backfires almost every time.

Motivation experts William Miller and Stephen Rollnick ask us to try a thought experiment where we choose something we've been thinking about changing, then imagine someone telling us to change, telling us reasons to change, telling us how to change, then telling us to get to it. Here's what they say will happen:

We have used this exercise all over the world and people's responses are remarkably consistent. A few find it helpful, perhaps one in twenty (just enough to keep helpers doing it), but most often, the "helped" person feels some if not all of the following:

- Angry (agitated, annoyed, irritated, not heard, not understood)
- Defensive (judged, justifying, oppositional, unwilling to change)
- Uncomfortable (ashamed, overwhelmed, eager to leave)
- Powerless (passive, one-down, discouraged, disengaged)

In fact, sometimes the person being "helped" concludes that he or she actually doesn't want to make the change![72]

Think back to Paul. He saw reasons to reconcile with Robert, but also reasons to keep fighting. He was caught in the middle, weighing things out.

So when someone with a directing style launches into reasons to change, Paul voices a case for the other side: "Yeah, but you don't see how Robert has been treating me," he says. The helper inadvertently encourages an opposing view.

Imagine a "helper" confronting someone about smoking: "You've got to quit," they say. "You're going to die of cancer." They expect this to work. They imagine the smoker saying, "Oh, I didn't know that. Thank you for telling me. I'll quit right away."

But that never happens. To bring balance to the discussion, the smoker voices reasons to keep smoking. "Smoking calms my nerves and keeps me trim," he says. "That's a health benefit. I know people who smoke and live to a hundred. I'm not sure the risk is as high as people say."

The helper turns up the pressure. "Good grief, that's ridiculous. Here, let me look at your cigarettes. See the label? It reads, 'Smoking causes lung cancer, heart disease, emphysema, and may complicate pregnancy.'"

Again, the helper imagines the smoker saying, "Oh, I never saw that. Now I'm convinced."

But the smoker says, "Yes, but…" He voices more reasons to keep smoking, and feels angry, defensive, uncomfortable, or powerless.

And more convinced to keep smoking.

"People learn about their own attitudes and beliefs in the same way that others learn them: by hearing themselves talk," write Miller and Rollnick. "From this perspective, if you as a helper are arguing for change and [they are] arguing against it, you've got it exactly backward."[73]

MAXIMUM GOOD, AS WE SEE IT

The ultimate human goal is *maximum good, as we see it*. We're all the same in that we all pursue this goal, all the time.

When we see things the wrong way, our ultimate goal gets hijacked for mediocrity instead of excellence. Or evil instead of good. And because we don't often question our way of seeing, the wrong direction can feel like the right direction. There's a sense that we're being true to ourselves, even doing right in a situation, when we're doing wrong. Perhaps horribly wrong.

This leads me to believe Andrea Corr was right. We are the same. Deep down, we all want the same things.

When we look at people, we should see them as similar to us, constantly pursuing *maximum good, as they see it*. Even when they're opposing us. Even when they're doing things we think are crazy or evil.

People aren't senseless idiots or monsters.

They're all just like you and me.

Except for the way they see.

CHAPTER 9

Automatic Evil

"There is a way that appears to be right, but in the end it leads to death."

— Solomon, Israelite king

When I was in college, someone on the freeway pulled a gun on me. I was almost the victim of what local news says is a "senseless crime."

But I was there and can tell you, it wasn't senseless at all. It was just one more piece of proof that there aren't near as many senseless crimes as we imagine. They only seem senseless on the surface.

It all started one evening at an on-ramp to the Interstate 5 freeway in downtown Seattle. I sat in my car in traffic, behind an old truck at the Olive Way freeway entrance, on my way to the University of Washington.

The old truck wasn't moving, so I honked my horn.

Still not moving. I honked again.

In that moment, here was my See-Feel-Act progression. I saw that the trucker guy wasn't paying attention, and I saw myself being delayed unnecessarily. I felt impatient and irritated. So I acted by honking twice.

SEE ▶ FEEL ▶ ACT

Trucker delaying me unnecessarily.	Impatient and irritated.	Honk twice.

My See-Feel-Act progression at the Interstate 5 on-ramp.

Then I discovered I was seeing the situation wrong. Trucker-guy wasn't moving because there was a mom pushing a stroller in the cross-walk ahead of him.

Yikes.

When I saw the mother and child, everything changed. No more irritation or impatience. Definitely no more honking. I felt terrible and wished I could apologize.

Consider the automatic influence here. When the way I saw the situation changed, the way I felt and acted changed automatically.

Now, trucker guy didn't know this, of course, so he gave me the finger and sped down the ramp. No doubt, *See*, *Feel*, and *Act* were progressing for him too. He saw me as an impatient jerk who didn't care about women and children. And because he saw me this way, he felt angry and acted.

 SEE ▶ FEEL ▶ ACT

Impatient, careless jerk behind me.	Angry.	Give him the finger.

The truck-driver's See-Feel-Act progression at the Interstate 5 on-ramp.

This should have been the end of it. But stupid kid that I was, I thought, *I should catch up to him on the freeway to apologize.* The least I could do is roll down the window and shout, "I'm sorry!" as we drove along.

But it was twilight. He wouldn't see my facial expressions. All he would see was an angry guy speeding up to him and rolling down the window. But I didn't think about that. I was locked into my own view.

Within a minute, I caught up. I rolled down the window and saw him pointing a gun right at me.

Good Lord!

I braked and almost swerved off the road.

Fortunately, he kept driving and that was the end of it. I drove home, my heart pounding out of my chest.

Think about the incident from the trucker's point of view. *Some jerk just honked at me. Doesn't care about people at all. Yeah, I gave him the finger. He deserved it. Someone's got to put jerks like that in their place.*

Then a minute later on the freeway, think about his view of me speeding up on him. *Am I seeing this right? Look at him, he's coming after me. Must be crazy. Better get out my gun. Look, he's rolling down his window, gonna shoot me. What a lunatic! I'd better be ready to protect myself and shoot first.*

The way the trucker felt and acted naturally followed his view of the situation.

The problem is, both our views were wrong. We both had mischaracterized each other. It almost killed me and almost earned trucker-guy an orange jumpsuit.

When we don't accurately see a person or a situation, our emotions and behaviors are wrong. The graphic shows how *See-wrong* automatically influences *Feel-wrong* and *Act-wrong*.

| See wrong. | Feel wrong. | Act wrong. |

When we see things the wrong way, this automatically influences us to feel wrong and act wrong.

APPEARANCE AND REALITY

What if we think we see right when we're really seeing wrong? Then we'll feel the wrong ways and do the wrong things, while believing we're feeling and doing the right things.

Misperception is a root of evil.

It's like a poisonous weed that a gardener believes is a valued plant. The gardener cultivates the plant, fertilizing and watering and caring for it, in what he or she believes is the pursuit of maximum good. In this way, evil flourishes.

Baumeister, our expert social scientist, tells of a woman's "brush with evil" in an airport cafeteria:

Susan bought a bag of chips and a diet cola. Then she looked for a table. None were free. She'd have to share with somebody.

So she sat down next to a reasonably well dressed man who was by himself, reading a paper. As she sat, they briefly made eye contact; he seemed to nod slightly and went back to his paper.

Nervous about the close encounter, she busied herself with her snack. She set down her diet cola, took a sip, then grabbed a chip.

The man looked up suddenly from his newspaper. He looked angry, and fixed his eyes on hers, like a predator seeing prey. Amazingly, he slowly reached his hand into her bag of chips and ate one.

Her heart pounded in fear. What kind of person is this? And what should I do? She didn't want to make a scene, so she forced herself to take another drink and nervously took another chip from the bag.

He glared at her again. It was a hostile, motionless, evil glare. When she first sat down, he struck her as a calm gentleman. But now, a psychopath maybe? He reached out again and took another of her chips. Now she knew he wasn't just helping himself one time, as if to say she owed him a chip for sitting at his table. He was totally out of bounds.

They didn't speak a single word, but intently took turns drawing chips, until the bag was empty. She never felt so violated in her life. He looked at her the whole time, one stolen chip after another.

Finally, she'd had enough. She grabbed her bag and walked out.

She got to her gate a few minutes early, heart still pounding, unable to grasp what manner of person she had just encountered. What sort of people just help themselves to a stranger's food in a restaurant?

She learned the answer sooner than she expected. When she reached into her bag to get her ticket, she discovered her own bag of chips. Somehow, when she paid for the snack, she put her chips into her bag. At the table, she and the mysterious stranger shared his chips, not hers. She herself was the sort of person who just helped herself to a stranger's food in a restaurant.[74]

Susan saw wrong. She saw the food as hers and the man as a thief, so she felt anger toward him. Then she acted wrong and stole his food. Her misperception triggered the wrong emotion and behavior.

Later, she realized she was seeing wrong. But what if she had never found her chips? What if she had put them on the ground instead of in her purse? To this day, she'd be under the impression that the man had wronged *her*. She'd feel justified in what she'd done.

Susan's misperception was the root of the wrong things she did. She did wrong, all the while believing she was doing right.

INSIDIOUS INTEGRITY

Our sense of integrity, ironically, can inspire a lot of evil.

That deserves explanation, because integrity, last I checked, is a completely good thing—a sense of consistency and soundness, the opposite of dishonesty, duplicity, and deceit. People of integrity are complete, undivided, and true to themselves.

In See-Feel-Act terms, integrity is alignment between the elements. We're true to the way we see things. We're honest about our feelings, not two-faced. We say what we mean and mean what we say. There's a sense of alignment between our perceptions, feelings, and actions.

When we're in alignment, it feels right. There's a sense of soundness that we often interpret as confirmation we're doing the right thing.

Even when we're doing the wrong thing.

Perhaps this is what is meant by the saying, "The road to hell is paved with good intentions."

When we carry around wrong views of people and self and life and situations, but believe we see right, *doing wrong feels right*. We sense the right alignment in our gut, but overlook the misperception. Misperception gets smuggled in under the guise of good alignment.

I call this *insidious integrity*. Integrity in and of itself is good, but when combined with misperception, integrity promotes evil. When we are insistently consistent, but unwilling to question the way we see, we do evil while thinking we do good.

LEXUS, AUDI, AND SELF-DECEPTION

Imagine we're buying a new car and are torn between two models: Lexus and Audi. The Lexus has better gas mileage and a better warranty. The Audi has a better look and a better price.

We compare feature after feature, the pros and cons of each, yet we're still dead in the middle. We can't decide. But our lease is up and we need a car, so almost impulsively, we choose the Lexus. We sign papers and drive it home.

After the decision, our opinion about Lexus and Audi changes. We start playing up the benefits of the Lexus. *That warranty is fantastic. I love the gas mileage. These seat heaters are really cool.*

At the same time, we start playing down the benefits of the Audi. *The Audi styling isn't that great from behind. The interior isn't as practical. The Audi cost less, but when you think about overall expense, the savings disappear.* We feel better and better about our choice over time. It seems obvious that Lexus is better than Audi.

Before we made a choice, we saw Lexus and Audi as equally good. But then we made a choice and created a misalignment. We felt good about Audi. We came very close to choosing Audi. But we didn't. There's a sense of loss in this, a sense that something's wrong and needs to be made right. We're out of alignment, and we need to restore alignment.

There are a couple ways to do this. First, we can change our choice. We can tell ourselves *that was a bad decision* and return the car. Or we can go back and buy the Audi too—one for daily driving, the other for the weekend. But if we don't change our choice, we tend to change our mind to accommodate our choice.

Here's the big question: Before we chose the Lexus, were we seeing both cars accurately? Pretty much. We were torn between the two because they were equally good.

Then, after the choice, did we see more accurately or less accurately?

The answer is, *less accurately.* We distorted our view to feel better about our decision.

Whenever we make a bad decision, and don't immediately acknowledge it, the need for consistency encourages self-deception. It motivates us to change our minds to justify the choice instead of admitting it was a bad one.

Let's say Janine runs the sales team at Henning Design. She fires Emily, a top salesperson. The true reason was envy. Emily made more money than Janine, and people liked Emily more. So Janine wanted to cut Emily down to size.

But Janine won't admit this. She won't call Emily back, apologize, and rehire her. So, what does she do to feel better about her choice? She plays up negatives about Emily and plays down positives. *Emily wanted too much time off. Emily's success was a threat to the company. Emily wasn't all that successful, anyway. There are better salespeople out there, and releasing Emily makes room for new people.*

Janine made a bad decision, and deep down she knew it. But the more she plays Emily down, the better she feels. What didn't seem right before seems perfectly right after.

COGNITIVE DISSONANCE

"Inconsistency among beliefs or behaviors," writes Stanford social scientist Leon Festinger, "will cause an uncomfortable psychological tension."[75] He called it *cognitive dissonance*.

If two things don't fit together in our minds, our system goes to work to cure the misfit. We want things to make sense. We want things to be consistent. To be right.

When the picture frame is cockeyed on the wall, we want to straighten it out. Same with our psychology. We want things to be right, properly aligned, consistent, and fair.

Think about the type in this book. It all lines up on each side. It has straight edges. It's what we call "justified" type. Justification feels good to us.

But when things don't seem to line up, we feel uncomfortable.

Consider the psychological tension caused by the "Stroop Effect." To create this effect, researchers first ask a participant to read a list of words like this: GREEN, RED, BLUE, PURPLE.

But these aren't just words. They are *colored* words. In the experiments, each word's color is matched with the type. The word "GREEN" is set in green-colored type, "RED" is set in red-colored type, and so on. These are easy lists of words to read.

But what happens when researchers switch the color of the type? How well does the participant read the word "GREEN" when the type for the word "GREEN" is colored red?

The answer is, not very well. It takes longer to read the words right, and participants often misread the words entirely, because there's a misfit between the name of the word and the color of the word.

I've tried Stroop tests. They're irritating! I'm not comfortable reading the misfit words. I think, *If I find the idiot who did this, I'm going give him a piece of my mind.* These words are contradictions and we're uncomfortable reading them.

This is cognitive dissonance.

Then, when a misfit becomes a fit, there's a sense of relief. What felt wrong now feels right.

The problem is, alignment isn't the only thing that matters. Truth matters too. Good judgment is based on *alignment and truth*. When we believe a lie, but feel alignment, things might seem right when they're wrong. Misperception and good alignment can lure us to believe we're thinking right and feeling right and doing right when we're doing the exact opposite. We've fallen prey to *automatic evil.*

Solomon the Israelite king described this trap. "There is a way that appears to be right, but in the end it leads to death."[76]

THE GAME OF LIFE

When we look out at the world, or look into our company, or look at our relationships, what do we see?

- Cutthroat competition?
- A dog-eat-dog world?
- Survival of the fittest?

Do we see life as fundamentally *competitive*? Or do we see life as fundamentally *cooperative*?

- A rising tide floats all the boats.
- There's more than enough for everyone.
- When we help others, we help ourselves.

These two ways of seeing have a profound impact on our motivations, our behaviors, and our sense of right and wrong.

I can illustrate this with a game of ping-pong. Imagine two people playing in front of an audience that they ask to keep score.

The first serve leads to a long volley, back and forth between the players. Then player one misses the ball.

Then in the second volley, player two misses the ball.

Then in the third volley, player two misses the ball again.

They stop the game.

What's the score? And who won?

The audience says the score is two to one. Player one wins.

But the players disagree. They ask a judge, who had been standing at the sideline, to tell them the score.

The judge simply says, "Fourteen."

The judge is right.

Seems senseless, doesn't it?

It turns out the audience misunderstood the game. It was "high volley" ping-pong, where the players scored the times they could hit the ball back and forth without a drop. It was a *cooperative* game, not the *competitive* game we normally play. The first volley was fourteen shots back and forth. It was the longest of the three. The second was ten shots. The third, seven.

Same ping-pong table. Same paddles. Same motions. But a different way of seeing the game. And a different sense of what behaviors are right and wrong.

In high-volley, slamming the ball is stupid. It's the wrong thing to do. But in traditional ping-pong, it is expected.

In the same way, we can see life as a cooperative or competitive game. Our different views automatically influence different emotions and behaviors.

PLAYING THE RIGHT GAME

Life offers both competitive and cooperative situations. When we mistake a cooperative situation for a competitive one, we do a lot of evil "in the name of the game."

- Work teams compete against each other instead of supporting each other.
- Co-workers backstab each other in the name of competition.
- People hide helpful information from each other.
- People compare themselves with each other, grappling for psychological status.
- Husbands and wives compete for the attention of their children instead of ditching insecurities and working together.

There are so many situations in life where it's just plain wrong to take a competitive mindset.

Contrary to what many believe, life is mostly cooperative. In most social situations, be it a conversation between friends, or a work environment, or a marriage, everyone benefits from cooperation. When two people smile at each other as they walk past, each one gains goodwill they didn't have before.

Even the free market, which is usually seen as competitive, is mostly cooperative. Whenever there's free trade, there's cooperation. Say we go to the store and buy a banana. What do we say to the clerk? *Thank you.* What does the clerk say to us? *Thank you.* We both win because the clerk wanted the dollar more than the banana, and we wanted the banana more than the dollar. Cooperation helped us both.

But we tend to believe the opposite: *Store owners are greedy; all they think about is taking my money.* Maybe the store owners see us the same way: *Customers are greedy. All they think about is taking my bananas.*

In the cooperative mindset, there's more than enough good to go around, because everyone contributes. But in the competitive mindset, there's not enough good to go around, so you've got to take what you can get from people. The competitive mindset sees life as a pie. There's only so much. The cooperative mindset, on the other hand, sees life as a potluck. Everyone makes and brings their own pies. There's more than enough for everyone, because pies are created, not just consumed.

Some people confuse the competitive for cooperative view when it comes to business, so they think *making money is taking money.* Wealthy people get wealthy by taking from the poor.

This is one reason screenwriters portray business people as evil. When we see making money as taking from others, it's easy to make business leaders into villains, because they're the biggest makers and takers of them all. But if we see business leaders as givers as well as takers, the view changes. Now they're the biggest givers of them all.

My point is, the game of life is mostly high-volley ping-pong, not traditional ping-pong. If we misunderstand the game, we'll do wrong things, thinking all along we're doing right things. We slam the ball when we should be lobbing it.

Here's a way we can check our mindset: Do we withhold information, praise, involvement, and encouragement from people? When others win, and it's not at our personal expense, are we happy for them? If we live in a cooperative mindset, we want them to win. Their win is our win, because they're our friends. But if we live in a competitive mindset, we want them to lose.

We fall into the trap of automatic evil when we confuse cooperative realities with competitive ones.

THE HEAT OF EMOTION

Another reason for automatic evil is the heat of emotion. We get angry and do something we regret. We feel a flash of fear and do something rash. It seemed like the right way to act, but later on we saw we were wrong.

Why does this happen? Much of it boils down to the way emotion influences perception.

Prior to this point, I've only been saying that perception influences emotion, not the other way around.

But now it looks like I'm reversing position, because I'm saying that perception doesn't just influence emotion, but emotion also influences perception. The arrow of influence goes both ways.

Here's how we sort it out. Perception is the *initial trigger* of emotion. But emotion can have a powerful influence on the way we see things *next*. Emotion intensifies our focus, changing the way we see things after the emotion has been triggered. The graphic below shows this reverse influence.

Even though perception is the initial trigger of emotion, emotion can have a follow-on intensifying effect on perception.

Whenever we perceive a threat, our brain triggers a psychological fire alarm, releasing a flood of chemicals into the bloodstream that changes our physiology so we're prepared to fight, flee, or freeze. It also intensifies our focus. We give full attention to the threat at hand. Say we open the mail and find we were massively overcharged for something. Instantly, our body reacts to the perceived threat. Our heartbeat quickens. Our skin temperature rises. We perspire. We're alert. We feel anger or fear. We're *intensely focused* and ready to act.

This flood of chemicals is like a fire drill in an elementary school. All the kids stop their studies and stream out of the class, filling the halls and milling around. It's mayhem, and the only focus is the alarm. It takes several minutes for the alarm to stop and for teachers to herd the kids back into class. In the same way, it takes some time before the chemical spike in our bloodstream goes back to normal.

When the threat is real, this flood of neurochemicals is good. If mother bear and cubs suddenly appear, we should be focused, because distraction means death. When face to face with a bear we don't suddenly remember we have a doctor's appointment, or that a faucet needs repair, or that we need to pick up milk at the grocery store. The only thing in view is mother bear and staying alive.

But when the threat isn't real, or isn't near as threatening as it seems, the fire alarm limits our perceptions. We can't see anything but the threat. We can't break out of our current frame of mind.

The key is to wait until the fire alarm is over before doing or saying anything. Get all the neurochemical kids back in class, then re-evaluate.

A couple years ago, I got a series of emails from an aggressive critic. Every time I read them, my mind pulled the fire alarm. Just the sight of his name in my inbox spiked my heart rate.

By this time, though, I was wise enough to know, *now isn't the time to write a response. Wait until you settle down.*

I remember reading that Mark Twain's wife would watch him write scathing letters to critics, then offer to mail them so she could secretly throw them away. Some letters are better left unsent.

Rarely have I felt or said or done something helpful during a fire alarm. It's a terrible time for conflict resolution. If I'm in a contentious conversation, I'll try as quickly as possible to ask for time to settle my soul. I'll say, "Can we take a thirty-minute break? I need some time to calm down so I can see better. Why don't we reconvene at 11:30?"

Every time I do this, I'm in a better place to work through the challenge. So is the other person.

Some people believe they should talk out the tough stuff right away. "We're going to keep talking this out until we get it settled," they say. This is good intention, but seriously misplaced. It only leads to more regrettable words.

Much of the things we later see as evil are done in the heat of emotion.

THE FOLLOW-ON INFLUENCE OF BEHAVIOR

The emotional alarm, and the way it influences our perception, is easy to detect. We all know when it goes off, and how it changes the way we see things. But there's another reverse-influencer that's even more sinister because of its subtlety. That influencer is *behavior*.

We saw this in our look at *choice-supported bias*. We make a decision, then change our minds to fit our choice, like we did with the Lexus and the Audi.

When we do wrong and fail to immediately admit and correct the error, we take a step toward misjudgment. We change our view to justify our behavior, then carry that distorted view into the next situation, where we behave wrong again, and further cement the distorted view. Pretty soon, we're so committed to the wrong belief we can't get ourselves to admit the truth.

So, while perception is the *initial trigger* of emotion and behavior, our emotions and behaviors can create a *follow-on influence* on our perception. They can influence the way we see things *next*.

This chapter is about automatic evil, so I'm offering mostly negative examples of follow-on influence. But there are positive influences as well. When we posture our body in positive and powerful ways, this helps us see ourselves as more powerful and feel more powerful, automatically. When we make good choices, choice-supported bias can work to support our good choices and lead to more good choices. The point is, our behaviors and our emotions can influence the way we see things, for better or worse.

Here's a graphic that shows the initial influence of perception, along with the follow-on influence from emotion and behavior.

Follow-on Influence

👁 SEE ➡ 💗 FEEL ➡ 📢 ACT

Initial Influence   Initial Influence

The way we see is the initial influence. But once triggered, emotion and behavior have a follow-on influence on the way we see.

HOW DO WE ESCAPE?

The idea of automatic evil scares me and humbles me at the same time. It also gives me hope, because understanding it is the first step to escaping it.

As soon as I discovered my blindness back in the mid-1990s, I started feeling the power of automatic humility. I was instantly more circumspect. I got wiser.

Then, once I started understanding the power of automatic evil, it transformed me even more. I started to see myself as easy prey for error and therefore, easy prey for evil. Without others to help me watch my back, the forces of evil would trap me. Without an outside standard for good and bad that could hold me accountable and keep my inclinations in check, I could easily do evil things.

What's the cure for automatic evil? How do we escape our self-deception? The key is to *see right, every moment of sight*. When our perceptions and imaginations and memories are accurate, when our standards are set the right way, when our goals match our potential, we're much more likely to feel right and do right. But when the perceptions and standards and goals are off-base, all our emotions and behaviors will work in the wrong direction.

The challenge is that self-deception is so deceiving. We often don't see how we see wrong, and therefore believe we're doing right even as we do wrong. How do we break out of the deception?

One way to is to *be accountable to wise people and proper standards*.

In the same way that Weight Watchers does weekly weigh-ins and peer group encouragement, we can measure our behavior against objective moral standards and be accountable to people doing the same.

Then, when we discover we've done something wrong, we can admit it quickly and completely. We know what happens if we fail to admit. Our need for consistency lures us into self-justification. Every choice is between something like the Audi and the Lexus, and when we choose one or the other, we'll automatically reshuffle the cards, redefining what is good and bad, not as they really are, but as we'd like them to be to better fit our choices.

It gets even more intense when we think about the long-term effect of our bias. We don't just create biases with bad choices. We also carry those biases forward to the next situation. Years later, that bias might still be guiding us. Back when we made the choice for Lexus, we didn't just change our mind about Audi that day. We carried our bias against Audi into the future. *We're Lexus people now.* We reshuffled the deck about these two brands to fit our choice, then stored our distorted way of seeing into our minds, and kept it there for ready reference long after the choice. We solidified our self-deception.

Which means there could be hundreds of bad beliefs boxed up in the basement of our minds, distorting the way we see and creating automatic evil.

We'd better get down there and clean house.

CHAPTER 10

The Root of Happiness

"All men seek happiness. This is without exception. Whatever different means they employ, they all tend to this end. The cause of some going to war, and of others avoiding it, is the same desire in both, attended with different views. The will never takes the least step but to this object. This is the motive of every action of every man, even of those who hang themselves."

— Blaise Pascal, French philosopher[77]

This opening quote is a headful. So let's break up what Pascal said into smaller bites.

First, he says,

All men seek happiness. This is without exception.

No matter which side of the political fence we're on, no matter if we're the terrorist or the peaceful citizen, no matter our moral standards, we all want the same thing—to be happy.

"Everyone who has observed human behavior for more than thirty continuous seconds seems to have noticed that people are strongly, perhaps even primarily, perhaps even single-mindedly, motivated to feel happy," writes American psychologist Daniel Gilbert, echoing the founding father of psychotherapy, Sigmund Freud, who described happiness as *the one and only thing we want.* "What do [people] demand of life and wish to achieve in it? The answer to this can hardly be in doubt. They strive after happiness; they want to become happy and to remain so."[78]

We all strive after happiness. But Pascal says we employ "different means" to achieve it, driven by "different views."

> Whatever different means they employ, they all tend to this end. The cause of some going to war, and of others avoiding it, is the same desire in both, attended with different views.

Some want to go to war, while others don't, and the crazy thing here is that no matter which side of the war issue we fall, we're all seeking the same thing. Everything we want, every motive of the heart, every means to every end, is a pursuit of happiness.

Even when people kill themselves. The suicidal person believes they are *better off dead.* In their distorted point of view, suicide is self-help—a way to be happier.

WHAT IS HAPPINESS?

One step to greater happiness is to get clear on what it is and where it comes from. We need to understand the *nature* and *origins* of happiness.

Problem is, most people are confused about happiness because it's something they know in their hearts but often can't grasp with their heads. They say things like, *happiness is a warm blanket, a sense of purpose, true friends, and good food.* But these are just the things that make them happy. It's not a clear sense of the word itself.

I've read dozens of books on happiness and find the authors almost always struggle to define the word. Most just assume we all know what the word means and plow ahead.

Arthur Brooks wrote a book about happy cultures, titled *Gross National Happiness,* but on page four he tells us, "The harder you think, the less clear the subject becomes."[79]

Nick Powdthavee wrote an entire book titled *The Happiness Equation,* yet doesn't get around to defining happiness.

My point isn't to throw authors under buses, but rather to show how difficult this word can be. It's like Supreme Court Justice Potter Stewart's attempt to define the word *pornography* in 1964: "I know it when I see it," he said.

"There are thousands of books on happiness, and most of them start by asking what happiness *really* is," writes Gilbert in his recent book, *Stumbling on Happiness*.

> As readers quickly learn, this is approximately equivalent to beginning a pilgrimage by marching directly into the first available tar pit, because happiness really is nothing more or less than a word that we word makers can use to indicate anything we please. The problem is that people seem pleased to use this one word to indicate a host of different things, which has created a tremendous terminological mess...[80]

Gilbert attempts a way out of the mess by outlining three basic areas of happiness—emotional happiness, moral happiness, and judgmental happiness—but there's no doubt, it's a mess.

I've had my chance to muck around in this mess for a while, and I've landed on a working definition that not only describes happiness, but more importantly, where happiness comes from. It reveals the root of happiness. Here's the definition:

> *Happiness is a pattern of positive emotion that comes from seeing good things happen at a good pace.*

How did I get to this definition? With a few tools: a standard dictionary; a look at etymology; the See-Feel-Act progression; and the universal goal of *maximum good, as we see it*. Let's invest this chapter to break out the tools and get clear about happiness.

HAPPINESS: A PATTERN OF POSITIVE EMOTION

The dictionary definition of the word, *happy*, is, "feeling pleasure or contentment." When we're happy, we experience *positive emotion*.

Here's my working definition of happiness again, with "positive emotion" in bold:

*Happiness is a pattern of **positive emotion** that comes from seeing good things happen at a good pace.*

Then I jump from the word *happy* to the word *happiness*, which dictionaries describe as a "state of being happy." Interesting phrase, "state of being." What does it mean? That we feel a certain way or act a certain way *on a regular basis.* There's a pattern of emotion or a pattern of behavior that becomes characteristic of who we are, not just how we felt one time, or what we did one time.

We can lie once, and only once, and not *be* a liar. But if we lie repeatedly, meaning, there's a pattern of lying, it's fair to say we *are* a liar.

So I describe happiness as "a pattern of positive emotion." When we feel consistently happy, we're experiencing *happiness.*

Given this, take another look at my definition, with the established phrase in bold:

*Happiness is a **pattern of positive emotion** that comes from seeing good things happen at a good pace.*

HAPPINESS IN THE SEE-FEEL-ACT PROGRESSION

Now let's break out the See-Feel-Act progression to show where happiness comes from. Is happiness mostly about seeing, feeling, or acting?

The answer is, feeling. *Happiness* is *emotion*, which puts it squarely in the *Feel* stage of the progression, seen here.

 SEE   FEEL   ACT

Something here triggers happiness.	Happiness: a pattern of positive emotion.	

Happiness lives in the second stage of the progression, which means it is driven by something in the first stage.

Happiness is a *second-stage reality*, driven by the way we see. The way we see *precedes* happiness and *causes* happiness. Which means happiness isn't the deepest thing. There's a deeper root. When we figure out how to cultivate this deeper thing, we trigger automatic happiness.

Imagine happiness as a flower. What does it take to grow a flower? A seed. The flower automatically grows when we plant the seed. In the same way, there's something else we must do to experience happiness. There's something deeper in human nature that grows happiness just like a seed grows a flower.

What is this seed of happiness? What is this deeper thing that creates automatic happiness?

Let's see if etymology can help. Etymology is simply the study of word origins, and the origin I'm most interested in here is the word behind two extremely similar-sounding words, *happy* and *happen*.

Look at these two words. The first four letters are the same. The only difference between them is that one ends with a *y* and the other with an *en*. They share the same four starting letters because they both come from the middle-English word, *hap*. It means, "that which happens."

The word *happy* describes an *emotion*, as we've seen above. But the word *happen* describes an *event*. What is an event? It's a thing that didn't exist before but now does. Whenever something enters existence, it *happens*.

So what's the connection between the emotion (happy) and the event (happening)? When we experience something we see as a "good happening," we instantly and automatically feel good about it. When we see our football team win (a good happening), we feel happy. When we see the birth of our first child (a good happening), we feel happy.

The graphic below shows how *good happenings* automatically influence happiness.

Good happenings.	Happiness: a pattern of positive emotion.	

When we see good things happen, we feel happy. Happiness is a pattern of positive emotion that comes from seeing good things happen.

Given these ideas, let's look at our working definition again, with the established phrases in bold:

*Happiness is a **pattern of positive emotion that comes from seeing good things happen** at a good pace.*

GOOD PACE

Finally, let's look at the *good pace* phrase. Good happenings have a shelf life. If something good happened a year ago, it's not going to have the same effect as a good thing that happened a minute ago. Good happenings are much like a good meal. Meals are good, but we can't live long on one good meal. In the same way, we can't feel happy for very long on one good happening. We need good happenings at a good pace. We need good happenings morning, noon, and night. We need good happenings today, tomorrow, and the next day. We need a continuous series of good happenings to get happiness. There's a *pace* to happiness.

In See-Feel-Act terminology, when we see good things happen at a good pace, we feel happiness. The graphic below shows the connection.

👁 SEE ➤	💕 FEEL ➤	📢 ACT
Good happenings, at a good pace.	Happiness: a pattern of positive emotion.	

*When we see good things happen **at a good pace**, we feel happiness, a pattern of positive emotion.*

I remember a *Seinfeld* episode where George Costanza admitted he felt like a loser. But he felt instantly happier by changing the timing of the good happenings of his life. "You know, if you take everything I've ever done and condense it down into one day, it looks decent," he said.[81] When good happenings are too far and few between, we don't feel like our lives are going well.

So, what is happiness? We've finally explored the full working definition: *a pattern of positive emotion that comes from seeing good things happen at a good pace.*

This idea of happiness fits perfectly with the goal of *maximum good, as we see it*. Happiness is the emotional response to the pursuit of this prime goal. The pursuit of happiness and the pursuit of maximum good are two sides of the same coin. We're constantly striving for good and when we see good consistently happening in our lives, the result is a feeling of happiness.

HAPPINESS FROM SEEING GOOD

Since happiness is the result of the way we see good, it means that happiness depends, not on the situations of life itself, but on the ways we see the situations.

Remember Danny—and how his coworkers reacted to his promotion? Henry was the only one who was happy about what was happening to Danny that day. All the others had negative or neutral emotion. Susan was sad, Frank was afraid, Anna was angry, and Nick felt nothing. The reason they responded differently wasn't due to the situation itself. Rather, it was the way they saw the situation that triggered their emotions. Each one saw good and bad in different ways, and this way of seeing drove their emotions.

Remember, happiness is a trailer, not a truck. It's a second-stage reality. It depends on the first-stage reality, which is the way we see good things happening in our lives.

"Happiness appears to be relative," writes Baumeister, "in particular, relative to the standards set by various expectations and norms....You appraise your circumstances and then compare these against what you had expected or wanted....Put another way, happiness is achieved when reality lives up to your desires and expectations."[82] What Baumeister describes as "standards" and "desires and expectations" we can also describe as "maximum good, as we see it."

Our view of the good drives our happiness. Happiness doesn't drive and it can't drive. Happiness rides shotgun.

WHY HAPPINESS SHOULDN'T DRIVE

Happiness is vital for the road trip through life, to be sure, but it should never get into the driver's seat because it's sure to run us into a ditch.

Here's what I mean. Happiness is a second-stage factor in the See-Feel-Act progression, driven by the way we see. When we see good things happening at a good pace, we feel happiness.

But when we see wrong, meaning, we think we see good things that really aren't good things, *we still feel happiness.* Happiness isn't an indicator of true goodness. It's an indicator of *perceived goodness.* That means we can feel happy about the wrong things.

- Men use "being happy" as an excuse to commit adultery and break up their families.
- Juvenile vandals feel happy as they break into a house and smash all the mirrors.
- People often feel happy when they put others down or when they see others fail.

Should we validate these sorts of behaviors because they make us happy?

Absolutely not.

We make a major mistake to think happiness is our purpose in life. *Maximum good, seen right* is the purpose, and happiness is the natural response when we are truly making good things happen at a good pace.

But when we see things wrong, like Pascal's suicide victim, and pursue happiness for its own sake, we're happy about the wrong things. If we let happiness become our standard of living, we run our lives from the wrong box in the See-Feel-Act progression, which means we can feel happy while living a lie and doing evil.

The Dalai Lama once wrote, "The purpose of our lives is to be happy." I respect all the good Dalai does for the world, so it's tough to take issue here, but there's that subtle but critical error in making happiness our purpose, or any other emotion for that matter.

The purpose of our lives is to see things that are *truly good* happen at a truly good pace. When we make happiness our purpose, and then see in the wrong ways, we could be making evil our purpose by accident. We go with our feelings, and fail to question the misperception that creates them. That's a gateway to evil, and a lot of people open that gate.

I'm all for happiness. As long as we're all happy for the right reasons.

PART 4
THE ROOTS
OF SUCCESS

CHAPTER 11

Penny Thick

"A champion is someone who is bent over, drenched in sweat, at the point of exhaustion, when no one else is watching."

— ANSON DORRANCE, AMERICAN SOCCER COACH

If there's a poster boy for excellence, it's twentieth-century American educator and author John Erskine. He excelled in education, getting his Ph.D. from Columbia University. He excelled in music, playing the piano with the New York Philharmonic his entire career. He excelled in leadership, serving as president of the Julliard School of Music.

Oh, and along the way, he wrote more than *forty-five* books.

How does someone like Erskine excel in two careers at the same time? And how does someone so busy in two careers find time to write *one* book, let alone *forty-five*?

Seeing Erskine's life triggers a train of thought like,

Wow, I'm a loser compared to that guy.

Sure, people with loads of natural talent and intelligence can do that.

But not normal people like me.

Most people believe they could achieve like John if they just had the same gifts.

But contrary to the common view, research shows no correlation between gifting and success: People don't succeed because they're more talented or more intelligent.

When I discovered the real reason for Erskine's success, it changed the way I saw myself…and the way I see you.

It gave me *a new view of potential.*

This new view automatically influenced the way I felt and the things I did. It gave me new hope and energy. It gave me new patience for the growth process. I started working harder, longer, and better.

SMARTS AND SUCCESS

To get this new view of potential, let's start with the idea that success is about smarts. Author Malcolm Gladwell has much to offer on this topic: "Over the years, an enormous amount of research has been done in an attempt to determine how a person's performance on an IQ test translates to real life success," writes Gladwell. He cites intelligence studies that classify people below 70 IQ as "mentally disabled," while "normal" people score around 100. University graduate students score on the higher side of normal (about 115), and "very superior" testers score above 130.

"In general, the higher your score, the more education you'll get," Gladwell continues, "the more money you're likely to make, and—believe it or not—the longer you'll live. But there's a catch. The relationship between success and IQ works only up to a point…having additional IQ points doesn't seem to translate into any measurable real-world advantage."[83]

Gladwell cites IQ expert Arthur Jensen, who writes that "beyond [115], the IQ level becomes relatively unimportant."[84]

So intelligence matters, up to a point, and that point is close to *average levels* of intelligence. Which means every one of us reading this book has all the innate intelligence we need to succeed.

NATURAL TALENT AND SUCCESS

How important, then, is natural talent?

The best person on earth to ask about this is Swedish psychologist K. Anders Ericsson, the world's foremost expert on expertise. For over forty years, Ericsson's field studies have centered around one question: What makes people with extraordinary talent differ from the rest of us? He's invested his entire career researching peak performers, from athletes to musicians to software programmers. He served as editor of the massive collaborative work, *The Cambridge Handbook of Expertise and Expert Performance*, overseeing over eighty contributors to create eight hundred dense pages of summarized research.

After surveying the spectrum of achievement, Ericsson concludes that natural talent is not the key factor. "When experts exhibit their superior performance in public," he writes, "their behavior looks so effortless and natural that we are tempted to attribute it to special talents.... However, when scientists began measuring experts' supposedly superior powers of speed, memory and intelligence, no superiority was found."[85] Ericsson says there's got to be enough natural talent to cross a threshold and get in the game, but once we're in, extra talent doesn't correlate to extra success.

While we're talking about success, let's be clear. There are thousands of equally important ways to succeed. We started the chapter with John Erskine's achievements as a writer, musician, and leader, which are equally important as someone taking care of the infirm, or serving food, or processing paperwork. Every occupation has purpose and value.

We also need to get clear about what success truly is. Some people think it's fame and fortune and followers. They think success is power and prestige. In my experience, however, this is a mismark on the treasure map, because there's no treasure there. People who only seek these things find suffering and disappointment instead of success.

Success is more about service and less about status. It's more about creating value, and less about being in charge. It's about great love and great character and great relationships. It's about great purpose and great teams. It's about great products and services that give people joy and relief.

In my experience, working with a spectrum of people from Fortune 500 executives to addicts off the streets, I find that we're all at our best when caught up in pursuit of the greater good, when *serving* in some way. In this sense, success is "our best in service to others."

WHAT'S THE SECRET?

If world-class achievement isn't about natural talent and intelligence, what's the key factor?

It surfaced for Ericsson in the early 1990s, when he and his team studied violinists at the Academy of Music in Berlin. They separated the group into three tiers of expertise—top performers, middle performers, and lower performers—then asked each one, "Over the course of your career, ever since you first picked up a violin, how many hours have you practiced?"

Although everyone in the group started near the same age, their practice differed. The top performers had accumulated about ten thousand hours of practice, the middle performers eight thousand hours, and the lower performers four thousand. Those who practiced the most were the best, without exception.

Intrigued by the pattern, Ericsson did similar comparisons between amateur and professional pianists and found the same thing.

The more Ericsson searched, the more he found this pattern. He couldn't find an exception to the rule. There were no "naturals," meaning, top performers who got there without top investments in practice. Neither were there any "grinds," people who practiced more than anyone but failed to reach the top ranks. There was a perfect correlation between "deliberate practice" and ranking.

So, if natural talent and intelligence are not the deciding factors, what's the key to success? The answer is, *persistent effort*. "The differences between expert performers and normal adults," writes Ericsson, "reflect a life-long period of deliberate effort to improve performance in a particular area."[86]

Many see success the wrong way. They think successful people are born with talent, while unsuccessful people aren't. They see smart people as smart from birth, and successful because of it. But decades of research upends that view. For almost every area of expertise, from playing music and chess to creating works of literature and world-class art, talent and intelligence are being shown to be *developed* traits, not *innate* traits. We aren't born with talent and smarts as much as we grow them through *persistent effort* over a long period of time.

Which brings us back to the secret behind Erskine's achievements. According to Erskine, a piano lesson in childhood changed the way he saw success, and created a ripple effect of excellence that flooded every area of his life.

"How many times a week do you practice, and how long do you practice each time?" his teacher asked him.

"I usually practice once a day, generally for an hour or more," John replied.

"Don't do that," the teacher said. "When you grow up, time won't come in long stretches. Practice in minutes, whenever you can find them."

Erskine started finding the minutes. His baby-step approach made practice so fresh and frequent that it never sapped his vitality. He did this in music and eventually became one of the top pianists in the world. He did this in learning and eventually earned his Ph.D. He did this in writing and eventually finished book after book.

Erskine spent a lifetime baby-stepping without burnout. He filled his schedule gaps with persistent spurts of productive effort. He wrote the bulk of his book *Helen of Troy*, for example, on train commutes between his home and the university.

FROM SPECKS TO SAHARA

The Chinese built a five-thousand-mile wall one brick at a time. The Giant Sequoias of the Sierra Nevadas reach towering heights growing the thickness of a penny each day. In the day-to-day, nothing much happens. But add it up over time and we get something big, like specks of sand adding up to a Sahara Desert.

This is Erskine's secret. The daily stuff is penny-thick. No big deal. But Erskine kept adding up the days and, eventually, the days added up.

Funny thing is, we tend to see achievement the opposite way. We think we can make great strides day-to-day, so we bite off more than we can chew. *I'll get the whole back yard in shape on Saturday*, we think. But we barely finish cutting the grass. *I'll finish the client's project in three days*, we think. Then we start in and realize there's no way to get done in a week, let alone three days.

So we lose heart.

Eventually we draw a lesson from our experiences: *I always think I can do more than I can. I'm not going to fall for that again.* We hype ourselves up for big-day achievements and big-week achievements, make big plans, overpack our schedules, then look back at the end of the day or the end of the week and see how much we fail to do. Then we get discouraged and pessimistic.

The crazy thing is that we do the exact opposite when the time span stretches out. In the same way that we tend to be too optimistic about our short-term ability, we're too pessimistic about our long-term ability. We underestimate the way small things add up to big things over time.

Take reading books for an example. One-third of adult Americans won't read a single book in a year.[87] Some haven't read a book in decades.

What's the reason? Sometimes there's no interest. But many fail to read because they think reading is too hard. They look at a thick book and think, *I can't do that.* Reading makes them tired (it does for everyone by the way) and they don't have the time.

So I sometimes ask a person, "Could you read just one page of a book in the next three minutes?"

"Of course," they answer. Then I pull a book off a shelf and have them read while I wait.

When they're done with a page, I ask, "Could you do that every day, make a habit of it?"

"Sure, that would be easy."

"Then there you go. That's two books a year."

The same is true for people who want to *write* a book (and almost everyone wants to write a book). I ask, "Could you write a half page of something?"

"Sure."

"Well, just a half page a day of writing, every day, becomes an entire book of writing over a year."

Same for losing weight. "Can you take a thirty-minute walk?" I ask. "Sure."

"Well, a thirty-minute walk for the average woman, every day, adds up to losing thirteen pounds in a year. It's even more for men."[88]

Over time, small things add up to big things.

But we don't see it that way. Why? Because penny-thick growth is invisible. Try watching a giant sequoia grow for a day. Get out a chair, sit in front of the tree, and stare. Will you see anything happening? Nope. Growth is too slow to notice.

No one goes to the gym one time and friends think, *Wow, what a transformation.* One visit doesn't do much. We can't see any results.

This is why we underestimate what we could accomplish in a year. We don't see how small efforts add up to big results over time.

The graphic below shows these two basic ways to see success, and how they automatically influence emotion and behavior.

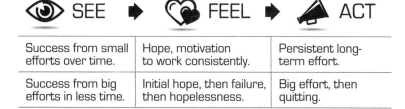

👁 SEE ➤ 💗 FEEL ➤ 📣 ACT

Success from small efforts over time.	Hope, motivation to work consistently.	Persistent long-term effort.
Success from big efforts in less time.	Initial hope, then failure, then hopelessness.	Big effort, then quitting.

When we see success coming from small efforts over time, we feel hope and motivation to work consistently, leading to persistent long-term effort. Big efforts in short timeframes often lead to failure and quitting.

GROWTH, TIME, AND ACORNS

Imagine an acorn in the palm of your hand. What do you see?

When I ask this in seminars, half the room says, *an acorn.* The other half says, *an oak tree in the making.* Then a few go wild and say, *a forest of oak trees in the making.*

It all boils down to the different ways we see *growth* and *time.*

Some people tell themselves, *We are who we are. People don't change.* They don't believe in growth. But others believe. *Give us time. We can overcome that weakness with new habits.*

There are different ways of thinking about *time* as well. Some people only see the present. *The only thing that matters is right now.* Lunch is as far out as plans go. Others see longer-term. Still others see really long-term: *In twenty years, with just a bit of my paycheck, I can save enough for retirement.*

It's not just different ways of seeing growth and time. It's the choices we make as well.

Think back to our acorn. Put an acorn in the ground and it grows automatically and continuously. It does the penny-thick growth-work, on time, every time. But we human beings don't grow that way, and that's why some of us turn out to be towering oaks while others stay acorns for life. We either choose to grow or we don't.

Think back to the violinists at the Academy of Music in Berlin. For the previous fifteen years, they made day-by-day, hour-by-hour, and min-ute-by-minute choices. Every day is about a thousand waking minutes, so they each had over five million waking minutes to use however they liked. They either used the minutes like Erskine, investing in growth, or they used the minutes for something else. In this way, some chose more practice than others did. Minute by minute, hour by hour, day by day, month by month, year by year, these different choices of minutes added up to thousands of hours of difference in accumulated growth, which marked the difference between those who were towering oaks of excel-lence and those who weren't.

THE TEN-YEAR, TEN-THOUSAND-HOUR RULE

It takes sixty years to grow an oak from an acorn. How much does it take to grow world-class performance? Is there a timeframe on excellence?

In every area of expertise Anders Ericsson studied, from computer programming to public speaking to professional sports to music, he final-ly concluded that the "magic number for true expertise" is ten thousand hours, usually accomplished in about ten years.[89] Superiority in any field comes from a *lot* of growth and time.

Once this number was known, the researchers began looking for exceptions. Are there any short cuts to world-class skill? What about prodigies like Mozart? Didn't they reach expertise sooner? The more the researchers looked, the more they found that even the prodigies fit the Ten-Thousand-Hour Rule.

Chess "prodigy" Bobby Fischer put in nine years of deliberate prac-tice before achieving grandmaster status at age seventeen.

Same is true for Gary Kasparov, the grandmaster who reached the top rank at age twenty-two. Kasparov's story is interesting because he's celebrated for superior intelligence, but when researchers tested him, they found he was just as intelligent as the rest of us. It wasn't his intelli-gence that made him a grandmaster. It was a massive investment of effort over time.

The great eighteenth-century composer, Wolfgang Amadeus Mozart, is a tougher one, because he exhibited superior ability early on. He started composing at four years old. By six, he was so skilled on the harpsichord and violin that he traveled Europe as a paid performer. Doesn't Mozart violate the Ten-Year, Ten-Thousand-Hour Rule? Cognitive psychologist Michael Howe, author of *Genius Explained*, writes,

> He did indeed begin creating music at an exceptionally young age, but by the standards of mature composers, Mozart's early works are not outstanding. The earliest pieces of all were probably written down by his father (a skilled musician) and perhaps improved in the process. Many of Wolfgang's childhood compositions, such as the first seven of his concertos for piano and orchestra, are largely arrangements of works by various other composers.
>
> Of those concertos that only contain music original to Mozart, the earliest that is now regarded as a masterwork (No. 9, K. 271) was not composed until he was twenty-one.[90]

Howe estimates that Mozart studied music for over 3,500 hours with his father, an expert instructor, by his sixth birthday.

Mozart's "genius" was the direct result of growth over time. Far from establishing the prodigy myth, Mozart's story debunks the myth, and further establishes the Ten-Thousand-Hour Rule. "No one has yet found a case in which true world-class expertise was accomplished in less time," concludes neuroscientist Daniel Levitin. "It seems that it takes the brain this long to assimilate all that it needs to know to achieve true mastery."[91]

THE REAL X-FACTOR: OBSESSIVE INTEREST

Let's be clear about the Ten-Thousand-Hour Rule. It's for world-class excellence in certain fields. It's not the only timeframe for excellence.

In other areas, like breaking a habit, change only takes a few weeks. Getting in shape may take three months to a year. Learning a new skill may take three weeks, or it may take three years. There are many time-frames for mastery, but the key is to respect the time and do the work. Any one of us can develop skill, even world-class skill, if we want to.

The key words are, *if we want to.* It takes persistent drive to invest ten thousand hours of deliberate practice over ten years. Think about Mozart, for example. What kind of persistence does it take for a four-year-old boy to invest at least four hours of practice a day for several years? What's extraordinary about Mozart isn't his genius, but his commitment to growth over time. "The true expertise of geniuses, the research suggests," writes talent expert Daniel Coyle, "resides in their ability to deep-practice obsessively." Exceptional talent flows from what psychologist Ellen Winner calls "the rage to master."

How do we unleash this obsession, this rage to master?

It starts with the way we see success itself. When we see ourselves as qualified to succeed, and when we see how growth happens penny-thick, we get a new view of potential, which automatically influences us. We feel hope and motivation, and we're inspired to work.

The trick is keeping this new view in mind, long term. We must keep our focus on the fact that success is penny-thick. We must learn to be patient in the process.

That's how I wrote this book, by the way. I whittled away, every day, for almost two years. It was relatively easy. I kept stacking the pennies until the work grew into a Giant Sequoia. I knew that eventually I would succeed.

Same with you. You can develop your intelligence and ability over time. It doesn't take herculean effort. It takes persistent effort. It takes long-term commitment and focus.

CELEBRATING THE WORK

One way to keep focus is to celebrate *the work that creates talent* more than celebrating talent itself. Carol Dweck, a Stanford psychologist who's been researching motivation for more than three decades, did a series of studies with four hundred New York fifth graders, showing that this subtle difference in thinking makes all the difference in performance.

The studies began with a series of easy puzzles. After the children finished, a researcher showed them their scores and added a quick encouragement. To half the children, the encouragement emphasized their *talent*: "You must be smart at this." To the other half, the encouragement emphasized their *effort*: "You must have worked really hard."

The next stage of the experiment shows the big effect of the small difference. When tested a second time, researchers gave children a choice—a harder test or an easier test. The majority of those praised for effort took the harder test. But a majority of those praised for intelligence took the easier test. It's a pattern Dweck has confirmed hundreds of times. "When we praise children for their intelligence," Dweck writes, "we tell them that's the name of the game: look smart, don't risk making mistakes."

Then the third stage of Dweck's experiment shows the effect even more. When the puzzle difficulty went up equally for both groups, the "effort group" got more involved, worked harder, and liked the experience. But the "intelligence group" hated the tougher puzzles. "They took it as proof that they weren't smart," Dweck concluded.[92]

A small difference in emphasis had a big impact on behavior.

SLOW AND SWEATY WINS THE RACE

"One of the most unfortunate things I see when identifying youth players is the girl who is told over the years how great she is," says University of North Carolina soccer coach Anson Dorrance. "By the time she's a high school freshman, she starts to believe it. By her senior year, she's fizzled out. Then there's her counterpart: a girl waiting in the wings, who quietly and with determination decides she's going to make something of herself. Invariably, this humble, hardworking girl is the one who becomes the real player."[93]

The key is the work, the work, the work. Not just a spurt of effort here and there. Persistent effort, for years.

When people believe success is about natural talent or intelligence, they imagine success without work. If schoolwork or a sport comes easy to someone at first, they think they can slack through the whole journey. They make a little early progress as they coast along, but fail to develop the work ethic and the patience that it takes to reach the finish line miles ahead.

This steady-work factor is one reason that *the easier it is to be good, the harder it is to be great.* A student may be honored for their aptitude and get good grades without much effort. But since they didn't work hard to get there, they'll falter when work is required. Those who keep at it, on the other hand, have an obsessive interest that keeps them working day after day. Eventually, they learn to love the work. They embrace the process. "The vision of a champion," says Dorrance, "is someone who is bent over, drenched in sweat, at the point of exhaustion, when no one else is watching."[94]

The great inventor Thomas Edison was right to quip that genius is one percent inspiration and ninety-nine percent perspiration. World-class talent and intelligence come from sweat. Erskine and Fischer and

Kasparov and Mozart were sweaty achievers, running the miles until the miles added up.

Take a minute and consider the things that come easy to you. Have you settled for *good enough* when you could be working toward *great*? Do you love work? Are you running the marathon like you could be?

The bottom line is, *the work*. When the work continues, so does the transformation.

Contrary to what we often believe, there's something deep inside us that *loves* the work. We *love* to improve. The process of identifying and achieving potential triggers a deep sense of happiness. Whenever life hands us a challenge we feel we can tackle, we come alive. It's the reason we challenge ourselves in sports and hobbies and video games. We love to drive forward, develop our skills, and win in life.

THE NEW VIEW

Remember our first look at Erskine and all his achievements? Forty-five books? Ph.D.? Concert violinist? Leader of Julliard?

Our first thought was, *Wow*.

Our second thought was, *I'm a loser compared to that guy.*

Our third thought was, *Sure, guys with loads of natural talent and intelligence can do that. But not normal people.*

This first look at Erskine was a distorted view. We saw him as The Great Man, descended from the gods with god-like endowments of intelligence and ability.

But now we see differently. We have a new view that busts the myth, that remakes the Great Man into the Sweaty Man. We see talent and intelligence as *developed traits* more than *innate traits*. We see achievers like we see towering trees—as slow and steady growers.

Because of this new view of potential and success, there's new hope. We too can slow-grow. We too have the ability to develop world-class skill and become great achievers. We all have extraordinary ability to develop our ability, in almost any area of life.

If we're willing to think and grow penny-thick.

CHAPTER 12

Automatic Sabotage

"One of my greatest fears is not being able to break out of a rut; or becoming a prisoner to my ways, unable to change course."
— Matt Dillon, American actor

A friend of a friend of mine ran a Lexus dealership that struggled in the middle of a market downturn. Customers weren't coming in.

While other dealers languished, this dealer innovated. He drove fleets of cars to where the people were instead of waiting for them to show up at the dealership. His sales team took cars to marinas, country clubs, and upscale malls to offer test drives.

The strategy worked, and he flourished. "Just because everyone is going through a downturn doesn't mean we need to," he said.[95]

There's a saying, *necessity is the mother of invention*. But why do we wait for necessity? Why don't we invent before the downturn? And why does our inventiveness always seem to get us to the same place we were before? Why does it feel like we're running into a wall?

Because we are. There *is* a wall.

What is it? Why is it there? How do we move it?

This chapter offers answers.

DYNAMIC STABILITY AND MAXIMUM GOOD

When driving on the freeway in the United States, good speed is around sixty-five miles per hour. If we're driving eighty, that's not good. *We need to slow down.* On the other hand, if we're driving forty, that isn't good either. *We need to speed up.*

This is the Inverted-U concept I explained several chapters back, showing how our sense of good maxes out somewhere in the middle of a curve. I showed how pepper on mac and cheese is good, and more pepper is better, but after some point, more pepper becomes worse. Same with freeway speed. Up to a certain point, more speed is better. But after that point, it's worse.

Here are the Inverted-U graphs for freeway speed and pepper.

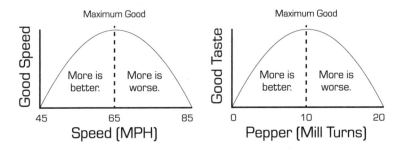

Inverted-U graphs for freeway speed and pepper on mac and cheese. Our sense of good increases with quantity up to a certain point, then decreases.

This sense of maximum good is unconscious. We don't deliberately tell ourselves how much speed is best and how much pepper is best. We just know. We don't think about these goals, these standards, these ways of defining maximum good. We just have them and live by them.

We're always aligning to these unconscious standards. Think about the freeway commute. We're always working to keep our speed at the peak of the curve, despite the circumstances. It starts at the freeway on-ramp. *This isn't good. I need to go faster.* We pedal down to reach sixty-five miles per hour. But then a car slows in our lane, so we slow down. Then it gets out of the way, so we speed back up. Then we hit a hill section of the freeway and our speed slows. *This isn't good.* We step on the gas to reach our goal again. Then we hit a downhill section and go too fast. *This isn't good.* We coast to get back to the right speed.

In this way, over and over, we work to reach and stay at maximum good. Even when it looks like we are "maintaining" speed, we are micro-achieving our goal, over and over, as we press and release the gas pedal.

This idea of holding a steady speed in traffic is what I call *dynamic stability.* Like a toy top that spins in place but looks like it's not moving, dynamic stability is our tendency to hold steady to the peak of the U in a changing environment.

Consider Beth the salesperson. She's used to making $5,000 per month, and she's been steady there for a few years now. Whether she knows it or not, $5,000 per month is maximum good, the peak of her U, her unstated standard, her unconscious goal.

What happens when Beth only makes $2,000 in one month? Her performance drops back from the peak of the U. *This isn't good. I gotta get things going and make it right.* She steps on the gas. She doubles up her sales calls. She thinks of new ways to recover the lost money for the month. She increases her performance.

Then what happens when Beth lands a $10,000 commission in one month? In this situation, her performance goes past the peak of the curve. She's excited, but also relieved. She takes her foot off the gas. She stops making her daily quota of calls. She schedules the vacation she's been putting off. *It's time to relax. I deserve it.* She decreases performance the same way she'd coast on the freeway when her speed got too high.

This is dynamic stability.

STABILITY IN AN UNSTABLE WORLD

When we think of steady things, like steady speed or steady income, it's easy to think nothing's happening, but that's not true. Steady states in a changing world require loads of work. What looks like passivity is actually a lot of unconscious effort to hold us in place.

Think about the thermostat and furnace system in our homes. It pursues a target room temperature in changing weather conditions. All the behind-the-scenes technology, all the effort, and the big utility bill every month, just to keep temperature steady at 71 degrees.

It takes a lot of work and smarts to keep status quo.

In the same way, we work to keep dynamic stability around our views of *maximum good* in a changing world. We seek steady incomes, relationships, environments, and more. When the world changes things, we counteract the changes, just like the thermostat and furnace system corrects up and down to stay at the target temperature.

The need for steady states is wired into our biology. As warm-blooded human beings, the only way to survive is to keep our core temperature steady at 98.6 degrees Fahrenheit, and our body does this for us automatically, signaling us to put on clothes and take them off, shiver and sweat, take shelter or get outside for fresh air.

The same is true with our blood chemistry. We work to keep certain amounts of things in our body, and when these amounts are different than they should be, our body signals us to act. We crave certain foods, we breathe lighter or heavier, we speed up or slow down our heart rate, and so on.

Scientists call this steady-state regulation *homeostasis*, from the Latin word *homeo*, which means "similar to," and *stasis*, which means "standing still." Homeostasis is all the work the body does to keep things "similar to standing still," meaning, make it look like nothing is happening at all.

The point is, again, that a lot is actually happening when it looks like nothing is happening. For every external factor, there's an internal reaction to offset it and hold steady at maximum good. What looks like "serenity" from the outside is a vigilant, dynamic, internal regulation that happens so quickly and so perfectly that it looks like nothing is happening at all.

SABOTAGING HIGH PERFORMANCE

Take a look at the Inverted-U illustration below.

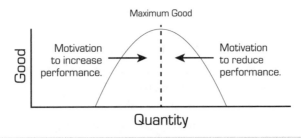

An Inverted-U showing forward and backward motivation.

When performance is left of the peak of the Inverted-U, meaning below what we feel is maximum good, there's discomfort, tension, and anxiety to bring performance forward to the peak. But when we're ahead of what we feel is maximum good, there's an urge to bring performance back, mostly through coasting, but also through active effort. Forward and backward, there's *unconscious motivation* to adjust performance to get us to the peak and keep us there. We're always self-regulating to reach and maintain *maximum good, as we see it.*

Our sense of maximum good might have little to do with our potential, because it is usually set by default. We don't even know we have it. We pick up standards and stick with them, usually without question. And once a standard is set, perhaps surprisingly, we automatically sabotage performance beyond the peak of the U. We hit a plateau, we run into a wall. We can't get past the vertical line in the Inverted-U.

It's not that we couldn't perform better, but we won't...until *the way we see maximum good* changes. In this way, our sense of maximum good has the power to hurt us, because it limits our performance to the top of curve.

Think about the Lexus dealer who worked to offset the dip in sales. All that effort got them back to their target income, but not beyond it. Even as they innovated in a down market, they were limiting themselves to an unconscious standard.

We tend to innovate when we've fallen behind, but think about what might happen if we kept innovating that way? Instead of coasting when we're ahead, what if we set the bar higher so we naturally perform at a new level?

The key is in the way we define maximum good. When our view of maximum good matches our potential, we've got it right. But when our view of maximum good is below our potential, we're creating automatic sabotage.

Let's say Paula works out five days a week and gets her cardio in three of those five days. She's in shape, and that's what feels good to her. That's maximum good, as she sees it. That's her unstated goal, her habit, her standard. Her view is pretty close to her potential, unless she wanted to become a bodybuilder or fitness competitor.

What happens when Paula goes a few days without exercising? She feels anxiety. Something is off. She sees herself performing behind the peak of the U, so there's forward motivation, as seen in the graphic below.

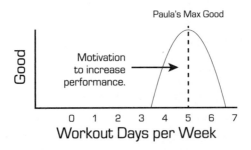

Paula's Inverted-U. Five days a week is the peak of her curve, so when she goes a few days without exercise, she feels forward motivation to get to the peak of the U.

That's not the case for average Joe, who doesn't work out at all. Joe's sense of maximum good is zero workouts per week. *Dang, I forgot to go to the gym today,* Joe thinks. *That's eight years in a row now.*[96] So when Joe doesn't exercise at all in a week, there's no motivation to change.

Say someone asks Joe to meet him at the gym one morning and he agrees. Joe gets up and goes, but there's resistance. Joe has backward motivation to return to his sense of maximum good, which is staying in bed. *This is not you. Get back to where you belong.* The graphic below shows this backward motivation.

Joe's Inverted-U. Zero days a week is the peak of his curve, so whenever he exercises, he feels backward motivation to get to the peak of the U.

Let's say Paula and Joe both worked out two days this week. Paula feels forward motivation to return to her peak, while Joe feels backward motivation to return to his peak. Even though they're both performing the same, their motivations are opposite, because of the different ways they see maximum good. The graphic below shows how this works.

Paula and Joe's Inverted-U, along with their actual performance (two workout days this week). Paula feels forward motivation to get to her peak, while Joe feels backward motivation to get to his peak.

Why wouldn't Joe change his standard? Why wouldn't he redefine maximum good at five workouts a week?

Now think back to Beth the saleswoman. Why would she pass up more money? Why wouldn't she start expecting $10,000 per month instead of staying at $5,000 per month?

There are several reasons, but the ones I want to show here are our deep need for stability, our automatic self-regulation to maintain this stability, and our unconscious definitions of maximum good. We pick up standards by default, and we're wired to stabilize around them. That's just human nature.

If we're unaware of this self-regulating penchant, we have no way of seeing how we correct backward just as we correct forward. So the first step to changing things is to understand our unconscious standards and how we self-regulate to them.

It's like learning how the thermostat and furnace system works so we can change the settings. If we don't know what a thermostat is, it's going to be hard to change room temperature. We might turn on a fan or open a window, but the system will offset it. Eventually, the temperature will settle back to the settings on the dial.

Ever feel that way? Ever make a resolution, whip up resolve, then peter out and go right back to where you were before? When we try to change performance but fail to change the view of maximum good that's self-regulating the performance, we're wasting our time. We need to figure out how to change our unconscious goals and standards. We've got to figure out how to move the peak of the Inverted-U, because once we do that, all the self-regulating power of human nature works for us instead of against us.

CORRECTING BACKWARD

When maximum good is set to excellence, like it was for Paula with fitness, our self-regulating system works in our favor. But when the way we see maximum good is off, that same system works against us.

Think about how this happens in our relationships. Many of us hang out with people because it "feels right," only to find later that they aren't right for us at all. There's a standard type of person we see as good to be with. We're comfortable with certain types of people, and not others, because of the way we see. Janice tells her friend, "I keep picking the wrong guy," but chances are good that Janice is picking the same guy with a different name. When our view of maximum good is wrong, we keep returning to the wrong places, doing the wrong things, and hanging out with the wrong people.

We are all goal-setters by nature, even though few of us see ourselves that way, because we set goals unconsciously and automatically. We pick up standards without knowing. We view maximum good in particular ways, without conscious thought. If we don't set goals purposely, defaults take over.

Whenever any view of maximum good becomes dominant in the mind, the mind works to achieve it, automatically. More importantly, if we don't give our mind a new view, the mind works hard to maintain the default view.

This is why outside-in approaches to change fail so quickly. If we don't change our standards, we'll get back to the old ways again and again. A misplaced view of maximum good creates *automatic sabotage*.

CHANGING THE VIEW

The key is to define maximum good as it really should be. There's a difference between *perceived maximum good* and *actual maximum good*, and the sooner we recognize the difference, the sooner we start unleashing our power to perform.

A friend of mine, Sharee, worked for some time as a lawn-care saleswoman. Within six months of starting the job, she was a top performer. Over the years, she continued to raise her numbers and became one of the top sellers in the company.

Sharee did this because she had a different goal, a different definition of maximum good, than Beth did. Remember Beth, the salesperson who self-regulated her income at $5,000 per month? $5,000 per month was her unstated standard. But Sharee's standard was different. It was sixty cold calls a day. Every day. Her leaders had told her that making sixty calls a day would maximize her potential.

Sharee followed their advice and got to work. Whenever she made less than sixty calls, she was uncomfortable. There was forward motivation to get her to the right call volume. Eventually, she built a rock-solid habit. Rain or shine, she'd make her quota.

When her sales rose, she kept calling. She kept her foot on the gas. She didn't coast when others did, because she had a better standard.

Unlike Beth, Sharee escaped the power of automatic sabotage. She continued to speed ahead while others were throttling back.

CHAPTER 13

Automatic Energy

"If you don't get up every morning with a burning desire to do things, you don't have enough goals."
— LOU HOLTZ, AMERICAN FOOTBALL COACH

"How long since your last cigarette?" asked the researcher.

"Almost four years," said Lisa, "and I've lost sixty pounds and run a marathon since then."

In his book, *The Power of Habit*, Charles Duhigg tells the story of Lisa Allen, a woman who had so transformed her life that she was one of a couple dozen subjects in a program studying how people change.

> According to her file, [Lisa] was thirty-four years old, had started smoking and drinking when she was sixteen, and had struggled with obesity for most of her life. At one point, in her mid-twenties, collection agencies were hounding her to recover $10,000 in debts. An old resume listed her longest job as lasting less than a year.
>
> The woman in front of the researchers today, however, was lean and vibrant, with the toned legs of a runner. She looked a decade younger than the photos in her chart and like she could out-exercise anyone in the room. According to the most recent report in her file, Lisa had no outstanding debts, didn't drink, and was in her thirty-ninth month at a graphic design firm.

She'd just bought a home and started her master's degree as well. Somehow, Lisa was able to escape her former life, and break into a new life of freedom and power. What was her secret?

"It all started in Cairo," said Lisa, explaining her transformation. The vacation to Egypt was a hasty response to trouble at home—her husband was leaving her for another woman. Four months earlier, he'd broken the news, and since then she'd been binge eating, crying, and drinking. She couldn't sleep. She felt helpless and angry. She had to change something, get out of there, anything to distract from the despair. "I had always wanted to see the pyramids," she said, "and my credit cards weren't maxed out yet, so I went."

Her first morning she woke up in a jet-lagged haze in her hotel room, fumbled for a cigarette and tried to light it, only to discover she was burning an ink pen. "A wave of sadness came over me," she said, "I felt like everything I had ever wanted had crumbled. I couldn't even smoke right. And then I started thinking about my ex-husband, and how hard it would be to find another job when I got back, and how much I was going to hate it and how unhealthy I felt all the time. I got up and knocked over a water jug and it shattered on the floor, and I started crying even harder. I felt desperate, like I had to change something, at least one thing I could control."

She took a taxi to visit the pyramids of Giza, where she saw the ancient monuments surrounded by vast seas of desert. There in the taxi, looking across the ripples of sand, it hit her. *I'm going to come back here and trek through this desert.* Duhigg writes,

> It was a crazy idea. Lisa was out of shape, overweight, with no money in the bank. She didn't know the name of the desert she was looking at or if such a trip was possible. None of that mattered though. Lisa decided she would give herself one year to prepare. And to survive such an expedition, she was certain she would have to make sacrifices.
>
> In particular, she would have to quit smoking.[97]

GOALS AND ENERGY

What triggered Lisa's transformation?

Yes, habit change was vital to her transformation. The nuts and bolts of habit change are important to understand, which is why I highly recommend Duhigg's book.

But habit change wasn't Lisa's trigger. Habit change *followed* the trigger. Lisa started building new habits because of the driving power of something else: *a compelling goal.*

Perhaps for the first time, Lisa had something she felt was big and worthwhile to accomplish. Next year's desert trek was more than a walk through the sand. It represented a new start, an escape from the past, and a way to regain control of her life. It triggered the energy Lisa needed to change everything.

"If you want to be happy," said industrialist Andrew Carnegie, "set a goal that commands your thoughts, liberates your energy, and inspires your hopes."[98] Notice Carnegie's words: A goal *liberates your energy.*

The United States Navy's Sea, Air, and Land Teams, SEALs for short, are recognized as some of the most intense fighting units in military history. Their training programs are the stuff of legend, pushing the boundaries of physical possibility.

What drives such intense training and transformation? The "Big Mish," short for a "big mission." It's SEAL lingo for *a compelling goal*, like the mission to kill Osama bin Laden.[99] Day after day, soldiers talk about the Big Mish. They train with intensity because the Big Mish is ahead.

AUTOMATIC ENERGY

Think of the thermostat and furnace system I described in the last chapter. It has a goal: get the room temperature to 71 degrees. When the room temperature is too low, the system fires up. Then once the room reaches the right temperature, the system shuts down. The system fires up when it perceives a goal and shuts down when it reaches the goal.

Same with human nature. We fire up to achieve goals. There's an instinctive energy-goal connection within the makeup of human nature, driven by the ways we perceive things to be maximally good for us.

Recall my description of Paula in the last chapter. Her view of maximum good was five workout days a week. That was her goal, whether she knew it or not. Call it her habit, her standard, her goal, or her view of maximum good in that area of her life, it's all the same thing. It was an energizing force. When she missed a day, she felt energy, in the form of discomfort and motivation, to increase her performance.

When there's a mismatch between our current performance and our view of maximum good, we produce energy (motivation) to increase performance and reach the peak of the U.

We tend to release just enough energy to achieve our goals, which means big goals release big energy, small goals release small energy and when we have no goals, there's no energy.

Our energy patterns mirror our goal patterns.

Which means a compelling goal has power to change the way we see, feel, and act. "When I'm training for a stunt and I have a goal, I change everything," says illusionist David Blaine. "I have self-control in every aspect of my life. I read all the time. I eat perfectly....I have a whole different energy....But as soon as I'm done with [the stunt], I go to the opposite extreme, where I have no self-control, and it seems to spread through everything."[100]

Let's relate this back to the See-Feel-Act progression. A compelling goal is simply a view of something extremely good we'd like to achieve or something extremely bad we'd like to avoid. This new view triggers new emotion, which motivates new behavior. Compelling goals hit the power button, instantly generating emotional energy.

SEE →	FEEL →	ACT
A compelling goal.	Compelling energy.	Compelling action.
Nothing good.	No energy. Boredom.	Inaction.

Energy and the See-Feel-Act progression.

Imagine we get home and flop on the couch. We're too tired to even reach for the remote. But there's a letter on the coffee table, and we open it to find the message, "You've just won a ten-thousand-dollar shopping spree!" It's for real—not one of those "You've just won" scams. But the deadline is *9 p.m. tonight* at the nearest mall.

What would happen? We'd fly off the couch. "Let's go! Get the keys, let's get out of here!"

Before reading the letter, our energy was low. But now we're frantic for our shoes. Energy is high.

Or imagine how the couch coma might change if we heard our spouse scream *Fire!* from the kitchen. Suddenly we have a compelling goal—*save the house from burning down*. We'd rush in and put out the fire with our shoe. We'd have new energy.

Well, not really. The energy was always there, but our system didn't have a reason to surface it.

With a new goal, though, there's new energy. Automatically.

In the case of the shopping spree and the fire, the circumstances set a compelling goal for us. But we don't need to wait for circumstances. We can choose compelling goals. We can build a case for a compelling goal, then let it energize us.

Of course, energy runs out, even in the pursuit of compelling goals. We can't go for more than a couple days without sleep. No matter how compelling a goal might be, and no matter how strong we are, there's a limit. It's like doing push-ups. A normal person might do ten, a strong person might do a hundred, and a super-strong person might do five hundred. But no one can do ten thousand push-ups without stopping. Eventually we all flop in exhaustion.

We can't go beyond our physical limits. If we imagined a one-to-ten scale for our physical strength, we can't go past ten.

Here's the big idea: Most of us are living at a five or less on the scale. We're not even close to our limits, but we feel we're out of gas—not because we're out of strength, but because we're out of goals. We're not goal-setting in a way that liberates energy. Our standards are too low to inspire performance. We haven't given ourselves a good enough reason to power up, so there's all this untapped power in the gap between five and ten.

MANAGE GOALS, MANAGE ENERGY

"If you are bored with life, if you don't get up every morning with a burning desire to do things," says football coach Lou Holtz, "you don't have enough goals."[101] If we aren't feeling energy, it may be that we haven't given ourselves reason to surface it.

This means our "couch coma" is more often a goal problem than an energy problem. Our goal was to get home to the couch, so when we reached the goal, no more energy was needed. Our system shut down just like a furnace switches off when room temperature reaches the goal temperature.

The better way to stave off after-work exhaustion is to goal-set *through* the evening instead of *to* the couch. If we plan to "play with the kids" or "fix the sink, sweep the garage, watch *Survivor*, then read for fifteen minutes," or "get home, eat quickly, then head over to Katie's house to enjoy a study group with friends," there's a different energy.

I set goals to get energy. I set small goals and larger goals, short-term goals and long-term goals.

I also make goals more compelling with the right type of reward. If there's something I want to do, I make it a finish-line reward for doing something else. Say I want to look at something online that I plan to buy, but Sandra just asked me to get the recycling out to the curb. That's not the most exciting job in the world, so I tell myself, *Finish the recycling, then look at that thing you want online.*

Another example is in the kitchen. I put food in the microwave for three minutes, then play a "kitchen-cleanup countdown." I push the start button and clean, wipe, and do dishes. I'm full of energy. I get a lot done in three minutes. My reward is hot food from the microwave and the satisfaction of a cleaned-up kitchen.

ENERGY FROM VALUES

While we're talking about the energy-creating power of goals, we should talk about *values* as well, because values *are* goals. They are abstract goals, higher-level goals, *goals for goals*, so to speak.

Let's say Edwin has a goal is to get a degree. We ask him, "Why do you want a degree?"

"Because I want a solid career," he says.

"Why do you want a solid career?"

"Because I want financial security."

The value here, meaning, the higher-level goal, is *security*. Security is a really good thing for Edwin, and the college degree and the solid career are good ways to get that really good thing. College and career are smaller, more concrete goals that serve his higher abstract goal.

Same is true of values like truth, freedom, and integrity. They are all high-level goals that govern lower-level goals.

This means values energize us. When we sense that our values are being threatened, or when we see a way to realize our values, we're energized. When we invest time thinking about our values, and why they're important to us, they restructure our motivation. They redirect our automatic energy.

Remember, values, goals, standards, habits, they all serve and support the constant functional goal in human nature—*maximum good, as we see it*. Values are abstract forms of maximum good.

JUST ENOUGH ENERGY

Too many people live with a "go with the flow" philosophy of life. They accept whatever is as the way it should be, so they have no compelling goals. As a result, they don't have much energy either. They're bored and tired all the time.

When we're going with the flow, we don't give our system reason to create any energy. It's like changing the thermostat setting to match the outside temperature. Now there's no reason for the system to fire up.

Boredom is a goal problem, not an energy problem.

When we set big goals, big energy emerges for the challenge. When we set less compelling goals or goals that require less work, our system delivers less energy.

- A homeless man may create just enough energy to work the cardboard and get his daily dose of drugs, alcohol, and food.
- A working mom may create just enough energy to take care of business and her two children.
- An entrepreneur may create just enough energy to build a company up to a million dollars in profit.

Our system releases just enough energy to reach the goal.

A TIME TO SHUT DOWN, A TIME TO FIRE UP

There's a time to shut down, and a time to fire up. The Israelite king Solomon wrote about this sense of timing and balance:

> There is a time for everything, and a season for every activity under the heavens.
> A time to be born and a time to die,
> A time to plant and a time to uproot,
> A time to kill and a time to heal,
> A time to weep and a time to laugh,
> A time to mourn and a time to dance.[102]

If we're constantly full-fire, we'll burn out. If we're constantly shut off, we'll rust out. There's a balance point, a natural rhythm to our goal pursuit.

Whenever we complete a goal, there's a drop in energy. Our system shuts off. We might describe the shut-off as boredom or slack. But we can also describe it in positive terms like peace and contentment.

It's good to have these peaceful times.

I think it's interesting how the Genesis account describes God working to create the world, then looking with satisfaction on His work. "And God saw that it was good."[103] God achieved, then rested and celebrated His achievement.

We could benefit from that practice. Unfortunately, it's human nature to pass too quickly on our accomplishments to appreciate them. We fail to do them justice, and undermine the winning feeling. When we move on to the next problem without celebration, we undermine our vitality.

ENERGY: EVIDENCE OF INVISIBLE GOALS

Our lives are filled with invisible goals and unstated standards. We're mostly unaware of these Inverted-U's buried in our minds. Whether by design or by default, the goals are everywhere, and we pursue them automatically.

We can discover these goals using energy as a clue. Since there's a natural connection between our goals and our energy, whenever there's energy, there's a compelling goal in the mix. Whenever we experience an intense emotion, a goal is driving it.

As we see in the graphic below, energy in the second box implies an energy-creator in the first box.

What is here?	Compelling energy.	Compelling action.

Since there's a natural connection between the first box and the second, we can discover compelling goals by asking ourselves, why am I energized?

What sorts of tasks and situations energize us? What angers us the most? What excites us the most? When we find these high-energy situations, we know there's a compelling goal buried nearby.

Consider the story of Martin Luther King, Jr. By eleventh grade, he was still physically small but something unique happened to his voice. It had been transformed, writes biographer Stephen Oates, "into a rich and resonant baritone that commanded attention when he spoke in class."[104] His powerful voice and remarkable vocabulary impressed both students and teachers, and they encouraged him to develop his abilities. Martin read constantly, studying the way great authors and speakers put words together. "My most constant interest," King said, "was the eloquent statement of ideas."

"I traveled from Atlanta to Dublin, Georgia," King remembered in his autobiography, "with a dear teacher of mine, Mrs. Bradley." The Negro Elks sponsored an oratorical contest on April 17, 1944, in Dublin, about a hundred miles southeast of Atlanta. King spoke on "The Negro and the Constitution," and won the contest.

That night, he and his teacher traveled back to Atlanta on a crowded bus, happily discussing the events of the day. But happiness would soon give way to rage. "Along the way," King recalled, "some white passengers boarded the bus." There were no empty seats, so the driver walked back to King and Mrs. Bradley, and in front of fifty quiet onlookers, demanded they get up and give the white passengers their seats. When King hesitated, the driver flew off the handle. "Get up, you black son-of-a-bitch!"

"I intended to stay right in that seat," said King, "but Mrs. Bradley urged me up, saying we had to obey the law. We stood up in the aisle for ninety miles to Atlanta. That night will never leave my memory. It was the angriest I have ever been in my life."[105]

Martin was excited the most about speaking…and was angered the most by prejudice. So he connected the two and became a speaker against prejudice. His anger revealed a compelling goal.

In her book *The Path*, Laurie Beth Jones asks readers to list three things in the world that anger them the most, alongside three things in the world that excite them the most. The answers can reveal one's life mission. She asks, "How can you use what most excites you to affect or change what most angers you?"[106]

Jones's strategy connects the dots between high energy and high purpose.

GETTING UNSTUCK

Sometimes we feel like we're out of gas, stuck by the side of the road. We can't muster the energy. Here are some practical ways to recharge and get back on track.

The first is to see the search for goals as a goal in itself. You might think, *I'm so tired and don't have any energizing goals. What do I do?*

I say, *Make finding a goal your goal.*

You didn't have a goal just one second ago. But now you do. And just having this new goal might energize you for the search.

Another problem is not knowing how to achieve a goal. You might think, *I don't know how to achieve my goal. What do I do?*

Whenever we want to achieve a goal but don't know how, we actually have two goals. The first goal is, *learn how to achieve the second goal.*

Let's say our goal is to complete a spreadsheet forecast of the company's growth, but we don't know how to use a spreadsheet. We could give up, saying, "I don't know how," or we could agree to tackle two goals: learn to use a spreadsheet, then forecast the company growth.

Another way to recharge is to use what I call the *fire builder* strategy. Think of your motivation like a campfire. When the fire is strong it can burn a big log, but when the fire is weak, a big log smothers the flame and makes things worse. Weak fires need kindling, small sticks, and twigs—things that burn quickly and easily. Save the logs for when the fire is blazing.

Think of goals as various sizes of wood for the fire. Small, easy goals are small pieces of wood—kindling and twigs. Big, challenging goals are big pieces of wood—logs. When the fire of motivation is hot, burn the logs. Tackle the big tasks. When the fire of motivation is low, build it up by burning the small sticks—the easy tasks.

NEW GOALS, NEW VIEW

Goals don't just energize us. They open our eyes to things in the world around us, which means we must set goals to expand our awareness.

This is a challenge, because we want to take the opposite approach. We want to know if a goal is realistic, then set it.

That approach doesn't work. It just traps us in the status quo.

The crazy truth is, people who claim to be "realistic" are actually the opposite. They're more unrealistic than the most delusional optimist they can imagine.

Really? The next chapter explains.

CHAPTER 14

Automatic Alert

"All of us seem to come equipped with filters on the floors of our minds, and all the filters have differing sizes and meshes. What catches in my filter may run right through yours. What catches in yours may pass through mine, no sweat."

~STEPHEN KING, AMERICAN NOVELIST

There's a mother on the edge of a noisy playground, talking with her friend. Hundreds of kids are playing and screaming. Her child is in the middle of it. He falls and cries, and though she's not looking in his direction, she instantly hears and runs to help.

There's a mother emperor penguin on an open plain of ice in Antarctica, packed in a colony of ten thousand birds. Her chick wanders off, and despite the noisy din, she instantly recognizes its cry.

There's a couple planning for marriage. It seems like all they see are ads for wedding venues and honeymoon spots. A year later, they're expecting a baby. Now it seems everyone is pregnant and all the ads promote baby strollers and diapers.

There's a man who recently bought a car. At first, it seemed like he was the only one who owned it, but now he sees them on the road everywhere.

What's happening in all of these similar situations?

INFORMATION OVERLOAD

As I mentioned in the chapter on *Automatic Humility*, we live in a busy, buzzing, dynamic world. There's a billion drivers in a billion cars swerving through roads all over the globe. There's ten billion billion (yes, billion billion) insects scurrying, scampering, flapping, and fluttering over the face of the earth. There's a Japanese manufacturer trying to land a can of sports drink on the surface of the moon,[107] a brash billionaire running for political office in America, and two hundred Russians digging for diamonds a thousand feet down in Yakutia. The world is abuzz with diversity.

On top of the natural buzz, there's a constant spray of outside information, a rain of info-confetti we can never wave out of our faces. The media industry offers thousands of television channels, packed with twenty-four hours of programming a day. The advertising industry serves up millions of ads each day, everywhere we look. Then there's social media, where we crank out the confetti for each other—31 million Facebook messages, 350,000 tweets, and 50,000 Instagram posts *every minute.*[108]

Then there's the inner spray of imagination, like a Blue Man Group flinging paint-water and toilet paper in the theater of our minds.

Even when we escape the mayhem to the serenity of the Zen garden, we're still overloaded because of the limits of our perception itself. Take a Zen moment right now to listen. What do you hear? A computer fan? Someone talking? A radio blaring in the next room?

Right now, I hear the hum of a television, a pressure washer gunning outside my window, a computer fan, a slamming car door.

While it seems like we're hearing these sounds for the first time, they've been there all along, tapping our eardrums. They don't get our attention, because there's too much information competing for too little mind-space.

SEARCH AND CATCH

We handle this overload by filtering. Our minds are wired to work in this crazy-busy world by catching information we believe is important and passing the rest through.

Think about what a filter does. It catches some things and lets other things pass. Our mind does the same, snagging things we unconsciously think are important and letting everything else go.

Several years ago, I was home and remembered that guests were coming over in just a couple of hours. Suddenly it became important to get the house clean, and I started seeing things for the first time, like a black Ethernet cable running across the kitchen floor and down into the basement. *What the heck?* I found out my son Grant had strung it from the kitchen to the game room to play Xbox Live—last week. It had been there the whole time, but I'd not noticed it until getting the house in order became important.

When our sense of importance changes, so does our filter.

Whenever we take up a new goal, we establish a new sense of importance, which changes the things we see. We catch new things related to our new goal—new resources, new ways to reach our goal, new problems to solve to reach the goal. It's as if we were completely blind to entire worlds of possibility before, but now we see these worlds clear as day.

This is what happened with the car buyer who started seeing similar cars everywhere or the couple having a child who now see all the baby product ads.

As soon as something becomes important, it also becomes visible. It changes the way we see.

This alerting attribute isn't just a "catch" feature. It's a "search" feature as well. The mind not only waits for information; it looks for it too. We're always looking for things that help us reach our goals and confirm our beliefs.

A WORLD OF INVISIBLE REALITY

Our mental filter separates reality into two categories: *perceived reality* and *ignored reality*.

Let's say we're filtering out ninety-nine percent of the reality around us and letting one percent in. That means one percent is *perceived reality*. The other ninety-nine percent is *ignored reality*.

Here's how I illustrate these two categories.

■ Perceived reality   □ Ignored reality

Our perception is filtered, so we see only bits and pieces of reality.

That's a lot of ignored reality.

There's a good chance that ignored reality contains information we need to better lead our lives, which means we're working without it. So we're unaware and ineffective.

Then consider the one percent that's getting in—our *perceived reality*. Is it the right one percent? Are these specs of reality going to help us be our best? Probably not. There's a really good chance that we're seeing the wrong things, that our way of seeing is sabotaging our highest and best, because we don't have the right information.

Back in the *Challenge of Change* chapter, I described the subtle power of complacency. What drives it? *Blindness*. We can't see the opportunity in making a change, nor can we see the danger in staying as we are. So we're okay with things when we shouldn't be.

Our decisions are only as wise as our ability to see the right way. If we're seeing wrong, or failing to see, this automatically influences our emotions, behaviors, and eventually the outcome of our lives.

This is a good place to make a subtle but important point. It's possible to see a situation right while we see it different from someone else. Think back to the five ways each worker saw Danny's promotion, and let's assume for a moment that they all saw different aspects of the situation in accurate ways. They saw right, but they saw different.

When I think about ways we perceive, several categories come to mind. Here are three:

- See-right. This is when we see some aspect of reality in an accurate way. Keep in mind that our seeing is always limited, so we see bits and pieces, but our view can be accurate, much like someone could accurately see a piece of a puzzle but not the whole picture.
- See-wrong. This is when we see some aspect of reality in an inaccurate way. We mischaracterize reality.
- See-different. This is when we see a different aspect of reality as someone else. Our filter catches different bits and pieces, which means we can see right but see different. This is why it's vital that we seek diverse feedback.

These categories combine as well. We can *See-different* and *See-wrong*, just like we can *See-different* and *See-right*. Sometimes people see things different because one person is wrong and the other is right.

Other times, people see different because they have two accurate but different perspectives.

Whenever we think about perception, we should keep these categories in mind.

THE LAW OF ATTRACTION?

The "law of attraction" was all the rage a few years ago, this idea that we could tell the universe what we want and instantly start seeing good things happening.

I think the mental filter offers a better explanation. Whenever we declare a new intention, it changes the filter, which creates a new awareness. Perceived reality changes when our goals change. New ideas and resources and opportunities that previously lived in *ignored reality* suddenly enter *perceived reality*.

This process feels miraculous, which is why the law of attraction idea was so popular. People started declaring their intentions, then seeing new opportunities and new ways to achieve their intentions surfacing out of the woodwork. They took this as proof that the law of attraction was indeed a law.

I'm saying there is a law, and it does have "miraculous" power. But it's a law of perception, not a law of attraction. New intentions create new perceptions that surface in new ways to achieve our goals.

UNREALISTIC REALISTS

Given this insight about our mental filter, it makes perfect sense to do something that previously didn't make sense at all: set goals without knowing how to achieve them.

When we set a goal, we change the mental filter. We start catching new things and searching for new things. Suddenly we find new resources and ways to reach the new goal.

Let's say the new goal is to grow our company's revenues ten percent. If we refuse to accept the new goal, thinking, *I don't see how that can be done*, we won't change the mental filter. So we won't find any new ways to achieve a goal.

If, however, we accept the goal and let it simmer in our minds, we'll start seeing new ways to achieve it, much like the car dealer found a new way to sell cars with test drives.

People who claim to be "realists" hold a philosophy of life that locks them into the one percent of *perceived reality* they already search and catch. This means they keep ignoring *ignored reality*. They stay blocked off from the ninety-nine percent of the reality outside the limits of their current awareness.

As strange as it may sound, realism is unrealistic.

When we only set goals we know how to achieve, we lock ourselves in a small, unchanging perceptive prison.

This false philosophy of "realism" says *we'll believe it when we see it*, but the right philosophy switches things around to say, *we'll see it when we believe it*. By first putting faith in a new goal, we start to see things differently. New believing leads to new awareness.

WHAT FIRST, THEN HOW

The strategy is, *what first, then how*. We must be goal-minded first, method-minded second. Goal-minded first, resource-minded second. The low-performance mindset is, "Show me how, then I'll buy in." The peak-performance mindset is, "Show me what, then I'll figure out the how." *How-to* is important. But it cannot get ahead of the *what-to*. We need both, in that order.

Think of it like a locomotive and a boxcar, where the locomotive is the *what-to*, and the boxcar is the *how-to*. The high-performance sequence is to keep the goal in mind, then let the goal change the mental filter, so we find previously unseen resources and methods to achieve the goal.

LOOK BEFORE YOU LEAP

How do we balance what we've just said about the "what first, then how" approach and the wisdom to "look-before-you-leap"?

First, let's admit that it's irresponsible to set impossible goals and waste time trying to achieve them. So there's a risk that this "what first, then how" approach could trick us into embracing impossible goals. This is what the realists fear, and they have good reason to be afraid. We think we can do something, then set out blindly, only to find out it's impossible, and we've wasted a whole bunch of time, money, and opportunity in the process.

So how do we prevent ourselves and our organizations from getting into impossible goal situations? How can we keep our realism and still follow this new way?

One answer is a "feasibility approach," which is an attitude that believes that the answers are out there and we're going to find them, so we'll act as if the goal is real and start scouting out the land. We're willing to experiment with a goal, to hold on to it long enough to reset the mental filter and see the new reality it shows us. Then, once the scouting is done from the new awareness, we can make a good decision.

There's another factor to consider. Some decisions are risky and that's just the way it is. There's nothing we can do to reduce risk any further; we have to make a leap if we want to get to the other side. Life requires we take risks—measured risks, to be sure—and while there are many risks that are irresponsible to take, there are also many risks that are irresponsible to pass up.

THE FULL PICTURE OF AUTOMATIC INFLUENCE

To this point, we've had a solid survey of automatic influence and how it works in many areas of our lives. Here's what we know…

> Perception is power, because the way we see automatically influences the way we feel and act. When we change the way we see, our feelings and behaviors change automatically.
>
> There's a huge difference between the situation itself and the way we see the situation. When we discover this difference, we discover our power. We can choose the way we live by choosing to see situations, people, life, and so on in the most constructive ways. The goal is to *see right, every moment of sight.*
>
> Change is easier when we change the way we see. Change is harder when we try to change attitudes and behaviors without first changing perceptions.

Then, after we'd learned about our power, the next step was to learn how it worked. In the next set of chapters, we saw how new ways of seeing automatically change our attitudes and behaviors.

> When we see change as paddling the river, with no place for a neutral attitude, we get inspired to go after life and resist drift.
>
> When we see how blind we are, we instantly become more circumspect, more open, more willing to question our point of view. We get *automatic humility.*
>
> When we see people as people, of equal high value as ourselves, instead of overlooking them, or seeing them as less important, or seeing them as tools and barriers to our goals, we feel differently and act

differently. We're ten times better at solving "people problems," because we trigger *automatic love*.

When we start seeing how all of us pursue the same basic goal, *maximum good, as we see it*, we see human nature as much more sensible than we believed before. We approach "people problems" in ways that lead to mutual understanding and mutual benefit.

When we see wrong but think we see right, we fall prey to *automatic evil*. But when we realize we're susceptible to misperception, we can take steps to counteract it. One way is to abandon happiness as our purpose in life, and embrace true goodness instead. Happiness is a secondary and subjective reality that can lure us into thinking we see right when we aren't. Which means we can do evil in the name of happiness. The goal is to be happy about the right things, which means true goodness should be our goal.

When we see success as coming from persistent effort, driven by obsessive interest and not from innate talent or intelligence, we get new hope to succeed. Instead of counting ourselves out of the game, we know we can win the game…if we want to.

When we discover *automatic sabotage*, we see how every standard sets an upper boundary for our performance. We have just as much motivation to correct down to the standard as we have to correct up to the standard. Our standards of maximum good define the upper limits of our performance, and many times those standards are set below the level of our potential.

When we discover how our goals create *automatic energy* to achieve them, we become more willing to set big goals. We see how big goals tend to create big energy, while small goals create small energy. By setting goals the right way, we can manage our energy.

When we see how our mind works as a filter to give us only the information that's relevant to our current goals, we get a new willingness to set goals, because new goals change the mental filter, helping us see new ways to achieve our goals in what was previously ignored reality.

Given this power, where should we go with it? There are all sorts of directions to take, as unique to every one of us as our fingerprints. But there are also directions that are common to every one of us.

In the next section of chapters, we'll explore two of these common goals: *total freedom* and *complete fulfillment*.

PART 5

FREE AND FULL

CHAPTER 15

Total Freedom, Complete Fulfillment

"Ever since I was a child I have had this instinctive urge for expansion and growth. To me, the duty of a human being is the sincere development of one's potential."

— BRUCE LEE, AMERICAN MARTIAL ARTIST

A recent GEICO television commercial featured Pinocchio the bad motivational speaker in a hotel conference room, speaking to a sparse audience of misfits. "You have potential," he squeaks, pointing to a middle-aged man in a rumpled suit.

Pinocchio's nose grows. He can't get away with a lie.

Unlike the GEICO Pinocchio, I believe in potential, even for middle-aged men in rumpled suits. But I don't believe in what passes for potential in the world of motivation nowadays—the surface hype and quick-fix ideas that don't emphasize long-term growth. That brand of potential is a lie.

WHAT IS POTENTIAL?

One way to describe potential is that it's everything *possible* that isn't *actual*. It's everything that could be that hasn't yet been turned into reality. It's a vast landscape of unused ability and untapped opportunity, not just for us as individuals, but for our work teams, our families, and our culture.

Potential is a big idea.

However, it does little good to talk up potential when we don't believe we have it. It seemed better to hold off on this topic until we'd fully understood the power of automatic influence, because there's a barb-wired barricade of cynicism blocking the path. When motivators push, the inner cynic pushes back, instantly converting *Yes, You Can* talks to *No, I Can't*, because real-world experience has made it abundantly clear: *surface motivation doesn't work.* We need a deep, persistent power to get up, over, and around the obstacles.

Why do motivators talk potential so much? Because FOMO—Fear of Missing Out—is a big deal. We see our friends on social media having a great time, and we want to be there too. We see others with great families, great careers, and great lives, and we want that too. There's a deep desire to make the most of things, and a sense that things aren't happening like they could.

"There is no such thing," said UCLA basketball coach John Wooden, "as an overachiever. I think we're all underachievers to different degrees."[109] None of us is our best all the time. We're all *underachieving* and *underliving* in one way or another:

- Do we treat everyone with respect and love, all the time?
- Do we show up on time, all the time? Are we faithful to our word?
- Do we overlook every insult and forgive people immediately?
- Do we rebound quickly from discouragement?
- Are we developing our intelligence and talent like we could?
- Are we uninhibited by fear of failure or rejection?

Sheesh! We all have loads of room to improve.

OBSESSIVE INTEREST AND PERSISTENT EFFORT

In the *Penny Thick* chapter, we saw how achievement comes from *obsessive interest* driving *persistent effort*. Contrary to common belief, we don't succeed because we're naturally smarter or more skilled than others. World-class skill comes from a "rage to master," a burning, long-term desire to grow, which in turn creates intelligence and skill.

The only way to keep the desire burning is to develop our *intrinsic motivations*, meaning, the things that drive us from deep within. We all have unique interests and unique histories. If we're going to invest the effort to grow into our best selves, we've got to get a clear sense of these deep and unique drives.

Individuals and organizations are wired differently, and that's what makes life great. I'm thankful that the folks at Apple Computer are obsessively interested in smartphones and electronic gadgets. They invest their entire lives in pursuit of the best widget, so I can text and call and surf the web.

Then there's the guy at Mr. Appliance I met last year when he came to fix my fridge. He's an expert in all things appliance, obsessively interested in how they work and how to repair them. He's invested his entire life in one area so I can reap just a fragment of the benefit.

Hopefully you are benefitting from the ideas in this book. It's here in front of your face because of my obsessive interest in writing and researching it, which inspired more than a thousand hours of effort.

This is the division of labor. We all have *obsessive interests* in different things, so we can create maximum good in a variety of ways. When we all develop in our own unique ways, there's a multidimensional flourishing, as each person lifts the lives of others.

Again, the key is to find our unique obsessive interests. I have no interest in how fridges work or how to repair them. I have no interest in the way an iPhone is built. But I'm really glad that others do.

The key is to figure out who we are and where we fit in the big buzzing world.

WHO ARE YOU?

Imagine someone asking Fred the sales guy, "Who are you?" What would he say?

He might give his name, "I'm Fred."

But they say, "I didn't ask you what your name was. I asked, 'who are you?'"

Then maybe he'd give them his job title: "I'm a salesman."

"I didn't ask you what you do," they say. "I asked you who you are."

Fred is annoyed and confused, but hopefully you get the idea. We aren't our names. We aren't our job titles. Our sense of identity is bigger than that.

A true sense of identity helps us adapt in a changing world. There's a saying, *If you are what you do, then when you don't, you aren't.* Whenever we confuse role and identity, role changes become identity crises.

Think of how I struggled with identity after I lost my first business in 1998. It took losing this role to surface a deeper sense of who I really was. That deeper sense of potential eventually brought me here, writing this book, to a place far from where I was before.

Now I put it to you: *Who are you?*

Your answer must be bigger than a job description. It needs to transcend your roles, because roles change but you'll always be you.

Just a few months ago as I write this, I spoke with my close friend, Larry Ward, who works at Joint Base Lewis-McChord, a military base in the south Seattle area. Larry leads consultants who teach veterans' benefits to outgoing soldiers. "Identity crisis is a major problem," Larry said. "They see themselves as soldiers, and when they aren't soldiers any more, their whole sense of self is in question."

Larry told me about a former boss, a sergeant major, who had retired after thirty years but didn't take any transition leave, which is the vacation time he could have used to ease into his new life. Instead, he chose to cash it all out, which meant he was a fully active sergeant major one day and "nothing" the next day.

On his first day of retirement, the sergeant major showed up at the airfield to run physical training and corrected soldiers on how to wear their uniform—just like he'd always done. Then he went around base doing similar things. As the days wore on, servicemen complained about this sabotage of the chain of command, and finally the military police stepped in. "If you don't stop this," they told him, "we're going to have to arrest you for impersonating a military officer."

The sergeant major then came by Larry's office and confided in him, saying, "I didn't realize how unimportant I'd be after I retired."

When our sense of importance and identity is so intertwined with our job descriptions, we're destined for trouble.

Not only do we need a clear sense of identity, we need a bigger sense of identity. At least most of us do. Our sense of self needs to be bigger and better than we typically think, because of the complacency, useless fears, and imagined inabilities that stunt our sense of who we are.

A few chapters ago, our biggest question might have been whether we had potential at all. But now I hope that our biggest question is, *how will we develop it?* The new view of success, the new view of people, the new view of potential, offers a new view of self. It's a picture of a plant growing through the asphalt, unstoppable, pushing up little by little. The new view says we're not weak and helpless. We brim with power.

The question is, *What will we do with our power?*

This is why I like to help people and organizations get clear about their identity. There are tools that help us identify our key characteristics, personality type, strengths, interests, values, and so on. There are ways to depth-sound the heart and detect the things that matter most to us.

RAISING OUR STANDARDS

While we get a clear sense of who we are, we also need to get our standards right. It's so easy to lower our standards in the comparison game, defining them at *better than average* rather than *best*.

A few years ago, I had a chance to meet the current coach of the Seattle Seahawks, Pete Carroll, through a mutual friend, Lou Tice. I was in Lou's office when Pete came in and we chatted briefly.

One of the things I love about Pete is how he gets his players to think at the *best-self* standard, not the *better-than-others* standard. In the summer of 2014, in Pete's first meeting of the year with the new Seahawks team, he laid out this high standard. The Seahawks were fresh off a Super Bowl win, blowing out Denver 43-8 just a few months earlier in a game described by *Fox Sports* writer Kenley Young as "a rout of fairly epic proportions, the kind of lopsided affair we haven't seen in more than a decade."[110] Given the staggering win, Denver's poor performance, and the fact that the first preseason game was against Denver, I wondered what Pete would say to his players.

"Guys, I hope Denver plays their best game against us coming up," Pete said. "That's the only way we can discover what our best really is. The Super Bowl win was fantastic but it didn't test us. Denver played one of their worst games in years, and we can't raise our game playing guys who beat themselves. We've got to prove ourselves against the highest standard, not the lowest."[111]

Instead of playing to the level of our competition, why not play to the level of our capability?[112]

TOTAL FREEDOM

To be our best, we all must follow common principles. I sum them up with the phrase "free and full." We all benefit from the pursuit of *total freedom* and *complete fulfillment*.

First, let's talk about total freedom. The goal is to get completely free from every wrong way of seeing. Every wrong view of self, situation, life, others, and the world around us—it's all got to go.

In the *Challenge of Change* chapter, I described three barriers to freedom—*useless fears*, *imagined inabilities*, and *blindness*—with a metaphor for each. Useless fears are rubber snakes, imagined inabilities are plastic chains, and blindness is a blindfold.

Total freedom is *the way our lives look and feel when all the barriers are gone*. When our lives are free from blindness, useless fear, imagined inability, and every other self-imposed limitation. It's hard to dream and grow when we're blindfolded, bound with chains, and surrounded by what we think are deadly snakes. But when we realize that blindfolds can be removed…and that the chains are plastic…and that the snakes are rubber, we can break free and be our best.

How might our lives be different if we were completely free from useless fear, if every rubber snake were seen for what it is?

We'd be unstoppable.

Then imagine what our lives might be like if we were completely free from imagined inabilities? If every plastic chain were gone?

It would revolutionize our lives.

Then imagine what would happen if we broke the power of complacency by seeing the danger in the status quo and the opportunity in constructive change?

We'd have all the motivation we need.

Remember, perception has the power to free us. When we see right, our emotions and motivations fall into line and automatically influence our behaviors. Complacency, useless fear, and imagined inability all spring from misperception, as we show in this graphic from the *Change* chapter.

See	Feel	Act
Blind to danger or opportunity.	Complacency.	Do nothing.
Danger that isn't real.	Useless fear.	Avoid things that should be faced.
See self as unable.	Helplessness.	Do nothing.

These three reasons we resist change spring from seeing things wrong. The way to freedom is to correct our perception.

Anything less than total freedom is a tragic squandering of human nature, a waste of the inconceivably great endowments that make us who we are. That means every blindfold, every plastic chain, every rubber snake has to go. Every misconception and misperception has to go. Every belief that keeps us from seeing what we need to see and doing what we need to do to fulfill the purposes of our lives, has to go.

COMPLETE FULFILLMENT

Total freedom is such a compelling goal that it's hard to even imagine reaching it.

But as fantastic and profound as it is, total freedom is not the total goal. It's just one leg of the journey. Once we're free from the things that hold us back, we're positioned to achieve *complete fulfillment*—the full development of our skills, wisdom, intelligence, attitudes, and character.

First, we can be *full of wisdom*. We can develop our wisdom to the point where we're brimming with skill and diligence.

Imagine our lives like a vast country estate, with vineyards and vegetables and orchards all around. Wisdom is the green thumb that makes every field flourish. How can we create more good in our community, our career, our finances, and our relationships? It takes wisdom to flourish in all these areas.

Second, we need to be *full of optimism*, having a trained mind that focuses on constructive things and constantly works against the gravitational pull of negativity. While we must tend to problems to solve them, people are well past the healthy balance point here. The typical person spends ninety percent of their lives stewing over the ten percent of things that aren't working. They overlook a thousand good things to obsess about one bad thing.

Just like it takes constant use of our leg muscles to stand against gravity, we need a muscular optimism to stand against the negative bias in human nature.

Third, we need to be *full of love*. We need a deep-seated and constant mindfulness that others have equal value as self. The general human tendency is to diminish others in arrogance or disregard people in our self-obsession. But when we learn to see other people the right ways, everything changes.

Finally, we need to be *full of faith in others*. Once we understand these principles for ourselves, we need to pay it forward and believe for others as well. We need to see potential in people and talk them into it. We should believe in each other, root for each other, support each other. Success isn't just for the people we think are naturally gifted and intelligent. It's for anyone who will put in the work.

Imagine someone saying to you, "Most people see me for what I am. You see me for what I could be." Wouldn't it make you feel more fulfilled? Wouldn't it make you a more effective parent, a more effective leader? Anyone can nag and judge, and most do. Why not buck the tide? Why not believe the best for people? Why not set high expectations in a positive and inspiring way?

DORMANT TO DOMINANT

Our best selves are waiting to be released. But they're locked up. When perception is off, we automatically trigger complacency, useless fear, imagined inabilities, and a host of other limiting beliefs. When we think about the potential we have as fathers and mothers, husbands and wives, as friends and business partners, as workers, and as individual human beings, we find so many aspects of our best self are suppressed, locked away within.

How do we unlock our best?

It starts with better perspective. Perspective is the power button, and when our perspective of ourselves and our situation is *right, in every second of sight,* we've got optimal power to be our best. We lay the foundation for a better life.

Not just a better life but better work too. The *best organization*, just like the *best self*, is waiting to be released. Think about how much the work culture would change if everyone in it used the power button for the greater good. What would happen if workers were totally free and completely fulfilled?

Think about all the people problems that currently hold your business back. How effective would you be if your workplace were full of automatic love?

When people get along, companies get ahead. When people have a sense of purpose and power, companies benefit.

It starts with leaders believing in the people they lead. If you've been to business school, you've probably heard the story of "Sweeney's Miracle." In 1965, Dr. James Sweeney was a professor of management at Tulane University, responsible for the oversight of the Biomedical Computer Center. There James met George Johnson, the janitor at the facility, and the two struck up a friendship. Although George didn't have an education and tested at an IQ so low that experts believed he was incapable of learning, James Sweeney believed in George and insisted that he could train him to become a computer operator. George not only learned the skills, but eventually became so adept that Sweeney put him in charge of the whole computer center. George ran the center successfully for years after and trained many others as he was trained.[113]

When we believe in people, they rise to the occasion.

Same goes for ourselves. When we believe in ourselves, we find new power to unleash our best.

CHAPTER 16

Breaking Plastic Chains

"I began to feel that we were all prisoners of our own history."
— ROLAND JOFFE, FRENCH FILM DIRECTOR

In 1974, Converse did an ad campaign for its *PF Flyer* shoe, picturing a two-year-old boy in an athletic pose. He was just playing, but the moment the camera clicked, he looked like an Olympic athlete about to throw a discus. The headline read, "Many champions are born and then unmade."

"A kid is an athlete," the ad copy read, "even the tiniest kid. Maybe he doesn't call his games basketball or tennis, but he goes at them hard all day long, running, jumping, climbing, tumbling around." The ad went on to pitch tennis shoes for the athlete within, but in the process, made a powerful point: *We're wired to go hard at life.*

Early life is enthusiasm, wonder, and vigor. We learn with speed and intensity as we take our first steps, speak our first words, and explore the world—turning over every rock, digging up every ant pile, and using every crayon in the box.

DOES "LIFE" UNMAKE US?

But something happens as we grow up. We stop playing. We get an attitude against growth and learning. Something unmakes the inner champion.

What's the culprit? Most people believe the answer is life itself. "Growing up is *getting real*," people say. "The real world, unlike the kid world, is a tough place that unplugs our enthusiasm, one disappointment at a time."

I disagree. The problem isn't *life*. It's the way we *see life*. Imagine two people going through the same troubles, but one person keeps their vitality, joy, and zest, while the other person plunges into depression, cynicism, and despair.

Same circumstances, different response.

Studies of optimists and pessimists show that both have the same amount of troubles, but their different attitude comes from different ways of *seeing* those troubles. Psychologist Martin Seligman writes,

> I have been studying [optimists and pessimists] for the past twenty-five years. The defining characteristic of pessimists is that they tend to believe bad events will last a long time and will undermine everything they do....The optimists, who are confronted with the same hard knocks of this world, think about misfortune in the opposite way. They tend to believe defeat is just a temporary setback, that its causes are confined to this one case.[114]

The optimist and the pessimist both experience the hard knocks. But they see the hard knocks in different ways.

It's hard to get this into our thick skulls, because we're all heavily invested in the myth that bad circumstances make for bad lives. So we need to be reminded it's not that way.

Here's where amputee motivational speakers are a terrific help.

You heard that right. We need to spend as much time as possible with amputee motivators. People leave their talks transformed, not so much by what is said, but by what is seen: a happy person who the audience thinks shouldn't be.

It's been said that the best way to get a career as a motivational speaker is to lose a limb but keep your humor. Why? Because amputee motivators are living myth-busters. Their lives dispel the prevalent illusion that our circumstances are our problem. It's common to think bad attitudes come from bad circumstances. But they don't. *Bad attitudes come from the way we choose to see our circumstances.* These motivators prove that people can go through terrible things and keep their joy.

Consider Josh Sundquist, who lost his left leg to bone cancer at age nine and is now a paralympic skier and motivator. His promo video begins with a view of himself standing on his solo leg, dressed like a rap artist complete with a Flavor Flav clock around his neck, saying,

Yo yo,
let me tell you
what it's like to walk
a mile in my shoe.

He's not just coping with his lost leg. He's laughing about it!

Or consider Spencer West, born with a genetic disorder. He lost both his legs at age five, but says, "If you work hard with others, if you never ever give up, and you laugh a lot, you can achieve absolutely anything."

Then there's Nick Vujicic, the most inspiring motivational speaker I've ever seen. Nick is an amputee motivator and bestselling author who takes the illustrated message to the max because he has neither legs nor arms. He's just a torso and, if you can believe this, he still pokes fun at himself.

His promo video is titled "No arms, no legs, no worries." The opening scene is a soccer players' view of the net, ready to kick a ball in. And there's Nick, propped up between the goalposts where a goalie would stand. My first thought watching this was, *This is too much. A video portraying a torso as a goalie?* Nick has a small foot and can stand upright, but it's hard to see how he keeps his balance. But there he stands...or sits...whatever you want to call it, and the player kicks a ball toward him and the goal. The ball veers left of Nick and goes in the net, while Nick watches it pass. Then he says in mock anger, "I wasn't ready!"

Should we be laughing? Yes, that's how he wants it. There's another video of Nick out at a water park going down the slides. He hops out of the water and says, "It's freezing. I can't feel my hands."

Then Nick hits the core issue: the challenges of life.

There were times when I looked at my life and thought, "I can't do this and I can't do that." I kept focusing on what I *didn't* have and what I *couldn't* do. And I forgot what I *do* have and *can* do. Sometimes it's hard to be thankful. I remember being eight years old, thinking about my future: *I'm never going to get married. I'm never going to have a job. I'm not going to have a life of purpose. What kind of a husband could I be if I can't even hold my wife's hand?"*

By now, the audience is in tears.

Notice Nick's problem was *focus*. "I kept *focusing* on what I didn't have," he said. His problem wasn't circumstance. It was his *view* of circumstance. This gets back to our point from the last chapter about total freedom. It starts with *seeing right, every second of sight*.

"I love life," Nick continues. "People ask me, 'How come you smile so much?' Sometimes it's not easy. Things happen in life that we don't understand, and we don't know if we're going to get through it."

Today Nick has gotten through it and much more. He has a college degree from Griffith University. He married Kanae Miyahara in 2012, and they have two healthy sons. "I may not have hands to hold my wife's hand," he says, "but I don't need hands to hold her heart."[115]

In every presentation Vujicic makes, people are transformed. They get a counterintuitive view of life. They break the false connection between circumstances and happiness. Nick shows the *life-makes-us-miserable* lie for what it really is. You don't find people with folded arms at the back of the room, thinking, *Who does this guy think he is? He doesn't know my troubles.* Amputee motivators show-and-tell how "people are about as happy as they make up their mind to be."[116]

Life doesn't unmake the champion within. Our view does. But it's one thing to say, *misperception is the problem*, and it's another to explain exactly how the misperception works. We need to get clear on the details so we can change things.

In the last chapter, we described three major barriers to freedom: *blindness, useless fear*, and *imagined inability*. In this and the next two chapters, we'll learn how the mind makes and breaks these barriers, starting here with imagined inability—the plastic chain.

THE MISUSE OF INDUCTIVE REASONING

An entrepreneur is cheated by his business partner. He thinks, *You can't trust anyone.*

A college student is dumped by her boyfriend. She thinks, *Men are pigs.*

An eighth-grader struggles with algebra. He thinks, *I'll never be good at math.*

On the surface, this looks like wisdom from experience, but it's not. This is the misuse of *inductive reasoning*, a thinking process we've been using all our lives to understand the world around us. We use inductive reasoning to create general beliefs from specific experiences, and it works great in the simple, predictable, natural world. But it's terrible for the complex realities of social life and personal growth.

To better understand inductive reasoning, and how we misuse it, let's start with our early life experiences and the ways we built beliefs from them. We taste the Gerber blended peas—*yuk*. We cry and Mom comes to our rescue—*thank goodness*. We experience the physical world and develop beliefs like, *these peas are bad* and *my mom is good.*

Say we put our hand on a hot stove. Searing pain teaches us a lesson: *hot, don't touch.* In a millisecond, we believe two things we didn't before. First, this stove is hot. Second, it's bad to touch it. But we don't stop there. Our *inductive reasoning* kicks in to convert our specific experience with one hot stove into a way of perceiving all hot stoves. The logic is, *this hot stove burns, therefore, all hot stoves burn.*

Before we used our inductive reasoning, we believed, *this hot stove burns.* But thanks to inductive reasoning, we make a terrific leap from one instance of a hot stove in a particular time and place to a way of seeing all hot stoves in all places and at all times.

We are right to think this way, because we live in a world where things happen in predictable ways.

TIME, SPACE, AND CLASS

Inductive reasoning creates beliefs that span *time*, *space*, and *class*. First, think about how induction spans *time*. If touching a hot stove *yesterday* is a bad idea, touching a hot stove *today* or *tomorrow* is bad too. We don't wake up each day needing a new experience with a hot stove. We don't think, *this burned me yesterday, but it might not burn me today.* No, we believe our one-time experience represents all the experiences that we'll ever have throughout time.

Same with *space*. If touching *this* hot stove is a bad idea, touching *that* hot stove is bad too. If someone tried to convince us, *it won't burn you because it's a different hot stove in a different place*, we wouldn't believe them. It doesn't matter if the hot stove is in Seattle or Shanghai. In *all places and spaces*, hot stoves burn.

Not only time and space, but for similar *classes* of things. If touching a hot stove is a bad idea, then touching other hot things is bad too: hot curling irons, hot fireplace pokers, and hot toasters.

All it took was a millisecond of pain touching one hot stove, decades ago, along with inductive reasoning, to establish the way we see the whole world of hot things for all time. One experience helped us see every hot thing right, in every place we'd ever see them, for the rest of time. Armed with this new view, we make our way burn-free through thousands of future experiences.

In this way, inductive reasoning helps us perceive and predict what will happen here, there, and everywhere, now and for eternity. It massively expands our view of things and helps us adapt to the physical world.

INDUCTIVE REASONING IN ANIMALS

Believe it or not, inductive reasoning comes standard in the brain-box of virtually every living thing, not just human beings. Think about how animals learn by experience. A dog trainer delivers a reward for a behavior and the dog thinks, *I got a treat when I jumped through the hoop. So if I jump through the hoop again, I'll get another treat. And if I jump through other hoops, I'll get a treat. And if I jump through this other hole that's similar to the hoop, I'll get a treat.* The dog has just a few specific experiences, but its brain uses inductive reasoning to wire a sweeping belief that *hoop-jumps get rewarded at all times, in all places, and for all things similar.*

Western movies show the cowboy parking his horse outside the saloon. Ever notice how he doesn't really tie up the horse? He just throws the reins over a post and walks in. The horse stays.

Why doesn't the horse just pull away and leave? Because of inductive reasoning. Long ago, a trainer tied the horse to a post. The horse tried to pull away, but couldn't. After a few of these experiences the horse learned, *I can't pull away from this post.* Then the horse used inductive reasoning to develop a general view of reins and posts everywhere and at all times.

The horse accepted a lifetime of personal limitation from one specific experience.

It might seem crazy that animals can "reason" this way, but it's important to understand that animal nature, along with much of human nature, reasons unconsciously. The horse doesn't know its reasons, but that doesn't stop the neural programming. The dog has no clue about induction, but uses it anyway. Animal brains are massively sophisticated software and hardware, and the logic of induction comes standard.

THE WRONG LESSONS FROM EXPERIENCE

Enough about animals—let's talk about us. Are we reined to a post in some way? Are we bound by plastic chains?

Think back to the "lessons" learned from experience at the beginning of this chapter. The cheated entrepreneur is burned by a partner and believes, *You can't trust anyone.* From one experience with a dishonest partner, the entrepreneur misuses inductive reasoning to create a way of seeing people that spans time, space, and class. He encompasses time and space by seeing *all partners, in all places, and at all times as dishonest.* Then he encompasses class by believing *you can't trust human beings*, not just business partners.

Is he seeing things right? Not at all. He's bought into a massive misconception about the nature of humanity. Here's his See-Feel-Act progression.

SEE	FEEL	ACT
All people are dishonest.	Suspicious, afraid, and angry.	Avoid doing anything that requires trust.

The cheated entrepreneur sees all people as dishonest. This automatically influences suspicion, fear, and anger toward people, which influences him to avoid trusting people.

His view of all humanity is off, which means automatic influence works against him, triggering the wrong emotions and behaviors for every interaction with every human being. The entrepreneur plastic-chains himself to solo efforts all his life. He can't go after any opportunity that requires trusting people. Unfortunately, almost all opportunities involve trusting people. That's a massive mistake in the way he sees the world, and it has massive negative implications for his life.

Same with the heartbroken college student who believes, *Men are pigs.* She has one bad experience with one man, then misuses inductive reasoning to create a picture of all men, in all places, at all times. If she continues to see men this way, she'll push away every suitor from here on out, along with any hope of happily ever after. She'll spend the rest of her years living with cats.

Here's her See-Feel-Act progression.

SEE	FEEL	ACT
All men are pigs.	Anger and disgust.	Avoid men forever.

The heartbroken college student sees all men as pigs. This automatically influences anger and disgust, and motivates her to avoid men forever.

Same with the eighth-grader struggling with algebra. He struggles with algebra (all kids do) and forms a belief: *I'll never be good at math.* Then he extends his imagined inability to the whole class of mathematics, instead of just algebra. Years later, he continues to extend the class to *any hard thinking* and may end up convincing himself, *You're not good at figuring things out. Better just to stick with the simple stuff you know.*

SEE	FEEL	ACT
I'll never be good at hard thinking.	Fear and hopelessness in the face of problems.	Stick with easy stuff for life.

The boy who used to struggle in algebra views himself as unable to do hard thinking.

Induction has massive influence on our perception. When we misuse it, we make a huge mistake. I can't emphasize this enough. *We make a massive, life-altering mistake.*

Inductive reasoning is a simple tool for the simple stuff of life, but it doesn't work for complex stuff in social life and personal development. When we use inductive reasoning in the wrong ways, we get it wrong every time.

"For every complex problem there's a simple solution," wrote the American writer H.L. Mencken, "and it is always wrong." The business failure, the breakup, and the algebra struggle aren't simple physical experiences. They are complex experiences. They involve complex social factors, and a complex process of personal growth that involves trial, error, and the patience to keep trying until we stop erring. There's no place for inductive reasoning here.

The problem is we've been using the hammer of induction so well for so long, we think it should work for everything. "I suppose it is tempting, if the only tool you have is a hammer," wrote Abraham Maslow, "to treat everything as if it were a nail."[117] Since we've been using inductive reasoning wrong almost all our lives, we are loaded to the brim with self-sabotaging beliefs. The plastic chains are piled over us. We have hundreds of them in almost every area of our lives.

SHUTTING DOWN THE SOUL

Think about how free we were in our earlier years. Starting out, our lives were packed with possibility and opportunity, much like a bustling airport is packed with airlines and flights to all sorts of destinations.

Imagine a literal airport, like the Seattle-Tacoma International Airport near where I live. It has three main terminals and seventy-six gates, offering non-stop flights to ninety-five cities. Now imagine a bad experience, combined with the misuse of inductive reasoning, is like closing a route at this airport. Let's say Sea-Tac used to serve Los Angeles, but airport operators had a bad experience on a flight there, so they shut down the route. Now travelers can't go there.

Then say there's another bad experience, but this time on a landing in Denver, so the airport operators close all flights to that city.

Soon after, there's a bad experience with Newark and LaGuardia and JFK in New York, and the port authorities shutter those routes too. Eventually the airport is down to fifty cities, and the traveler traffic is a fraction of what it was before. This continues year after year, route by route. Eventually, no one goes to the airport anymore.

This is how limiting beliefs shut down our lives. This is how champions are born, then unmade. The wrong use of inductive reasoning shuts down our potential, one negative experience at a time, until the soul is a weedy shadow of its former self.

The sad truth is that we're all prey to this. Unless we've been trained to counter the induction tendency, we shut down possibility after possibility. Eventually, we've completely shut down our lives.

Is it any wonder so many of us struggle with depression?

DEPRESSION AND LEARNED HELPLESSNESS

In the fall of 1964, Martin Seligman arrived at the University of Pennsylvania to get his graduate degree in experimental psychology. An eager twenty-one-year-old, Seligman found his way into the lab of Richard Solomon, who was doing behavioral experiments on dogs.

But there was a problem with the dogs. They wouldn't do anything.

Over the previous two weeks, these dogs had been exposed to high-pitched tones and mild, brief shocks, paired together. The dogs would hear the tone, feel the shock, and attempt to escape, unsuccessfully. The researchers were trying to get the dogs to associate tone and shock just as Pavlov's dogs associated a ringing bell with food. (In later interviews, Seligman agreed that these experiments were a mistreatment of animals, but in the research culture of the mid-sixties, these sorts of experiments were business as usual.)

After the weeks of paired associations, lab assistants put the tone-shock-conditioned dogs in a large box separated in the middle by a low wall. The dogs could easily jump over the low wall to get from one compartment to the other, and lab assistants delivered tone-shock pairings only in one compartment.

Normal dogs quickly escape by jumping over the barrier into the other compartment. But these dogs weren't normal. Instead of jumping to escape the shock, they just lay there, whimpering. There was no way to continue the experiments.

Why wouldn't the dogs jump to safety?

The answer is, *imagined inability, triggered by the misuse of inductive reasoning*. The dogs had wrapped themselves in plastic chains.

"As I looked at the whimpering dogs," Seligman recalled, "I realized that something significant had occurred.... Accidentally, during the early part of the experiment, the dogs must have been taught to be helpless.... During Pavlovian conditioning they felt the shocks go on and off regardless of whether they struggled or jumped or barked or did anything at all. They had concluded, or 'learned,' that nothing they did mattered. So why try?"[118]

This insight set off a slew of additional experiments and decades of debate within the scientific community, eventually proving that when people or dogs experience repeated failure, they enter a state of *learned helplessness*. They become passive, in a way that mirrors the symptoms of depression.

ESCAPING THE CAGE

Seligman reasoned that if the researchers *caused* the helplessness using specific steps, they should be able to *cure* it by reversing the steps.

"We took a group of dogs that had been taught to be helpless," Seligman recounts, "and we dragged those poor, reluctant animals back and forth across the [compartmentalized box], over the barrier and back again, until they began to move under their own steam and came to see that their own actions worked. Once they did, the cure was one hundred percent reliable and permanent."[119] These dogs were cured of their "depression" when they saw that they were able to act.

Imagined inability gives way when we see things working.

If we imagine we're unable to trust people, or tackle tough problems, we won't try. We lose hope for change in these areas. And in the process, we shut down our vitality. We put ourselves into a depressed state. But when we unmask the imagined inabilities for what they are, we recover our sense of power.

REMAKING THE CHAMPION

How do we recover the former glory of what was once a Sea-Tac Airport of possibility? We've got to abandon the simplistic thinking that shuts things down and embrace a new wisdom to open things back up.

We must learn to identify and resist *the destructive inductive*.

We need to question every limitation, interrogate it, and see if it's real or self-imposed. We need to pull on chains, see if they're plastic, and break the plastic ones. Let's imagine ourselves as border patrols of our minds, watching thoughts stream through checkpoints, and arresting those with ill intent. Beliefs built by the misuse of induction are criminal, and we should treat them as such.

Wise thinkers resist the lure of induction. The wise entrepreneur is cheated by a business partner and tells himself, *Yes, my business partner cheated me. But that doesn't mean everyone will. In the future, I will be more selective.*

The wise woman in the bad relationship tells herself, *This man was a pig. But this man isn't all men. There's a better man out there for me.*

The wise student tells himself, *I'm struggling with algebra. But everyone does. If I keep at it, I can eventually learn this. I just need to be more patient and persistent.*

In 2007 and 2008, I had the privilege to help build a consulting practice for one of Harvard Business School's most celebrated professors, John Kotter. He's a world-renowned expert on leading organizational change.

When I first brought up the idea, John was open but hesitant. "Last two times I tried something, it didn't work," John said as we ate dinner one evening at Crewe Hall in northern England. He and I had just spent the whole day with the top managers at Bentley Motors, and I could see that they wanted more hands-on help. Why not John in a consulting role? Over two decades up to this point, John had earned a substantial income from speaking fees and book royalties. But he wanted to make a bigger impact.

The problem was the past and the lure of inductive reasoning. *I failed before, so I'll fail again.* John chose to resist the lure, and when I showed him how we could make it work, he agreed to try again. I brought in management expertise, built the plan, and within a few months, we had a viable business.

By January of 2009, the new company was in full stride, landing multimillion-dollar and multiyear consulting engagements. Experts estimated the new venture was worth ten times the value of John's previous company, because he was willing to question limiting beliefs and try again.

SPREADING BAD BELIEFS

As we question our own limiting beliefs, we also need to be careful about buying into other people's limiting beliefs as well. Whenever we have a bad experience, then use our inductive reasoning to hatch a false belief, we also spread the false belief. We want to warn others to avoid the same dangers we ran into.

Say we're the entrepreneur who got burned by a partner long ago and hatched the false belief that *you can't trust anyone.* Do you think we're going to keep that "hard-won wisdom" to ourselves? No, we're going to tell people. Every time we see one person take advantage of another, we'll say, "You see that? You can't trust anyone." We think we're being helpful, but we're wrapping people in plastic chains. Someone accepts our belief and the imagined inabilities that go with it, even though they haven't had the bad experience themselves. In this way, bad beliefs spread and imprison people.

It's possible that right here, right now, we're wrapped up in the self-imposed limitations of people who are no longer even alive, like parents, teachers, and friends who passed on what they thought was wisdom.

Our operating policy should be, *question all limitations.* Check the chains to see if they're plastic.

Another good policy is, *keep trying.* Remember the power of obsessive interest and persistent effort I described in the *Penny Thick* chapter. Keep trying in algebra. Keep trying in relationships. Help people jump the barriers like Seligman's team helped the dogs. Show people that their actions can work, that the limits are imaginary.

Here's the good thing. We're not dogs or horses. We don't have to spend our lives curled up in cages or hitched to posts. We can identify and eliminate the plastic chains. We can choose to believe different. Then, once free, we can see bad beliefs coming and put up a defense.

Let's say goodbye to plastic chains and never wear another as long as we live.

CHAPTER 17

Identifying Rubber Snakes

"There are very few monsters who warrant the fear we have of them."

— ANDRÉ GIDE, FRENCH AUTHOR

"For some reason, doc, I'm afraid when I see the sun in late afternoon," said a young man sitting across from an older man in an office. The young man was a soldier. He was strong, courageous, yet oddly anxious about the setting sun. The problem was so strange he had to ask about it.

The older man was Joseph Wolpe, a South African psychiatrist who, in forty years of study and practice, had become the world's foremost expert on fear. Wolpe not only understood the deep origins of fear but a proven way to eliminate it.

So, what was going on with this soldier?

THREE STEPS TO FREEDOM

We all struggle to make sense of our fears. We see things happening on the surface but we don't understand what's going on underneath. Why am I so afraid? What can I do about my anxiety?

We can get free in three steps. The first is to *identify fear and its source.* What are we afraid of? What is causing it?

The second step is to discern between useful and useless fears, sorting out rattlesnakes from rubber snakes.

The third step is to face our fears in baby steps until we acclimate.

STEP 1: IDENTIFY FEAR AND ITS SOURCE

Where do our fears come from? How do they develop? The answers are a first step in overcoming useless fear.

Fear is an emotional response to a perceived threat. Whenever we believe something bad is about to happen, we feel fear. There are many forms of fear, and many words to describe it.

- We can be *worried* that our friend hasn't called us since the camping trip. *Is she hurt, still stuck in the woods?*
- We can feel *guilty* for lying to the boss. *Is he going to find out and fire me?*
- We can feel *anxious* about traveling out of the country. *I've never been to England before. It's making me nervous.*
- We can feel *embarrassed* about asking someone out on a date. *If she says no, I'll make a fool of myself.*
- We can feel *panic* about layoffs at work. *These downsizing rumors are freaking me out.*

There are many ways to describe fear, but in all of them, the idea is the same. We believe something bad might happen, triggering the emotion of fear, along with physiological symptoms of rapid heart rate, muscle tension, and quicker breathing.[120]

Innate Fear

Some fear is hard-wired. We were born with it, and it is good for us. Experts call it *innate fear*. From just a few months after we're born, we have an instinctive fear of certain types of things that might cause us harm, like fast-moving objects and loud noises. If we clang pots and pans together, the baby is afraid.

As a baby should be. She's been designed with life-preserving, harm-avoiding intelligence, and fear is a key part of it. Fear keeps her alive in a dangerous world.

In a 1960 experiment at Cornell University, researchers Eleanor Gibson and Richard Walk set up what they called a "visual cliff" to test innate fear of heights in infants and animals.[121] The "cliff" was a setup similar to two dinner tables spaced several feet apart, each with a checked tablecloth that reached the floor. Researchers then placed a large piece of glass over the tables, creating several feet of canyon-like space between them that would look like a cliff from each side. Would babies crawl from one table to another to reach their mother? Would newborn rats scurry across for a reward? How about kittens or chicks or ducklings? The goal was to test "original endowments," meaning, unlearned responses to height.

Infants wouldn't cross, no matter how much the mother called them. Neither would rats, pups, kittens, or chicks. They would go to the edge, look down, then back away.

These were not learned traits. The subjects of the experiment hadn't fallen off any cliffs. They hadn't learned anything yet. Yet they all had the innate ability to discern depth and danger, feel the fear, and steer clear. Take baby goats, for example. Even though they were only one day old, they wouldn't step over the cliff.

But aquatic turtles had no problem going across. Which makes sense, because there's no place for aquatic turtles to fall in their natural environment—it's all water, all the way down.

It all goes back to design. In a 2008 article in *Psychology Today* titled "Are We Born to be Afraid?" Robert Leahy describes innate fears as a critical design feature. Innate fears are assets. They keep us alive and well. "Our fears have been built into us to keep us from getting killed," says Leahy.

Leahy describes several types of innate fears and shows how they help us survive. The cliff study showed fear of heights. Another is fear of water. Human beings are naturally afraid of water and should be. We could die in there. We're also innately afraid of poisoned food, so much so that all it takes is one bad experience with a certain type of food and we'll avoid it forever.

Another one, crazy as it may sound, is fear of starvation. This is the deepest reason for binge eating (though there are many other learned reasons). There's something in us that wants to make sure we get as many calories as we can while the getting is good.

Leahy describes fear of open spaces as useful design as well. Rats are hard-wired to fear open spaces, and there's some of that same wiring in us too. This is because we feel more vulnerable out in the open where predators might isolate us.

Then think of our fear of closed spaces. When we're in closed spaces and something bad happens, we might not be able to escape. So we're naturally wired to fear tight spots.

Then there's a child's innate fear of abandonment, something that's completely developed by their first year of life. A child is naturally wired to stay close to mom, because mom represents protection and provision. A closely related fear is fear of strangers. *That's not Mom, so that's not safe.*

The point is, we've been designed with innate fears, and these fears all have a useful function. They are *useful fears*.

We need to emphasize the normalcy of innate fear because people often feel ashamed of their fears. They imagine that strong people are fearless people and since they feel fear, they must not be strong. In their mind, fear is proof of inadequacy or inferiority.

This simply isn't true, and it's liberating to learn that fear is natural and in so many ways, completely appropriate. In a November 4, 2015, interview with Stephen Colbert, Elizabeth Gilbert discussed her most recent book, *Big Magic: Creative Living Beyond Fear*. When asked about what creative living has to do with fear, Gilbert replied:

> Everything. They are intricately connected. I think of them as conjoined twins. It's virtually impossible to step into a new creative endeavor without having to encounter fear. Every time you engage in creativity, your creativity asks you to walk into uncertainty. If you don't find some sort of way to work with and around and through your fear, then you can never do anything creative with your life. That's why the subtitle of my book is *Living Beyond Fear* not *Living Without Fear*. You have to go through the fire of fear. In my experience, the only truly fearless people I've ever met were sociopaths. Or three-year-olds.

Thankfully, we keep our innate fears as we grow up. I remember the day an Iraqi journalist threw a shoe at President George W. Bush. It was December 2008 and Bush, alongside Iraq's prime minister, was holding a press conference at a palace in Baghdad. Instinctively, Bush ducked as the shoe flew right through the space where his head was just a millisecond earlier. It was an instinctive response to *innate fear* of moving objects.

Learned Fear

As soon as we start experiencing physical or psychological pain as children, we start building *learned fears* on top of the foundation of *innate fears*. Something bad happens. We think, *this happened once. It can happen again.* So we learn to be alert to it.

Take, for example, touching the hot stove in the last chapter. It's a painful experience and thanks to inductive reasoning, we learn that *hot stuff harms*. We extend the lesson from one specific instance of a hot stove in one time and place to a general belief that spans all times, all places, and all classes of things. We learn to fear touching all hot things, everywhere.

As we should.

But what works well in the simple, predictable physical world doesn't usually work well in the more complex world of social life and personal growth. Personal growth requires doing things that initially trigger fear, like jumping off high dives and trying out for sports teams. Social life requires we do fearful things like exposing our weaknesses, resolving conflict, and overcoming rejection.

In the bumpy world of social life and personal growth, it's easy to have a bad experience, draw the wrong lesson, and adopt a useless fear.

Associated Fear

Not only are we pre-wired with *innate fears*, then steadily build a large set of *learned fears* from life experiences, but we also create *associated fears*, which are situations and settings and conditions that influence us when we're in fearful states. In the same way that Pavlov's dogs associated a ringing bell with food, we can associate almost anything to a fearful experience.

This type of fear explains the mystery of why the man was upset by the sunset. Joseph Wolpe writes about this in his book *Our Useless Fears:*

> [The man] had no idea why, but on investigation, I found that his fear dated from a troubled romance he had had several months earlier. He was working then in an army camp in Arizona. Each evening, just after

204 • AUTOMATIC INFLUENCE

work, he would walk to a telephone booth to call his sweetheart. Their relationship was disintegrating, as she had become attracted to another man. During these conversations, he would argue and plead with her to come back to him, but to no avail. As he spoke, the red setting sun was visible in the enormous sky over the desert. Because that image was so vivid, it became a trigger to his disturbed feelings, and these could still be set off each evening at sunset if he was out of doors, even though the romance no longer mattered to him.[122]

STEP 2: DISCERN USEFUL FROM USELESS FEARS

Once we've identified our fear and its source, then we need to figure out whether it's a rubber snake or a rattlesnake. Are we really in harm's way or does it only appear that way?

Whenever we think something might harm us in some way, we feel fear. If there's real harm, the fear is useful. If we're in the woods and step on a hornets' nest, we should be afraid and act fast. If we're inching too close to a ledge, we should feel afraid and back away. If the business is in jeopardy because of changes in the market, we should feel the fear and take action.

But if there's no real harm, that's useless fear. A rubber snake. We're afraid of what people might think, so we don't try out for the part, we don't ask for the date, we don't interview for the new job. We live in confinement instead of walking in freedom.

Type in "epic snake chase prank" on YouTube and you'll find three guys making mayhem with a large rubber snake attached to a ten-foot string. One guy walks up behind some girls on a path and clips the string to the back of one girl's backpack. Then he walks beside them, looks behind, and says, "Oh! Snake! Behind you!" The girls look back and there it is, wriggling and following. They shriek and run. The snake wriggles faster. It follows them. And follows them. And follows them.

It's an *awesome* prank. Based on a useless fear.

After a few seconds, the girls get the joke and stop running. It's just a rubber snake. There's no real harm, so there's no reason to be afraid. Terror turns to anger. Or laughter. Or both.

We can do the same. But it's not as easy for us as it was the girls, because in the world of the mind, rubber snakes can be extremely convincing, and we run so fast that we never take time to find out if they're real or not.

Imagine we are in dense jungle and someone pranked us with a rubber snake. We get a glimpse of it in the leaves and get out of there fast. So fast that we can't tell if it was rubber or real.

In the real jungle, this is good logic—better safe than sorry. But in the jungle of the mind, it's not good at all. When we don't face fear long enough to know if it's useful or useless, we have no way of dealing with it. We've got to look at the rubber snake long enough to identify it as such.

Get a Second Opinion

Another way to discern useful from useless fears is to *get a second opinion*. Many of our fears come from the unquestioned opinions of others.

- Gluten is terrible for your health.
- People will take advantage of you.
- Diet soda causes cancer.
- Bugs are dangerous.

People yell, *snake!* and we believe them.

Take the *gluten is terrible* idea, for example. In a January 25, 2012, article in *Slate* magazine titled "The Maximum-Gluten Diet," Brian Palmer writes, "Wheat gluten is healthier, tastier, and more versatile than tofu. Vegetarians should be eating it all the time." Far from being terrible, gluten is terrific. He calls it an excellent meat substitute, and suggests that people eat it pure. That's right, 100% pure gluten, baked or broiled, is a healthy, protein-packed main course.[123]

There are a few people who should avoid it—about one in a hundred who have celiac disease. There are a few more who might have a gluten sensitivity and might feel better avoiding gluten. But for the overwhelming majority of us, the experts say, eat away, it tastes great and is great for you.[124]

A second opinion is like a second-look at the rubber snake. It just might be all it takes to unmask and break the false fear.

Accurately Estimate the Chance of Harm

Another thing we can do to separate useful from useless fears is *accurately estimate the chance of harm*.

Once while teaching a seminar I talked to a woman, let's call her Rhonda, who admitted she was afraid to drive on freeways. "I always take the back roads," Rhonda said. "I ran into a car while merging on the freeway about a year ago, it almost killed me. Since that accident, I haven't been back on a freeway."

Was Rhonda facing a real threat? Sure. Could it happen again? Of course. But she had put a *high chance* on the threat, when the truth is her chance of another harmful accident like this is *extremely* low. She lives in Pierce County, Washington, and based on collision data collected by the Washington State Department of Transportation, her chance of being seriously injured or killed in a collision on any particular day is about one in three million.[125] In addition, freeway driving is twice as safe as the side streets.[126]

In a closing scene of the 1994 comedy, *Dumb and Dumber*, Lloyd Christmas (played by Jim Carrey) asks his love interest Mary Swanson (played by Lauren Holly) about the chances of starting a relationship. Lloyd grabs Mary's hands and looks in her eyes. "I want to ask you a question. Straight out. Flat out. I want you to give me the honest answer," says Lloyd. "What do you think the chances are of a guy like you and a girl like me...ending up together?"

"Well, Lloyd," says Mary, "that's difficult to say. We really don't..."

"Hit me with it!" he says. "Just give it to me straight. I came a long way just to see you, Mary. The least you can do is level with me. What are my chances?"

"Not good," says Mary.

Lloyd looks confused. His confidence sinks. "You mean, not good like one out of a hundred?"

"I'd say, more like one out of a million," says Mary.

Lloyd pauses, trying to grasp Mary's meaning. But it eludes him. His face brightens with hope and he whispers, "So you're telling me there's a chance." Bursting with enthusiasm, he shouts, "Yeeaaaahh!"

In a way, we're all a little bit like Lloyd Christmas. It's hard for the average mind to comprehend large numbers. *A million, a billion, a trillion, a gazillion—it all seems like the same to me.* We buy lottery tickets, even though our chance of winning is one in a million. We fear shark attacks even though the chances are even lower.

The problem is that even when chances are extremely slim, we think chances are good, which means we're afraid of things that will never happen.

This is where the media has a heyday playing up useless fears. They portray the world as much more dangerous than it is, and we believe them. So we learn to fear things we shouldn't.

We need to be more aware of why events get media attention. The media seldom report on common things—it's the *extremely rare* and tragic events that get media attention. Journalists scour a world filled with billions of people to find the most shocking things to report, which means virtually everything we fear in the news is, by definition, a useless fear—a rubber snake. Every local newscast promo should say, "Rubber snakes at eleven," because so much news is about useless fears.

Shark attacks are one of these non-threats. Michael Reilly of *Discovery News* wrote an article in 2010 on this topic. He lived for twenty-one years in Florida, a place he describes as "the shark bite capital of the world," and was *himself* bitten by a shark. But he believes that's not a good reason to fear, because the chances of attack are extremely low.

> Sharks always seem to be taking the rap as man-eating villains in the media, movies, and books. So let's get a little perspective. Your chances of being attacked by a shark are just one in 11.5 million, according to the University of Florida's International Shark Attack File. On average, there are about 65 shark attacks worldwide each year; a handful are fatal. You are more likely to be killed by a dog, snake, or in a car collision with a deer. You're also thirty times more likely to be killed by lightning and three times more likely to drown at the beach than die from a shark attack. Even digging a sand hole is more dangerous.[127]

Back when we lived in villages of just a few hundred people and didn't communicate much between villages, people didn't hear much about people being killed. There wasn't much danger in these "peaceful communities." But then modern life came along, and people started communicating beyond the village. Their ability to see what's happening around them jumped from a few hundred people to millions of people.

Stories of murder skyrocketed. Peaceful communities were shocked to hear all the terrible things going on outside their little world. *Murder,*

murder, murder, day after day. Everyone's killing each other. The world is getting worse and worse.

But that's an illusion. The world at large is just as peaceful as their little town, statistically speaking. It just seems more dangerous, because now they see what happens to millions of people, not just the people in their town.

The problem is, we see people getting shot in a theater in Colorado and think, *that could happen to us.* Statistically speaking, that's not true. We think our chances of danger are much higher than they actually are, because we see almost everything going in the lives of over seven billion people. Which means our lives are filled with useless fears and a false sense of threat.

The only cure is to see the news as it is—a systematic distortion of reality.

Get Comfortable with Uncertainty

Another thing we can do to separate useful from useless fears is *get comfortable with uncertainty.* We want to know what happens next, so we can avoid bad things. So we want certainty. A sure thing is a good thing.

But we can't be sure about everything, and if we only took the sure bets in life, we'd miss out…on a lot.

Say there's a fifty-fifty chance we'll get the job if we interview for it. Will we take the chance? People who take sure bets won't interview, so they'll miss out on advancement. Is that a good thing? Not at all. *We miss out on a hundred percent of the chances we don't take.*

But that's only good logic when the consequences are mild. When the consequences are severe, everything changes. For example, experts say there's a fifty-fifty chance of surviving a 135-foot leap off the Brooklyn Bridge. Should I take the chance? Heck no. Imagine a motivator encouraging me to jump by saying, *You only live once, man. Remember, we miss out on a hundred percent of the chances we don't take.*

You can't get any stupider advice. When it comes to thrill-jumps off high bridges, we should miss these chances.

When chances are fifty-fifty, and the consequence is death, we should pass. When the chances are one in ten, and the consequence is death, we should pass. Same is true for one in a hundred, and one in a thousand. Some risks aren't worth it because the consequences are too great.

But when the consequences are low, the game changes. A one-in-ten shot is worthwhile. Say a guy is contemplating asking someone out on a date. The consequence of her saying no is just a twang of rejection, and the chance of a yes is one in ten. Should a guy take this chance? If he wants to find love, he should.

So, the level of consequence matters. A lot. Here are a couple of good questions to estimate the consequences. The first is, *What's the worst that could happen?* The second is, *Is that worst thing really so bad?*

Let's say we ask for that date and she says no. Is that really so bad? We're right where we were before asking, but now we're better informed. If we sensed a glimmer of hope, now we know we can try again. Or if we felt the door slam shut, we can move on to more fruitful opportunities.

When the consequences are low, we should learn to get comfortable with uncertainty.

Identify Useless Fear of Failure

Another way to separate rattlesnakes from rubber snakes is to identify *useless fear of failure.*

- Ethan is afraid to put in for the new position because there's a chance he'll make mistakes as he acclimates to the new role.
- Nancy wants to introduce a better work process for her department, but *if it doesn't go well, I'll get the blame.* She tells herself it's better to stick with what works, and forgets about the change.
- David knows that going back to school would help him in his career. But he didn't do well in school last time, and even though he's a different man five years later, he fears that he'll get poor grades and feel even worse for the trying. He keeps putting off his education, and may never get his degree.

These are useless fears of failure, because there's nothing real to fear. The consequences aren't near as great as we think they are.

Of course, there are times when the consequences of failure are terrible, so our fear of failure is useful. Climbers rarely climb solo, because failure means death. They use ropes and harnesses and double-back their buckles in three places.

While we respect the useful fear of failure, we need to develop an immunity to useless fear of failure.

One way is to redefine failure. Failure isn't the end of the world. It's just part of the process. Imagine a child learning to walk, falling, then laying there and saying, "I'm afraid to fail and I'll never try again." That would be ridiculous. Failure is part of the *process*, not part of the *problem*. "If at first you don't succeed," the saying goes, "join the crowd." Everyone who eventually succeeds, fails. A lot. We need tolerance for useful failure, like the small failures in learning a new job, improving things at work, and taking tests in school.

Identify Useless Fear of Rejection

Another useless fear that prevents change is *useless fear of rejection*. We're so concerned with others' opinions we can't move forward. This fear starts in childhood when we see that we're loved when we perform well but not when we don't. Rejection is deeply personal, and fear of rejection roots in from an early age. *If I don't perform well, people will reject me.*

Most people hate public speaking and actually fear it more than death itself. One reason is because public speaking offers a solid chance of rejection from a whole lot of people.

Then think about starting a new habit, like a new diet. How many people don't tell other people when they're deciding to start, because they already feel like they're going to fail, and they're afraid of adding rejection and disgrace to it? The answer is, most people.

One way I see this fear in business is in our struggle with performance reviews and impromptu evaluations. Everyone hates them. One of the biggest challenges organizations have is giving and receiving feedback in constructive ways, because the usual ways are loaded with fear and strife. So there's little in the way of constructive information, and people have no idea how they're doing.

Companies need to get better at giving accurate feedback in a spirit of affirmation and approval. When we learn to coach people forward as I described in the *Word after Word after Word* chapter, the culture of an organization changes. People feel validated even as they're corrected.

But unlike the fear of the unknown and fear of failure, there's not nearly as many useful fears in this area. Most rejection-fears are useless, and the sooner we get over them, the better we'll live.

So, how do we overcome the useless fear of rejection? One way is to make a distinction between other people's opinions and our own self-belief. The American activist and former first lady Eleanor Roosevelt once said, "No one can make you feel inferior without your consent."[128] Whenever someone criticizes us or rejects us or tries to make us feel inferior, we have the choice to accept it or not. If someone believes we aren't valuable, that doesn't mean they're right.

Imagine someone saying, "Hundred dollar bills are worthless." The opinion doesn't change the value of the bill. The value is innate. In the same way, our self-worth can't be determined by selection committees, playground peers, and bosses. Other people's opinions aren't the deciding factor. Our choice to accept their opinions is. The moment we recognize the difference between other people's opinions and our consent to accept these opinions, we're on our way to freedom.

But it's a constant challenge, because we're wired for social approval. We've been deeply conditioned to appraise our worth in the social mirror, which means we need a stronger inner appraiser, because the social mirror is often a funhouse mirror, driven by other people's misperceptions.

Before we move on, let's clarify something about uncertainty, failure, and rejection. They're unavoidable, and they all go hand in hand with success. We're not trying to get rid of uncertainty, failure, or rejection as much as we're trying to get rid of *the useless fear of them*.

STEP 3: ELIMINATE EVERY USELESS FEAR

Once we've identified fear and its source, then discerned the difference between useful and useless fear, the third step is, *eliminate every useless fear*.

How do we do this?

There are times when simply acknowledging it as a useless fear is enough. Think back to the girls in the snake prank. The moment they saw the rubber snake for what it was, their fears died out. In this sense, just knowing that a fear is useless can eliminate it.

But what's true for some useless fear isn't true for all of it. Some fears, no matter how useless they are, are more resistant. They don't just go away. We have to do something else to eliminate them.

We have to learn how to handle the snakes.

CHAPTER 18

Handling the Snakes

"Always do what you are afraid to do."
— Ralph Waldo Emerson, American essayist

I'm not supposed to be out here.

In his recent book, *The Making of a Man*, my friend Tim Brown gets real about fear in football, from his early years playing in high school, to Heisman Trophy glory at Notre Dame, then sixteen seasons with the Oakland Raiders. Raising his game put him into one fearful situation after another.

"When I left high school and arrived at Notre Dame, everything in me wanted to go home," Tim told me. "It didn't matter how great the place was. It didn't matter that I was beginning what would become a celebrated career. Everything in me was saying, *Leave. Get on a plane and go home.*"

A couple of weeks into practice sessions, the anxiety died down but with the first game of the season, it returned with a vengeance. "In high school I never played in front of more than four hundred people," said Tim, "but in our opening game against Purdue, the stadium was packed with sixty thousand people. Sixty thousand! I thought, *I'm not supposed to be out here.*"

Tim's coach knew he hadn't played in front of a crowd that size and promised to "work him in slowly." But seconds before they left the locker room he yelled, "Tim Brown! If we win the kickoff, I want you to return it."

"I was so stunned that I left my helmet in the locker room," said Tim. "Mentally, I was out of it. On the sideline, I begged, *Please God, let us lose the opening coin toss.*"

Tim's team won the toss, of course, and elected to receive. "I gave myself a quick pep talk: *Tim, this is football. Catch the ball and run with it. It's not hard.*"

Purdue kicked a "squib," a line drive that bounced on the ground a couple times before Tim could pick it up. "To my relief," said Tim, "I was able to scoop it up, but by the time I did the Purdue coverage team was almost on top of me. I took two steps, ran into one of my teammates, and took two more steps before I realized I didn't have the ball. The collision with my teammate had knocked it out of my hands. I tried to recover the fumble, but it was too late. Purdue had the ball on our eight-yard line."[129]

Tim was devastated. "I couldn't have drawn up a less inspiring start to my career at Notre Dame. It confirmed what I felt: *I'm not supposed to be out here.*"

DELIBERATE DISCOMFORT

When Tim first arrived at Notre Dame, everything in him said, *go back home.* But he stayed, and after weeks of daily practice, the anxiety started going away.

While most people feel fear and try to escape it, high performers do the opposite. They hold themselves in the fear until the fear subsides. They deliberately put themselves into uncomfortable situations, because that's where the growth is.

Hall of Fame hockey player Wayne Gretzky always fell down in practice, even though he was one of the world's most coordinated and balanced skaters. Why? Because he pressed beyond his comfort zone. He used practice for deliberate discomfort, to acclimate to new levels of pressure and skill.

I remember moving to a new neighborhood in Tacoma when Sandra and I were first married, and the first night was uncomfortable. It was downtown. It wasn't as nice as our former neighborhood. It felt all wrong. We were anxious.

But within a few weeks, all was good.

This is the way we change. We put ourselves in uncomfortable situations, then, if we stay long enough, we acclimate.

The challenge is, we have to stay in the arena until the fear dies down, and most of us don't stay. "Most of us instinctively avoid struggle, because it's uncomfortable," writes peak performance expert Daniel Coyle, "It feels like failure. However, when it comes to developing your talent, struggle isn't an option—it's a biological necessity."[130]

We can also acclimate through *virtual experiences*, not just real ones. For example, the first time I thought about becoming an author, I felt uncomfortable. But as I continued to think about it, and hold myself there in my imagination, I started acclimating to the idea. Eventually, it became so comfortable that it became an expectation. Now that I'm releasing this book—my first—the thought is, *Why did this take so long?*

GETTING USED TO THINGS

Human beings have amazing capacity to get used to things, good or bad. Think about the last time we bought a car. That first few weeks were incredible. But over time, enthusiasm faded. What happened? We got used to it. Over time, new becomes normal. The new spouse becomes the normal spouse after the "honeymoon phase." The new furniture becomes the normal furniture once we've looked at it every day. The new job becomes the normal job once we've worked there for a year.

Think about how emergency medical technicians acclimate to gruesome accidents, or how morticians acclimate to working with the dead, or how addicts acclimate to life on the streets. The first experiences are uncomfortable. But eventually, the discomfort dies down.

In college, I lived in a men's house that housed about thirty students, much like a fraternity. About ten of the students were Indonesian, and they liked to cook an exotic rice in their rooms. I'd get home to the steamy foul smell and shout, "Someone's cooking socks up there!"

But within a few minutes I couldn't smell anything.

Acclimation is one reason I defined happiness the way I did a few chapters back: *a pattern of positive emotion that comes from seeing good things happen at a good pace.* Soon after something good happens, we acclimate. The "good happening" loses goodness over time. We can't rest on last year's accomplishments, because they don't seem that good to us anymore. We want a steady stream of good things, just like we want a steady stream of good food.

FEAR OF PUBLIC SPEAKING

In October 2014, Chapman University published a study of Americans' top fears. The top five fears were walking alone at night, identity theft, safety on the Internet, becoming a victim of a random shooting, and *public speaking*.[131]

As a veteran speaker, I chuckle to see public speaking make the fear lists. Random shootings, death, and public speaking? Yep, they go together. "According to most studies," said comedian Jerry Seinfeld in an opening bit for his show, "people's number one fear is public speaking. Number two is death." Then he pauses to let it sink in. "Death is number *two*. Does that sound right? This means to the average person, if you go to a funeral, you're better off in the casket than doing the eulogy."[132]

This fear of public speaking makes sense. Where else can you get so much public humiliation? Just this week I spoke to audiences of several thousand people. If I screw up my talk, thousands see me as incompetent. There's massive rejection risk. Even when I do well, there are those who disapprove. It takes thick skin to endure the process.

Early on, I was afraid to speak to groups. *Deathly afraid.* Everything in me said, *you don't belong here. Get back to where you belong.* In high school, I skipped all my oral reports. I'd rather get an F than endure that hell. I didn't feel I belonged in front of groups. It was better to fail the class than fumble and stumble in front of classmates.

After school I worked at Safeway, a grocery store which required I use the all-store intercom from time to time for "cleanup on aisle seven" sort of stuff. I was sixteen then, hitting puberty late, and my voice would crack right in the middle of announcements. My co-workers all laughed.

It was public humiliation. It said to me, *you don't belong on the intercom.* So I avoided the intercom as much as I could. It took me a long time to become acclimated to public speaking.

Today I don't feel the same anxiety I felt early on. I've acclimated. I've done a TED talk and shared the stage with some of the world's great leaders. I stand in front of thousands of people with confidence and poise. *I feel like I belong there.*

How did I go from skipping class and feeling like a complete failure to speaking comfortably to thousands of people? How did I get from those places of fear to the places of confidence I enjoy today?

Repeat exposure.

That's it. Repeat exposure.

I continued to speak in front of groups, whether it felt good or not. I held myself in discomfort and eventually, discomfort dissolved. For more than twenty-five years now, I've been repeating these experiences. Over time, with repetition, the discomfort goes away.

SYSTEMATIC DESENSITIZATION

Almost every discomfort can be eliminated through this process, described by scientists as *systematic desensitization*.[133] The word "desensitization" simply means "sensing less." At first exposure to something, we sense a lot of good (the thrill of the new car) or bad (the agony of public speaking). But with repeated experience, we sense things less. We acclimate.

Say we take a job washing windows on high-rise buildings. We're terrified at first, but eventually get used to the heights. Months later, hanging from a rope eighty stories up is all in a day's work—thanks to desensitization.

While "desensitization" is "sensing less," the "systematic" word in systematic desensitization describes the repeat exposure. One exposure isn't enough. There's a systematic process to inoculate us to fear that involves creating a sense of calm, then creating small doses of fear and consistent exposure, and stepping up the intensity over time.

Here's how our peak performance expert Daniel Coyle describes the desensitization process at a "Shyness Clinic."

> One of the first [tasks] for a Shyness Clinic client is to walk up to a stranger and ask for the time. Each day, the [tasks] grow more strenuous—soon clients are asking five strangers for the time, making phone calls to acquaintances, or chatting with a stranger in an elevator. After a few months, some clients are "socially fit" enough to perform the ultimate [task]: They walk into a crowded grocery store, lift a watermelon above their head, and purposely drop it on the floor, triumphantly enduring the stares of dozens of strangers. (The grocery store cleanup crew doesn't enjoy this quite as much as the clients do.)[134]

The key is to acclimate to each new level, embracing the anxiety until it goes away.

Using systematic desensitization, researchers have cured all sorts of phobias within several hours.[135] Using systematic desensitization, mixed martial artists get "comfortable" being kicked in the head or punched in the face. Using systematic desensitization, POWs acclimate to deprivation in prison camps.

TEN THOUSAND PUNCHES

Given what we now know about systematic desensitization, let's see how we might use it to help us at work. Say Jerry and I are co-workers, talking about a problem.

"Guess what I just found out?" Jerry said.

"What?" I asked.

"I'm going to be working with Darryl on an upcoming project with the dev team," said Jerry. "He's a total idiot."

"How so?" I asked.

"Last time I worked with him, he insulted me and everyone else. He ordered us around though he didn't have the authority, and he told me I was stupid," said Jerry. "I'd like to hit him with a shovel."

"It sounds like you're going to have a tough time on the project," I said. "Good thing it's only a month."

"Yeah, the project starts next week," said Jerry. "I'm dreading it."

"How would you like to be completely free from dread about Darryl?" I asked. "Imagine he could say all that without affecting you? In fact, imagine he could do what he does and you'd actually *like* Darryl despite his ways?"

Jerry looked confused. "Are you kidding me?" he said. "That's impossible."

"Well, it all pretty much depends on you," I said.

"What do you mean?" said Jerry.

"Do you think you could handle someone punching you in the face?" I asked.

"What? Of course not," said Jerry.

"Yes, I agree. But there are some people who get punched in the face and it doesn't affect them at all. Check out ultimate fighting," I said.

"There are guys in there, and girls even, who get punched in the face with bare fists, then smile, laugh even. Ever seen it?"

"Yes, I have," said Jerry. "Pretty amazing. But what's the point?"

"Well, at some point earlier in their lives these fighters got punched in the face for the first time," I said. "How do you think they reacted to the first punch?"

"They probably didn't handle it well," said Jerry.

"I agree. So why do they handle it well now?" I asked. "A punch is a punch, after all. Why would they respond any different to that first punch long ago versus today?"

"I guess it's because they trained so much," said Jerry.

"Exactly. They trained. What did trainers do?" I asked.

"They made sure the fighter got punched. A lot," Jerry said. "By the thousandth time they'd been punched in the face, they got used to it."

"Exactly," I said. "I bet they got ten thousand punches in training. Now they're used to it. That's why they can smile and laugh. It's nothing new, just business as usual."

"Now back to Darryl," I said. "What if you could imagine Darryl saying you're stupid, and see yourself taking it like you'd take a punch? With a smile? The mind interprets reality and vivid imagination almost equally, so maybe you could shadow box with an imaginary Darryl. You imagine him calling you an idiot. Then you overlook the insult. You imagine him treating you like a doormat, then imagine yourself treating him the exact opposite."

Darryl asks, "Why should I allow him to treat me that way?"

"Sure, you can confront him," I say. "When he does something wrong, you can call it out. But I'm talking about the attitude you take when you do it. If you practiced enough in your mind, you could get to the point where nothing he says can trigger anxiety or anger in you."

"There's a big difference between confronting an issue from a position of emotional strength and confronting it from emotional weakness," I continue. "When you feel offended and anxious and angry, that's weakness. You're letting him control you. When you're itching to get payback and insult him, that's weakness. He's in charge. You're not in control of yourself. He controls you.

"But when you can counter his insults with kindness and humor, that's proof you can take a punch. Get yourself to the place where you can take a punch and smile and laugh. Then, and only then, will you be able to correct Darryl in a way that is validating and effective. Strength is the way to peace."

ACCIDENTAL DESENSITIZATION

Desensitization has the power to help us or hurt us, depending on how it's used. Think back to the Houston pastor and his team of former prostitutes offering working girls an escape. Many of the prostitutes refused the help, thanks to systematic desensitization. They got used to the life. Comfortable with it. Happy with it, even. Prostitution used to be terrible. Later, it was normal.

Desensitization often hurts more than it helps because we acclimate to the lowest common denominators. We conform to the bad habits and bad thinking of those around us. We conform to the pessimistic mindset at the office. We conform to the way our friends might act. Systematic desensitization is often accidental or incidental because of repeated experiences at work or at home. Circumstances create patterns, and those patterns desensitize us.

Systematic desensitization can also happen accidentally because of our dominant patterns of thought. We think a certain way over and over, and what was bad at first doesn't seem that bad after the thousandth thought.

In this way, systematic desensitization can make people worse over time. It gets people used to living in squalor and abuse. It gets people used to living on the streets in cardboard boxes, or telling lies, or living in debt, or living alone. Repeated experience has a powerful conditioning effect for better or worse, and usually the default effect is for worse, not for better.

Not just for the sinister and blatant things. The small and subtle things as well.

Let's think about the situations of life that are conditioning us into mediocrity right now. What small things have we tolerated long enough to become normal? How about the culture of insults and negativity at our work? Have we joined right in, or are we strengthening ourselves to overcome it? Either way, we're acclimating.

How about that clutter in our garage? Or that extra fat around our waist? Initially we were uncomfortable with these things. But we acclimated. Instead of holding a standard of excellence that made us so uncomfortable we'd fix our problem, we ignored the problem and now it doesn't feel like a problem anymore.

This is the lure of desensitization.

IF IT FEELS RIGHT...

Most of us go with our gut. If something feels right to us, we're okay with it. But if it doesn't feel right, we're not okay. Whenever we're in a comfort zone, things feel right. And when we're out of a comfort zone, there's something inside that says, "Not right. Make it right."

The problem with this mindset is that feelings come second in the See-Feel-Act progression. The way we see drives our feelings. So when we see wrong but think we see right, our feelings betray us. We feel that things are good, but they aren't.

Social situations are major desensitizers. We tend to think things our friends do are all right. Our buddies get drunk every weekend, so it's okay with us too. Our friends talk about others behind their backs, so it's okay if we join in. Our community thinks it's okay for kids to spend five days a week in sports leagues, so we do too. There's a powerful social acclimation. Our sense of what is right and normal is, to a large extent, drawn from our social world.

Social norms can become subtle conspiracies, desensitizing us into patterns of mediocrity and destruction.

Then, once desensitized, our feelings betray us. Things are bad, but they don't feel that bad. Things feel good when they aren't good at all. Acclimation changes the way we see, creating feelings of happiness can't be trusted.

Back to the quote by the Israelite king Solomon, "There is a way that appears to be right, but in the end it leads to death." Just because something seems right or feels right doesn't mean it is, especially when we understand the conspiracy of acclimation.

When I first understood how systematic desensitization works, I started questioning my standards. I stopped trusting myself the same way I used to, because I know that I can get used to anything when I'm in it long enough. Eventually, mediocrity is acceptable. Bad things become good things. Good things become bad things. Repeated thought and experience conditions us. If we don't stay aware of this and make a change, we may be whistling our way down the highway to hell.

"I'M STAYING OUT HERE."

Used in the right way, however, systematic desensitization is the key to excellence. Think about how Tim Brown went from fumbling failure that day in Purdue to a Heisman Trophy winner (college football's greatest athletic honor) to a sixteen-year professional football career. He chose to stay on the field. He held himself in the fearful place, time after time, until the fear went away.

Walking back onto the field after his first fumble, he thought, *I'm not supposed to be out here.* But he stopped that thought and replaced it with another one. *I'm not going back to the sideline. I'm staying out here. I've got to make up for that fumble.*

"The play called for me to run across the middle," Tim said. "I didn't expect the pass to come my way, but I turned out to be the open man. Steve Beuerlein's throw was high and a little behind me, a tough catch even with the pressure of a tight game. But this time I came through. I reached back and was just able to close my fingers around it. We gained nineteen yards and got a first down that led to a score."

"The coaches didn't let me back in the game after that play," Tim said, "but I'd made my mark. For me, that catch meant everything. It was probably the most important play of my college career. The kickoff fumble had already raised doubts about my mental toughness with the coaches and my teammates, and maybe even in my own mind. If I'd dropped the pass too, I certainly would have gone into the next week questioning myself. Crazy as it sounds, I might have been a different player from that point.

"But in that moment when I was running onto the field and had to decide if I would keep going to the huddle or return to the sideline, I knew I had to try. I wanted to play. I wanted to prove I belonged. If the coaches weren't yet ready to give me a second chance, I needed to create one. The catch against Purdue solidified in my mind that I could play this game at the college level."[136]

Tim stayed in the arena until the anxiety went away.

The best way to improve our presenting skills is to present, present, present. The best way to get comfortable with difficult conversations is to converse, converse, converse. The only way to get comfortable with the new role at work is to work, work, work.

If I could convince you to do one thing that would change almost everything, it would be to face fear until it goes away. Progress begins when we stretch. People come alive when they embrace stretched goals and the fear that always goes with it.

Because that's where the adventure is.

CHAPTER 19

Removing the Blindfolds

"In the kingdom of the blind, the one-eyed man is king."
— Desiderius Erasmus, Dutch theologian

In 2001, I put in an offer on an old Spanish estate on a lake near where I live. It was a seven-thousand-square-foot mansion on five sprawling acres, with a vineyard and one hundred seventy feet of waterfront. It was one of the last big estates on this lake.

The estate sale was being managed by a trustee. The former owner, a Korean businesswoman, had recently died due to complications from a liposuction surgery. She had no heirs. I get a shade of sorrow thinking who she was and how she must have lived.

We finally agreed to terms—$1.1 million, closing in ninety days, subject to a feasibility study, because this was an old house, built in 1922. I had to figure out what I was dealing with.

My plan was simple. I'd slice off the edges of the lot and sell them to the neighbors, then live in the home. I have six children and at the time, they were all young, so we could have used the space. Then I'd resell it once it came time to downsize.

Each neighbor tentatively agreed to pay me around $300,000 for their slice. Now the estate would be four acres instead of five, and my cost would be $500,000. It seemed like a good play.

During the feasibility phase, I had a developer friend come out to see the property. He looked it over and said, "This is a dangerous deal. There's wetland on the back corner, and all sorts of underground pipes and tanks. You never know what might be under the surface. If I were you, I wouldn't buy it. You're taking a big risk."

I took his advice and backed out of the deal.

A couple years later, I had coffee with a guy I'd worked with, and wouldn't you know it, he was leasing that Spanish mansion. Someone else had purchased the property after I'd backed out and did exactly what I had wanted to do. They sold off the edges to the neighbors. They didn't want to live in the big house just yet, so they had leased it to my friend.

Then he dropped a bomb on me. "Just six months ago," my friend said, "I was looking out the back window and noticed that one of the patio tiles was tilted. I asked the gardener to fix it, and he said, 'There's something under that tile.' I had him dig it up, and it was a plastic bag of hundred dollar bills. Six hundred thousand dollars!"

I just about crapped my shorts.

"You're kidding me," I said.

"No joke, that's where the Korean businesswoman stashed all her savings."

It took me a while to process what he was saying. There were no heirs to this estate, so if I had purchased the home, that money would have been mine. I would have paid a net $500,000 for the home, only to find $600,000 under the patio.

I imagined it like someone handing me a million-dollar estate, along with an extra hundred grand, saying, "This is all yours. It's fully paid for. Enjoy." But I refuse the offer.

That's about as bad as it gets.

I immediately called my developer friend. "Hey, remember that estate deal on the lake that you came out and helped me with? Remember how you said, 'You never know what might be under the surface?' Well, there was *six hundred grand* under the surface. Hundred dollar bills, in a plastic bag under the back patio. Thanks for the advice."

"That is unbelievable," he said, laughing. "You missed it big time." We laughed because there was nothing else we could do. I had made what seemed like the best decision at the time, given what I knew. But no question, this was the big fish that got away. Today the house is worth about two million. So I would have gotten it for nothing, lived free for fifteen years, and gained another million in the process.

Instead, I got nothing.

It hurts to tell this story, even to this day, many years later. Of course, hindsight is 20/20, and there was no way to know that this would happen. But if there was a way to see what was really there under the patio, and all the good in taking the deal, *I would have done anything I could to get that house.*

Jesus tells a similar story in the Gospel of Matthew. "The kingdom of heaven is like treasure hidden in a field," Jesus said. "When a man found it, he hid it again, and then in his joy went and sold all he had and bought that field."[137] Why did the man sell everything to get the field? Why was he so motivated when everyone else was so complacent?

It's simple—*he saw something no one else saw.*

THE CAUSE OF COMPLACENCY

This is how I picture the cause and cure of complacency, that false feeling of self-satisfaction we have when we're *blind to danger* and *blind to opportunity.*

Here's the See-Feel-Act progression.

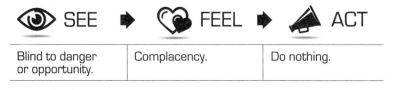

👁 SEE	♥ FEEL	📢 ACT
Blind to danger or opportunity.	Complacency.	Do nothing.

When we're blind to danger and opportunity, it automatically influences us to feel complacent and do nothing.

When we're blind, we can't feel motivated. But when our eyes open to the opportunity or danger that we didn't see before, motivation is automatic.

The issue isn't motivation. It's blindness.

The See-Feel-Act progression shows us how the way we see automatically influences the way we feel, which automatically influences the way we act. Perception is the root of our attitudes and motivations. So when we see things wrong, and fail to see right, our motivations and attitudes will be wrong. But when we suddenly see right, the motivations and attitudes change automatically.

Think about the man in Jesus's story who suddenly sees the treasure in the field. Think about my story and imagine me seeing six hundred grand in plastic under the patio. The only natural response is intense motivation. We'd do anything we could to get the field, to get the estate, and while our motivation may not make sense to people blind to the buried treasure, it makes perfect sense for those who see.

The key is to see.

To live our best life, we need a clear view.

BREAKING OUT OF THE DARKNESS

One big way to ensure our vision is clear is to get out and look around. Think of the man in Jesus's story. To find the treasure in the field, he had to explore. He wasn't going to find it in the confines of his village.

A few years ago a friend of mine, Eric Boles, trained the leaders at Hickam Air Force Base in Hawaii, where he met a colonel who told him how he grew up in the government housing neighborhoods of South Central Los Angeles. Early on, all this colonel knew was poverty, crime, and despair.

"When did you know you wanted to join the military?" Eric asked him.

"It was a field trip to Fresno I took in the tenth grade," he said. "Up to then, South Central LA was my entire world. I had no idea what was out there."

"Fresno?"

"Yeah, Fresno," said the colonel. "It doesn't sound like much. It was only two hundred fifty miles away, but it might as well have been an entire world away. I never saw hills like that. I never saw windmills before. I never thought there were possibilities for my life beyond the confines of the city. For the first time I realized the world was bigger than South

Central LA. I thought, *How can I see more?* That's when I started thinking about the military."

Everything changed when he changed his view.

So I say, go new places. Talk to new people. Get more friends. Read. Explore. Get curious about the world. Whenever I coach people, I ask them to get out and stretch the boundaries, because limited seeing leads automatically to limited living. To live better, we've got to see better.

BLIND TO OUR BLINDNESS

In past chapters, we talked about rubber snakes and plastic chains, meaning the useless fears and imagined inabilities that usually come from bad experiences.

But this third barrier to freedom comes from a *lack of experiences*, not bad experiences. It's a false sense of limitation that comes from limited exposure. It's blindness to our real opportunities and potential.

The problem with blindness is that we don't know what we don't know. Think about the colonel at Hickam. Before he left the projects of South Central LA and went to Fresno, his tiny little world was all he knew. He didn't know what he was missing.

Kerry Patterson and the co-authors of the book, *Influencer,* tell a story of an American manufacturing client struggling against Japanese competitors. The Japanese were outperforming the Americans' production by at least forty percent, so the bosses gathered the underperforming workers to say, "If we don't boost production, we're toast."

The workers didn't believe the bosses. They were already overworked and thought this was the latest ploy to squeeze out more productivity. "We see what this is," the union leaders told the bosses. "It's manipulation."

The bosses tried another approach, making detailed presentations to show workers the problem. They still weren't convinced.

Finally, management realized the only way to change things was to send a group of workers to Japan to see for themselves. When workers arrived and saw their Japanese counterparts performing at a pace they'd never seen before, they thought, *This is a ruse. Our bosses told them to pick up the pace.* Then one of them got the idea to sneak into the night shift to see how they worked without being watched. "Instead of catching their competitors plodding along and messing around (as they themselves often did back in the States)," writes Patterson, "the night shift employees appeared to work faster than the day-shift employees."[138]

The American workers went home convinced that if they didn't pick up their productivity, they'd be out of a job.

Before that trip, the workers not only were blind about themselves and their competitors. They were blind to their blindness. They didn't respond with an open mind because they were sure they knew the truth. They thought they had all the information they needed, even when they had no information at all.

WYSIATI

Psychologist Daniel Kahneman writes extensively about this tendency. "Jumping to conclusions on the basis of limited evidence," he writes, "is so important to an understanding of intuitive thinking, and comes up so often in this book, that I will use a cumbersome abbreviation for it: WYSIATI, which stands for what you see is all there is."[139]

- We accept one side of a story and make a snap judgment instead of waiting to hear both sides.
- We read stories on the Internet and believe them without double-checking.
- We judge our entire outlook on life from our current mood. *Yeah, life sucks.* Or, *Everything is awesome!*

"Our view of the world," writes Kahneman, "is limited by the information that is available at a given moment."[140]

When we're blind to our blindness, we're perfectly comfortable making blind decisions. Years ago, I advised an executive in a manufacturing company whose customer service team had recently clamored to change an entire product line and fire the product team based on *two* customer complaints. That's right, two complaints. They were blind to the *hundred thousand satisfied customers* who bought the product. They only saw the two complaints.

The executive had to stave off a lot of problems between the two departments (customer service and product development) for about a week, only to find that the real cause of the complaints was a botched batch on the manufacturing line. It only affected a couple dozen units, and the problem was solved right there on the line.

The customer service team didn't think about things that were beyond their sightline, because it's hard to take invisible things into account. The mind works with what it has and when we're not trained to consider invisible factors, we make blind decisions.

INVISIBLE AND UNINTENDED CONSEQUENCES

Politicians do this in spades, along with the people clamoring to have politicians fix social problems. The media reports an abuse, a problem, a safety hazard, and politicians and voters say, "Someone needs to pass a law." They think they have all the information about the problem they need, but they make a bad decision almost every time.

Why? Because they're working from inadequate information. They fail to account for the unintended and invisible consequences of the new law that might harm more people than it helps.

Take bicycle safety laws as an example. In 2013, 743 bicyclists were killed in crashes on the streets of America.[141] It's natural to think, *we should do something. There should be more laws.* Some states have already passed laws requiring riders to wear helmets.

But do these laws make the streets safe? They might do the opposite, claims reporter John Stossel, citing studies done by Ian Walker, a researcher at the University of Bath in England. Walker set up a distance sensor on bike handlebars and rode for miles, with and without a helmet. He found that drivers reacted differently when he wore a helmet. Here's the interview:

Walker: When I wore a helmet, there was a considerable tendency for cars to get closer. 23% more cars came within three feet of me.

Stossel: What's the reasoning? Is it, *Ahh, he has a helmet, if I hit him he'll live?*

Walker: No. When they see a cyclist who has all the gear, they think, *That's an experienced and skilled rider.* And there's another unintended consequence of helmet laws. Parts of Australia, Canada and New Zealand have made bicycle helmets a requirement. And what you see is the number of cyclists with head injuries drops off, which is good.

However, the number of cyclists is dropping off at the same rate. So there's no actual improvement in safety, but rather, less cycling. And when people don't cycle, they get less exercise. We know that not getting exercise and being sedentary is incredibly dangerous. You get heart attacks, you get strokes—proven killers that kill thousands of people. When people make helmets a requirement, with the best intentions, it may actually kill more people.[142]

We focus on things we see, and don't account for invisible things. Unless we're trained to do differently, we'll make snap judgments on the available information, as if that were all the information we needed.

SEEING THE POSSIBILITIES

Imagine the Hickam colonel as a young man in the projects, thinking about the possibilities for his life, *before his trip to Fresno*.

Would his thinking help him or hurt him?

No question, it would hurt him.

Why? He was still wearing a blindfold. He couldn't see clearly because he hadn't yet taken the trip.

When we invest time to look across the landscape of opportunity, and explore the vastness of the world around us, we find a thousand places to go and things to do. There are thousands of job descriptions for thousands of roles, and thousands of places to do those jobs. And that's just what's possible in our work lives. Our social lives, our community, our personal lives, all offer thousands of possibilities as well.

But if we fail to invest the time to look, we'll make blind decisions. We're like the Hickam colonel, deciding the course of our lives, before the trip to Fresno.

If we're missing vital information, we can't make good decisions. And we're talking about our lives here, not just a decision for a burger or a taco for lunch, or plastic or paper at the grocery store. The choices we make about our careers, our hobbies, the people we spend time with, and the things we do have long-term consequences, for better or worse. And the sad truth is that people are making life-impacting decisions with very little sense of what's out there.

But when we get out and look around, we discover things that completely change the course of our lives.

This is why we must expand our awareness as quickly as possible.

Consider how industrialist Henry Ford got out and looked around, and what it did for him. He was twelve when he and his father took a wagon ride to Detroit. Clopping along on the dirt road, they came up on someone who was driving a steam engine on wheels lumbering along the path, wheezing under its own power. It was the first "horseless carriage" he'd ever seen, and Henry was mesmerized.

"I remember that engine as though I had seen it only yesterday," Henry wrote, "for it was the first vehicle other than the horse-drawn that I had ever seen....I was off our wagon and talking to the [driver] before my father knew what I was up to."[143]

That day Henry discovered something profound in his widening world. But he also found something in his heart—his life's passion to build cars. "This encounter became a turning point in Henry Ford's life," writes biographer Steven Watts, "fostering a profound interest which would lead in new and fruitful directions."[144]

Henry's story is a pattern we find in all sorts of people who find purpose in their work. They explore. They expand their horizons. Then they find a sense of calling.

- Howard Schulz found the inspiration for Starbucks while exploring Europe, where he saw the local café as a social hub. *This is something I can bring to America*, he thought.
- As a teenager, Steven Spielberg bluffed his way into Universal Studios and eventually found a directing career.
- Amelia Earhart, the first female aviator to fly solo across the Atlantic Ocean, was a college student when she went to an air show with her parents in Long Beach, California. She took a ten-minute plane ride that changed her life.[145]

We should always be asking, "How can I expand my boundaries? How can I increase my awareness?" The world is bigger than we think, and there's more out there happening than is visible from our little cocoons. There's an explorer within all of us, a mini-Magellan, and if we don't give this little guy room to roam, we're guaranteed to miss out.

When we explore, we not only find new things, but we find ourselves too. That day when Henry Ford first saw the horseless carriage rattling along a dirt road, he found something deep inside him—a love for a machine, a magnificent obsession, that carried him through the rest of his life.

When Howard Schulz found the European café, he didn't just find something outside of him, but found something inside of him—a magnificent obsession to bring great coffee and community to America.

Exploring the world is exploring our hearts. It's like trolling the surface of deep waters, sounding the depths, until we hear the ping-back.

What's down there? Our calling. Our life purpose.

Solomon, king of Israel, said, "The purposes of a person's heart are deep waters, but one who has insight draws them out."[146] The more we troll the surface of the deep waters and listen, the more treasure we find in the depths.

Get out there and look around. Make a habit of doing new things. Meet new people. Listen to people who are different than you. Don't argue. Listen. Try to see how they see. Go to new restaurants and vacation spots. Travel to new countries. Read biographies. Watch the Discovery Channel. Get a new view of life.

A better life might be just one experience away. If we're willing to step out and have that experience.

CHAPTER 20

Full of Optimism, Love, and Wisdom

"We have always held to the hope, the belief, the conviction that there is a better life, a better world, beyond the horizon."
— FRANKLIN D. ROOSEVELT, AMERICAN PRESIDENT

Remember Nick Vujicic from a few chapters back? He had no arms or legs but, wow, he had humor. When we first heard Nick say, "I wasn't ready," when someone kicked a soccer ball past him or, "It's so cold I can't feel my hands," when he finished a water slide, we wondered if we had permission to laugh.

But the more we heard from Nick, the more we lightened up. We laughed, we cried, and felt so inspired. He had every reason to feel bitter, but gleamed with love instead. He loved people. He loved life. He was grateful for every moment.

When I think of qualities I admire, Nick's are at the top of my list.

Same with most people. In seminars, I invest time to discuss the qualities we admire in people around us. What comes up? *Optimism, humor,* and *love. Kindness* and *humility. Confidence, resilience,* and *commitment. Gratitude* and *compassion. Honesty, transparency,* and *integrity.*

In sessions like these, I find there's little mention of skill or intelligence. Of course, we admire skill and intelligence, but not nearly as much as *positive attitudes*.

ATTITUDE: A SETTLED WAY OF FEELING

Dictionaries define "attitude" this way:

> Attitude: a settled way of thinking or feeling about something or someone, typically one that is reflected in a person's behavior.

There's a See-Feel-Act progression in this definition. The "settled way of thinking" is how we see. Then there's the "settled way of feeling" that follows our seeing. Then these are "reflected in a person's behavior."

While attitudes involve all three elements of the progression, I believe they're mostly about the *Feel* part. Think about what people mean when they say, "*She has a good attitude*," or, "*He has a bad attitude*." They're usually referring to patterns of emotion that lead to behavior.

- Dan is always complaining, he hates his job, and he walks around with a sour look on his face. So we say, "Dan has a bad attitude."
- Paula, on the other hand, smiles a lot, likes her job, and is eager to learn. So we say, "Paula has a good attitude."

An attitude is a "settled way of feeling." That puts it in the center of the See-Feel-Act progression.

👁 SEE	💟 FEEL	📣 ACT
A settled way of seeing things.	A settled way of feeling things (attitude).	A settled way of doing things.

The See-Feel-Act progression shows how settled ways of seeing automatically influence settled ways of feeling (attitudes), which lead to settled ways of doing things.

An attitude is a *pattern* of emotion, driven by a *pattern* of perception. All the admired traits I see in seminar surveys are *settled ways of feeling good about people*. It's the dog vibe, as opposed to the cat vibe. It's *automatic love*. We don't admire intelligence or skill as much as we admire authentic, consistent expressions of love.

The See-Feel-Act progression shows how attitude originates in perception. Perception is the power source, automatically influencing our attitudes.

Austrian psychiatrist Viktor Frankl described this power as "the last of the human freedoms." Frankl, a Jew, had been imprisoned in Nazi death camps in the final years of World War II and watched how people coped with the brutal hardship of camp life. In his bestselling book, *Man's Search for Meaning*, he writes,

> We who lived in concentration camps can remember the men who walked through the huts comforting others, giving away their last piece of bread. They may have been few in number, but they offer sufficient proof that everything can be taken from a man but one thing: the last of the human freedoms—to choose one's attitude in any given set of circumstances.[147]

Frankl's suffering, and his insight from it, is so profound that it's a struggle to adjust his wording, but for the sake of clarity, I must. Truth is, we don't really choose attitudes. Attitudes are second-stage effects from first-stage causes—our perceptions. We choose the way we see. Then the attitude automatically follows. So I would describe the last human freedom as, *to choose one's point of view in any given set of circumstances*. We can choose how we see. This, in turn, automatically influences our attitudes.

This means we can transform our attitudes. We can invest time and effort to build great attitudes by building great ways of seeing self, others, and the situations of life. The only question, is, will we? We have the power to embody all the admirable attitudinal traits, but we must build these traits just like we build skill, with penny-thick investments of attention over time.

THE GOLDILOCKS ZONE

One powerful attitudinal goal is to be *full of optimism*. When we perceive life, others, and self in ways that are optimally good, and when we do this consistently, we automatically fill our lives with optimism.

Notice I didn't say *total optimism*. I said, *full optimism*. There's a balance point, even for something as great as optimism. People with extreme positive attitudes take excessive risks, plan poorly, and usually fail to count the costs. To promote pure positivity is to encourage delusional optimism and risky behavior. Pure positivity is out of balance.

But it's also out of balance to walk around with a hangdog face, caught up in the negatives of life. It's not healthy to steep our lives in drama and anxiety.

So, what's the balance? How much time should we be investing into the positives and negatives? What's the balance point between solving problems and celebrating solutions? What's the balance point between acknowledging negative realities and living carefree?

The first step is to admit a balance point. Life without any negatives is a delusion. Life without any positives is hell on earth. The best life is somewhere in between.

It reminds me of the fairy tale where a little girl, Goldilocks, goes for a walk in the forest and happens upon a house where three bears live. She knocks and the bears aren't home, so she goes in. At the table there are three bowls of porridge.

She tastes one, *too hot*.

She tastes the second one, *too cold*.

She tastes the third bowl, *just right*.

There's a Goldilocks zone for positivity and negativity. What's too positive? What's too negative? And what's just right?

RESEARCH IN POSITIVITY RATIOS

Several studies point to answers, but perhaps the best person to answer the question is University of North Carolina psychology professor Barbara Fredrickson, whose research on positivity to negativity ratios and their implications for human flourishing have created its own set of positives and negatives. Her initial 2005 study with Losada has been cited well over three hundred times, but it came under scrutiny in 2013 for technical errors, prompting Barbara to update her research.[148] The upshot of the new scrutiny is better-tested ratios that we can use to estimate our balance point.

One ratio came out of a study that recorded the conversations of sixty work teams as they developed their strategic plans. The research team recorded team meetings and identified positive and negative phrases in the conversations. Then they used business data to group each team into performance categories—high, medium, and low.

They found the ratio of positive to negative conversations for the high-performance teams was just under 6 to 1, while the ratio for the medium-performance team was 2 to 1, and the ratio for the low-performance team was 1 to 3.[149]

University of Washington psychology professor John Gottman studied this same positivity ratio in the conversations of married couples, and became so good at analyzing conversational styles that he could predict fifteen-year divorce rates at ninety-four percent accuracy in just a half hour of listening. His studies show the positivity ratio for healthy couples is about 5 to 1, where those on the way to divorce have ratios of about 1 to 1.

Another ratio-researcher is clinical psychologist Robert Schwartz, whose studies in depression recovery concluded that healthy positivity ratios were 4 to 1. He also found that "normal" people have a ratio of 2 to 1, while depressed people had ratios just under 1 to 1.[150]

These studies show that "equal balance" between positive and negative is terrible. Equal balance is a depressive condition, or a sign of divorce, or a lousy work culture.

Keep in mind as well that these ratios of 4, 5, and 6 don't show the peak of the curve. They just show that 4, 5, and 6 are healthier than the lower numbers. Frederickson herself suggests the peak of the curve might be as high as 11 to 1. So to say that 6 to 1 is optimal is a conservative estimate.

It also says that normal people, with a ratio of 2 to 1, are less than a third as optimistic as they should be. Here's an Inverted-U graph showing the peak of the curve.

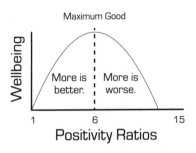

The Inverted-U for positivity ratios.

The more I looked into these ratios, and the more I looked at my own experiences, the more I realized, *I'm way out of balance.*

I like to solve problems. That requires paying attention to them. I like to be realistic because, as an entrepreneur, I've had my share of delusional optimism in my early years. So I pay attention to negative realities to offset over-optimistic tendencies.

In the name of problem-solving and realism, however, I was investing way too much of my time on negatives and way too little on positives. As a result, I didn't possess nearly as much of the positive attitudes we see in our seminar survey and in the example of Nick Vujicic.

I needed to boost my optimism, big time.

WALKING ON JUPITER

So does everyone else. So do you. In a world where 2 to 1 is average, and at least 6 to 1 is optimal, we're all way off the mark. The science is in, and it tells us we need at least three times more positivity than status quo.

Why are we so off the mark? Why such a bent toward the negative? Why does life feel heavy instead of light?

We could say it's because bad things happen, but we're back to the studies in optimism and pessimism that show it's not the circumstances that get us down, but our way of seeing them. We're back to the example of Nick Vujicic handling his circumstances, and we're back to the Greek philosopher Epictetus, who wrote, "Men are not moved by things, but the views which they take of things." The circumstances don't move us as much *our views of the circumstances.*

We also know from a previous chapter that limiting beliefs can weigh us down. There's the "destructive inductive" that massively magnifies our negative outlook, expanding bad experiences into beliefs about all things for all time.

But there's more to our imbalance than limiting thinking. Even when we're totally free from every useless fear, every imagined inability, and every limiting belief, there's still a persistent pull to the negative that I describe as *walking on psychological Jupiter*. We all struggle under a heavier psychological gravity that's the byproduct of a highly useful attribute of human nature.

I'll describe this useful attribute in a moment, but let's think for a moment about gravity. Say we weigh 150 pounds here on Earth. On Mars, which is smaller than Earth and has less pull from gravity, we'd weigh only 57 pounds. On the moon, which is even smaller and has even less pull, we'd weigh only 25 pounds. That's why we see those old pictures of astronauts bouncing around on the moon like half-filled helium balloons.

But on Jupiter, which is larger than earth and has more pull from gravity, we'd weigh 381 pounds. It would be like walking around in the fattest fat-suit we could imagine.

Human psychology has a gravity to it, but not like that of Mars or the moon. It's more like what we find on Jupiter. There's a constant and natural bent to pay attention to things that weigh us down.

- We spend ninety percent of our lives dwelling on the ten percent of life that isn't going right.
- We overlook a thousand good things to focus on a few bad things.
- Our positivity ratios are less than a third of what they should be, which means we're much closer to depression than optimal mental health.
- Fear is our most powerful motivator. We're way more alert to bad than good, and way more motivated by threats than benefits.
- Whenever we get a win, we fail to celebrate it enough to build a "winning feeling." We quickly overlook our wins, but obsess about our losses.

We miss the balance point of positivity because of an obsessive need to focus on bad things, driven by a safety feature in human nature called *loss aversion*.

LOSS AVERSION

Imagine we lost a hundred-dollar bill. We'd be alarmed. *My money's gone!* Scientists tell us the amount of misery we feel losing a hundred-dollar bill is about double the pleasure we'd feel finding a hundred-dollar bill. We hate losing roughly twice as much as we love winning.[151]

Loss aversion is this greater sensitivity to losses than gains.

Whenever something goes wrong, or whenever something bad happens, we're naturally more alert to it than when something goes right or something good happens. Say a teenager brings home their report card, showing three A's, two B's, and a D. The parent's knee-jerk reaction is, "Why'd you get this D?" They skim over the good and lock on to the bad.

- Loss aversion is the reason bad news travels faster than good news and why news producers say, "If it bleeds, it leads."
- Loss aversion is why we worry more than we hope. We waste truckloads of time imagining bad things happening, even though they haven't happened and most likely will never happen.
- Loss aversion encourages us to remember bad things longer than good things. It's why we remember the fish that got away more than the one we caught, or the spelling bee word we missed more than the one we got right.[152]
- Loss aversion also explains why we always seem to choose the slowest lane in traffic and the slowest line in the grocery store. When we're moving faster than average, we don't notice it. But when we're moving slower than average, we notice. We overlook the good (faster progress), but notice the bad (slower progress).

Loss aversion is a good thing. It keeps us alert to danger and free from harm. It goads us to protect the good. But it can also be a trap, because it constantly incites us to focus on negatives.

Think of the soul like you'd think of a garden, where weeds grow faster than flowers. We don't need to plant weeds. They show up on their own. That's human nature.

It's also human nature to overlook flowers soon after they bloom, thanks to acclimation. We experience something good, then we get used to it. The new car was great, but six months later it doesn't feel as great as it used to.

All this puts us way over on the left side of the Inverted-U. Negative forces constantly push us left on the graph, and the only way to find the balance is to *take deliberate daily steps to be more positive.* Just like we use our leg muscles to stand upright in constant physical gravity, we need a muscular optimism to stand against psychological gravity.

Studies show that people who are happiest are good at managing their attention. They experience more positive thoughts, more vividly, for longer attention spans than unhappy people. They control the way they see and what they say, and this automatically controls the way they feel and act. Happy people have more constructive thinking patterns and better habits of attention than those who are unhappy.[153]

Unhappy people, on the other hand, toss and turn in a clothes dryer of imagination. They "ruminate," holding themselves in destructive patterns of thought.[154]

BUILDING MUSCULAR OPTIMISM

Here are some practical ways to build the muscles of optimism.

The first way is, *recognize the distortion in negative attitudes.* Some people resist positive attitudes because "that isn't realistic." They see positivity as a denial of reality.

Actually, it's the opposite. The negative attitude is much more of a denial of reality than the positive attitude. The negative mindset ignores ninety percent of the good reality in an all-consuming focus on the ten percent that isn't going right. In this way, the negative attitude shrouds and distorts our view of reality.

A second strategy for building muscular optimism is, *solve problems faster.* We tend to spend too much time thinking about problems and too much time solving problems. We give problems a lot more airtime in the form of complaining and gossiping than they really need. Before marching into the problem-solving tar pit, we should ask ourselves, "How much time should we invest to solve this problem?"

Then we should try to hit our time budget. We need to solve problems faster.

Think of it like washing a dirty window. It needs about a minute of work, max. So if we spend more than just a few seconds complaining about the dirty window when we could be washing it instead, we're over-emphasizing the problem.

A third strategy for building muscular optimism is to *ignore unsolvable problems*. Most of the problems of life are out of our control. They're not our problems, and the worst thing we can do is make them our problems.

When a problem is unsolvable, drop it. Follow the advice in the Serenity Prayer, which reads, "God, grant me the serenity to accept the things I cannot change, the courage to change the things I can, and the wisdom to know the difference." Let's not give any attention to unsolvable problems, but use that time instead to focus on problems we can solve.

A fourth way to boost our optimism is to *journal our wins*. Keep a notepad of victories. Finish the day by writing down things that went well.

A successful recovery from a challenging situation is a win. So is a good response in a difficult circumstance. Overlooking an insult is a win. Refusing to pay back an offender is a win. Seeing self as bigger and stronger than the situation is a win.

In addition to what went well, we can list what we're looking forward to the next day, or week, or month. Then, when we wake up the next day, we can look again at what we wrote, further cementing a sense that good things are happening and good things are ahead.

We can also share our wins with friends and family. Instead of simply asking, "*How was your day?*" we can ask, "*What went well today?*" We can get the conversation going in the right direction. Instead of only writing wins in a diary, we can talk about them too.

The goal in all this is to *triple the positives*. Positivity ratios tell us the average person should be three times as positive as they actually are. Follow these strategies with vigilance and diligence. Read inspiring quotes out loud. Dispute and replace negative thought patterns. Listen to inspiring music. Watch motivating videos. Read jokes, tell jokes, and watch comedy. Do good things for people. Look for the good and talk about it.

Every one of us have moments of optimism. No matter how bad our lives may seem, and no matter how pessimistic we are, there are bright spots in the gloom, times when it seems like the sun shines in the soul.

We just need to create more of these bright spots. A lot more. In the name of "balance," we need to tip the scales way-way-way over to the bright side. We've got to overcompensate for the forces of gravity.

Before my new resolve for balance, life was cloudy with occasional sunbreaks. I spent most of my time focused on problems and deficiencies and negatives. Now, I'm resolved to clear the atmosphere and make a life that's mostly sunny, with occasional clouds and rain. I move mentally from Seattle to Scottsdale. I trade a life of pessimism, occasionally interrupted by optimism, for a life of optimism, occasionally interrupted by pessimism.

FULL OF LOVE

In the same way we can be full of optimism, we can be *full of love*. How do we know if we are full of love? The 6 to 1 positivity ratio gives us a way to measure optimism, but how do we measure the fullness of love?

Here's one way: remember who people really are, every moment they're in our airspace. "Full love" is to immediately and consistently keep in mind that people have equal value as ourselves. Then we let this profound appreciation automatically influence our emotions and decisions.

If we're out hiking by ourselves or immersed in a work project, we don't need to pay attention to the value of people. But when we're with people, we can be with them *fully*. While others diminish and overlook the people around them, we can be shining exceptions to the rule. We can give off the dog vibe instead of the cat vibe when people are present. We can be our best and loving selves, as we learn to see people right.

We can also can see people for who they could be, not just for who they are. We can remind ourselves that intelligence and skill and attitude are *developed traits* more than *innate traits*, which means that everyone can grow. We should always be encouraging people to grow, as we work to do the same.

Think about how it feels when others believe in you, when they see you for who you could become. You feel validated and inspired to be a better person. Why not do that for the people around you? Anyone can believe the worst, and most people do. Why not go against the flow? Why not stand out as an exception to the rule?

The key in all this is *see people right, every time we see them.* I use this thought-trigger: *Erik, remember, you're with people of equal value and needs as yourself.* This automatically influences me to be full of love.

FULL OF WISDOM

As we work to fill our lives with optimism and love, we can also work to be *full of wisdom.* We can listen and learn instead of just talking and ignoring. We can seek diverse points of view, instead of only listening to people who think like us. We can read biographies and wisdom literature, building up a library of vicarious life experiences as we watch people live out their lives. We can keep a constant zeal for understanding. We can become farmers of the soul, cultivating the fields of our lives with daily diligence and skill.

Just like there's a balance between positive and negative thoughts, there's a balance in the pursuit of wisdom. It's possible to spend too much time learning. As the Israelite king Solomon said, "Much study wearies the body."[155] But it's also possible to spend too little.

Unfortunately, most of us miss the balance on the little side. We neglect wisdom and harm ourselves. Consider Solomon's ancient depiction of wisdom as a female artisan, describing three common attitudes toward her.

> Blessed are those who listen to me, watching daily at my doors, waiting at my doorway. For those who find me find life and receive favor from the LORD. But those who fail to find me harm themselves; all who hate me love death.[156]

To help us remember these three attitudes toward wisdom, I'll call each person with each attitude *The Waiter, The Later,* and *The Hater.*

The first attitude toward wisdom is *The Waiter.* Waiters are those who "wait at wisdom's door." They want wisdom. A lot. They make wisdom top priority. They set aside time. They listen and learn. They observe self and life to understand and improve. They're not casual seekers. They're intense.

What is The Waiter's reward? Success. They flourish in life and work.

The second attitude is *The Later,* meaning, the one who puts off learning for later and fails to find wisdom. After years observing people,

I believe most put themselves in this category. So many of us go casually through life. We're more interested in leisure and trivia than wisdom.

What is The Later's reward? Self-harm. "Those who fail to find me harm themselves," says Lady Wisdom. There's no neutral ground with this lady. We're either for her or against her. What we think is a neutral, passive attitude is far from neutral. It is self-harm. Ignorance isn't bliss. Doing nothing isn't nothing. Negligence diminishes all the things we could be, do, and have.

Then finally, there's the third attitude, *The Hater*. Haters are those who reject wisdom. They don't just ignore wisdom. They despise it. They don't want anyone telling them what to do. They forsake feedback. They resent correction. They refuse to learn any way but the hard way, and they don't learn much that way either.

What is The Hater's reward? Death. "All who hate me," says Wisdom, "love death." The Hater plunges past self-harm into self-destruction.

Unfortunately, we live in a world where Laters and Haters are common, and Waiters rare.

But it doesn't have to be that way. We can change our attitude toward wisdom. We can stop Lating and Hating...and start Waiting.

CONCLUSION

The Electric Life

"Transformation is a process, a journey of discovery—there are moments on mountaintops and moments in deep valleys of despair."

— RICK WARREN, AMERICAN PASTOR

Humanity has known about the strange power of electricity for a long time. Egyptian papyrus texts from 2750 B.C. describe the electric catfish as the "Thunderer of the Nile."

Over two thousand years later the Greek philosopher, Thales of Miletus, studied static electricity by rubbing amber, a fossilized tree resin, while more practical-minded Greeks in Thales's era used electric shocks from torpedo fish to treat headaches.

Then, almost three thousand years after Thales, scientists like Michael Faraday and engineers like Alexander Graham Bell and Thomas Edison finally figured out how to harness the "power of the gods" for communication, light, and work.

That's a long time to put power to work. All the benefit of electricity was out there, bottled up in the universe, lying dormant for five thousand years.

The power of perception can lie dormant too. It's one thing to know how perception powers human nature. But it's quite another to harness that power, to put it to work like an engineer strings up power lines and makes places to plug in.

If we want a better life, a better workplace, better cultures, and a better world, information gets us only so far. Knowing what perception is and how it works isn't enough. It takes consistent and frequent investments, along with constant reminders, to hone our perceptions, manage our power, and change the way we feel and act.

Human nature is to start reading a book like this, get distracted, then stop. So most readers never get to here, where you're reading now, which is why I was tempted to put a creepy *The Grapes of Wrath* ending in just to see if anyone finished. (If you haven't read *The Grapes of Wrath*, check out the last page. *Way to leave it, John Steinbeck.*)

Don't get me wrong. Finishing a book is a commendable thing. But there's still a journey to take, a transformation to make. It's fantastic that we all understand the power of perception. It's great that we all know where the power button is, how it works, and how to press it. But that doesn't assure success. Success comes by *application*.

Which is why I encourage you to keep baby-stepping to freedom and fullness. Read this book again, slowly, just a page or two a day, while you hone the craft of perception. Work toward that place where you *see things right, every second of sight.*

Then I encourage a deeper dig into the resources that orbit this book: the seminars, the workshops, the workplace training, and the consulting. They will help you and your work teams translate *Automatic Influence* into reality.

Now that we've found the source of our power, and know how to use it, the electric life awaits. We just need to start stringing the wires.

About the Author

Erik Van Alstine is a leadership strategist, corporate problem-solver, and sought-after keynote speaker on a mission to transform people and organizations around the world.

After graduating with a Mechanical Engineering degree from the University of Washington, Erik started an advertising communication company and grew it to near–Inc. 500 status and multimillions in sales before the age of 30. He went on to create a publishing company that reached 1.5 million daily readers in over 180 countries.

Erik is the founder of several companies, including a leadership consulting firm figure headed by Harvard Business School's most recognized professor of leadership. Erik's other companies have served several *New York Times* bestselling authors, company executives, and the largest retailers in the world.

Erik is the author of *Breaking Free*, a personal finance video training program that is transforming people all around the world.

Erik's combination of experience in entrepreneurial leadership, applied science, and corporate learning provides a unique and compelling perspective into the dynamics of personal and organizational transformation.

He and his wife Sandra have six children, have been married for twenty-six years, and live in the Seattle area.

Endnotes

1. A 2005 commencement speech at Kenyon College, Ohio, first published as "Plain old untrendy troubles and emotions," *The Guardian*, September 19, 2008.

2. The scientific basis for the book will usually be revealed in the footnotes, where, for example, I rely on the "Appraisal Theory" of emotion initially proposed by American psychologist Magda B. Arnold to form the basis of the See-Feel-Act progression. Arnold's research in the 1950s and 1960s shifted the whole direction of emotion research into psychology's "cognitive revolution" and was further developed by Richard Lazarus in the early 1990s.

3. Sandra Hempel, *The Strange Case of the Broad Street Pump: John Snow and the Mystery of Cholera* (Berkeley: University of California Press: 2007). See also John Snow's story in the documentary, *Snow* (http://www.snowthemovie.com/index.html)

4. Henry David Thoreau, *Walden* (Yale University Press, 2006), p. 80. The original quote is, "There are a thousand hacking at the branches of evil to one who is striking at the root." I have adapted the quote for readability.

5. The story of the five workers was inspired by an example offered by cognitive therapist Aaron Beck in his book, *Cognitive Therapy and the Emotional Disorders* (New York: New American Library, 1976), p. 51.

6. Thank you, Jodi Cameron, for this analogy from a talk you gave in 2015.

7. My close friend Eric Boles, an executive coach, says this. So does self-help author Belinda Moss.

8. Richard S. Lazarus and Bernice N. Lazarus, *Passion and Reason: Making Sense of our Emotions* (Oxford: Oxford University Press, 1994), p. 199.

9. To "perceive" is to become aware of something through the senses, as opposed to imagination, which is to conceive of something without the senses. Throughout the book I'll use the word "perception" to represent any representation within the mind, whether from sensation or imagination or memory.

10. I changed the name to protect the identity of the disqualified golfer.

11. This quote is from General Electric's year 2000 Annual Report.

12. "The Serenity Prayer" is often attributed to Friedrich Oetinger (1702–1782) and to Reinhold Niebuhr (1934).

13. David Dubal, *Evenings with Horowitz: A Personal Portrait* (Cambridge: Amadeus Press, 1991), p. 130, Paul F. Boller, *Presidential Wives* (New York: Oxford University Press, 1988), p. 470.

14. Martin E. P. Seligman, *Learned Optimism: How to Change Your Mind and Your Life* (New York: Vintage Books, 2006), p. 4.

15. www.BrainyQuote.com, accessed April 2016.

16. Nina Colman, *The Friars Club Bible of Jokes, Pokes, Roasts, and Toasts* (New York: Black Dog & Leventhal, 2001), p. 316.

17. The phrase *useless fear* was coined by the world's foremost authority on anxiety, South African psychiatrist Joseph Wolpe. See Joseph Wolpe and David Wolpe, *Our Useless Fears* (Boston: Houghton Mifflin Company, 1981).

18. Proverbs 24:10, New International Version.

19. Lucien Tesnière, *Elements of Structural Syntax* (Paris: Klincksieck, 1959).

20. Steven Pinker, *The Sense of Style: The Thinking Person's Guide to Writing in the 21st Century* (New York: Penguin Books, 2014), p. 172.

21. Rips, L.J. & Marcus, S.L., "Suppositions and the analysis of conditional sentences," in M.A. Just & P.A. Carpenter (Eds.), *Cognitive Processes in Comprehension* (Hillsdale: Erlbaum, 1977), pp. 185-220.

22. AP, "'Jurors Will Disregard' Is Often Not Regarded," *The New York Times*, March 28, 1988.

23. Daniel Gilbert, "How Mental Systems Believe," *American Psychologist*, Vol. 46, No. 2, February 1991.

24. Daniel Gilbert, *Stumbling on Happiness*, p. 130; S. M. Kosslyn et al., "The Role of Area 17 in Visual Imagery: Convergent Evidence from PET and rTMS," *Science* 284: 167-170 (1999).

25. Job 3:25, NIV.

26. Christopher Bergland, "Why Does Overthinking Cause Athletes to Choke?" *Psychology Today*, August 8, 2013.

27. Robert Cialdini, *Influence: The Psychology of Persuasion* (New York: Harper-Collins, 2007), p. 57.

28. Ibid., p. 80.

29. Sigmund Freud, *Introductory Lectures on Psychoanalysis* (New York: W.W. Norton & Company, 1966), p. 20.

30. Wasink, B. (2004). Environmental factors that increase the food intake and consumption volume of unknowing consumers. *Annual Review of Nutrition, 24,* 455-479.

31. Robert Evans Wilson Jr., "The Most Powerful Motivator: How fear is etched into our brains," *Psychology Today*, September 23, 2009. See also Joseph Wolpe, *Our Useless Fears* (Boston: Houghton Mifflin Company, 1981), p. 8.

32. Robert Rosenthal, *Optimarketing: Marketing Optimization to Electrify Your Business*, p. 14.

33. Bernard J. Baars, *In the Theater of Consciousness: The Workspace of the Mind* (New York: Oxford University Press, 1997), p. 39.

34. If participants don't have watches, this can be done with a penny. Ask participants to draw a picture of a penny from memory. Invariably, they get the details wrong—the head pointed the wrong direction, missing date, and so on. There are a dozen different things that could go wrong. Then after they're asked to look at the penny design, ask if they know the year of the penny. Many miss it. They were looking for design, not dates.

35. Arien Mack and Irvin Rock, *Inattentional Blindness* (Cambridge: The MIT Press, 1998), cover text.

36. Christopher Chabris and Daniel Simons, *The Invisible Gorilla: How Our Intuitions Deceive Us* (New York: Broadway Paperbacks, 2009), p. 13.

37. Baars, *In the Theater of Consciousness*, p. 40.

38. George Johnson, "Sleights of Mind," *The New York Times*, August 21, 2007

39. Chip Heath and Dan Heath, *Made to Stick: Why Some Ideas Survive and Others Die* (New York: Random House, 2007), p. 64.

40. Kahneman, *Fast and Slow*, p. 201.

41. Samuel M. McClure, Jian Li, Damon Tomlin, Kim S. Cypert, Latané M. Montague, and P. Read Montague, "Neural Correlates of Behavioral Preference for Culturally Familiar Drinks," *Neuron*, Volume 44, Number 2, October 14, 2004, pages 379-387.

42. Marvin Minsky, *The Emotion Machine: Commonsense Thinking, Artificial Intelligence, and the Future of the Human Mind* (New York: Simon & Schuster, 2006), p. 152.

43. Nicholas Carr, *The Shallows: What the Internet is Doing to Our Brains* (New York: W.W. Norton & Co., 2010), p. 134.

44. Judith S. Beck calls this "the cardinal question of cognitive therapy." Beck, p. 10.

45. News brief, "It Pays to Know Your Opponent: Success in Negotiations Improved by Perspective-Taking, But Limited by Empathy," *Association for Psychological Science*, April 22, 2008.

46. Hannah Parry, "Man presumed dead after being found 'frozen solid' on side of the road recovers to become living medical miracle," *Daily Mail*, January 19, 2016.

47. Friedrich Max Muller (translated by George Putnam Upton), *Memories: A Story of German Love* (Chicago: A.C. McClurg & Co., 1902), p. 34.

48. Leo Buscaglia, *Speaking of Love and the Art of Being Fully Human*. DVD, KVIE Public Television.

49. Dylan Love, "16 Examples of Steve Jobs Being a Huge Jerk," *Business Insider*, October 25, 2011.

50. Atsuko Saito, Kazutaka Shinozuka, "Vocal recognition of owners by domestic cats (Felis catus)," *Animal Cognition*, July 2013, Volume 16, Issue 4, pp. 685-690, Elyse Wanshel, "Who Loves Their Humans More—Cats or Dogs? Here's The Answer," *The Huffington Post*, February 1, 2016. Wanshel cites a recent Claremont Graduate University study.

51. Duchenne de Boulogne, G.B., translated and edited by A. Cuthbertson, *The Mechanism of Human Facial Expression* (New York: Cambridge University Press, 1990), original publication 1862.

52. E. H. Hess, "The Role of Pupil Size in Communication," *Scientific American*, November 1, 1975, p. 110-119. See also Eckhard Hess, *The Tell-Tale Eye: How Your Eyes Reveal Hidden Thoughts and Emotions* (New York: Van Nostrand Reinhold Co., 1975).

53. Robert Rosenthal, Lenore Jacobson, *Pygmalion in the Classroom: Teacher Expectation and Pupils' Intellectual Development* (Bethel: Crown House Publishing Company, 1992).

54. J. Sterling Livingston, "Pygmalion in Management," *Harvard Business Review*, January 2003.

55. Rosenthal (1992), p. 6.

56. Johann Wolfgang Von Goethe, *Wilhelm Meister's Apprenticeship* (New York: The Heritage Press, 1959).

57. *Billboard* reviewer Mikael Wood described the song as one that "handily reduces [Currington]'s worldview to a memorable one-liner." Wood, Mikael (2008-10-18). *"Little Bit of Everything review." Billboard*.

58. I adapted this story from one told by Aaron T. Beck, *Cognitive Therapy and the Emotional Disorders* (New York: Meridian, 1976), p. 25-27.

59. Jonathan Haidt, *The Happiness Hypothesis: Finding Modern Truth in Ancient Wisdom* (New York: Basic Books, 2006), p. 26-7.

60. Magda Arnold, *Emotion and Personality* (New York: Columbia University Press, 1960), p. 73-4.

61. See Stephen R. Covey, *The Seven Habits of Highly Effective People: Powerful Lessons in Personal Change* (New York: Fireside, 1989).

62. The Wanted, *Glad You Came* (released 2014).

63. Proverbs 25:16, NIV.

64. For more about the light depression that comes from too much vacation and leisure, see Mihaly Csikszentmihalyi, *Flow: The Psychology of Optimal Experience* (New York: Harper & Row, 1990).

65. For more about "Jenny," an actual prostitute who made these actual claims on camera, see *8 Minutes*, A&E Networks.

66. Roy F. Baumeister, *Evil: Inside Human Violence and Cruelty* (New York: Henry Holt & Company, 1999), p. 34.

67. Heinrich Himmler's "Posen Speech," given to a secret meeting of SS Officers in Poland, October 4, 1943.

68. Baumeister, p. 13.

69. George A. Miller, "The Magical Number Seven, Plus or Minus Two: Some Limits on Our Capacity for Processing Information," *Psychological Review* 63 (2): 81-97.

70. NPD Group, "U.S. Total Restaurant Count Increases by 4,442 Units over Last Year, Reports NPD," January 23, 2013.

71. I adapted these principles from the work of William Miller and Stephen Rollnick, *Motivational Interviewing: Helping People Change* (New York: The Guilford Press, 2013).

72. William R. Miller and Stephen Rollnick, *Motivational Interviewing: Helping People Change* (New York: The Guilford Press, 2013), p. 11.

73. Ibid., p. 9.

74. Baumeister, p. 3-4.

75. Leon Festinger, *A Theory of Cognitive Dissonance* (Stanford: Stanford University Press, 1957).

76. Proverbs 14:12, 16:25, NIV

77. Blaise Pascal, "Pensées," in *Pensées*, ed. W. F. Trotter (1660: New York: Dutton, 1908)

78. Sigmund Freud, *Civilization and Its Discontents* (New York: W. W. Norton & Company, 1989), p. 25.

79. Arthur Brooks, *Gross National Happiness* (New York: Basic Books, 2008), p. 4.

80. Daniel Gilbert, *Stumbling on Happiness* (New York: Vintage Books, 2005), p. 33.

81. *Seinfeld*, season 8, episode 21, "The Muffin Tops."

82. Roy F. Baumeister, *Meanings of Life* (New York: The Guilford Press, 1991), p. 214.

83. Malcolm Gladwell, *Outliers: The Story of Success* (New York: Little, Brown & Company), p. 79.

84. Arthur Jensen, *Bias in Mental Testing* (New York: Free Press, 1980), p. 113.

85. K. Anders Ericsson, "Expert Performance and Deliberate Practice: An Updated Excerpt from Ericsson (2000)," accessed from the Florida State University website, August 25, 2014.

86. K. Anders Ericcson, Ralf Th.Krampe, and Clemens Tesch-Romer, "The Role of Deliberate Practice in the Acquisition of Expert Performance," *Psychological Review,* 1993, Vol. 100, No. 3, 363-406.

87. "POLL: 28 Percent of Americans Have Not Read a Book in The Past Year," *Huffington Post BOOKS*, October 7, 2013.

88. A 30-minute walk at 3 miles per hour for an average-weighted woman (166 pounds) burns 124 calories, for 365 days, is 45,000 calories. 3,500 calories is one pound of weight loss. That adds up to thirteen pounds.

89. K. Anders Ericsson (editor), *The Cambridge Handbook of Expertise and Expert Performance* (Cambridge: Cambridge University Press, 2006). For more about the Ten-Thousand-Hour Rule and the Ten-Year Rule, see also the research of Carnegie Mellon University cognitive psychology professor John Hayes.

90. Michael J. A. Howe, *Genius Explained* (Cambridge: Cambridge University Press, 2001), p. 3.

91. Daniel J. Levitin, *This is Your Brain on Music: The Science of Human Obsession* (New York: Plume, 2007), p. 197.

92. Andrei Cimpian, Holly-Marie C. Aree, Ellen M. Markman, and Carol S. Dweck, "Subtle Linguistic Clues Affect Children's Motivation," *Psychological Science* 18 (2007), 314-316.

93. Daniel Coyle, *The Little Book of Talent: 52 Tips for Improving Your Skills* (New York: Bantam Books, 2012), p. 30.

94. Ibid, p. 54.

95. Adapted from Jack Canfield, *The Success Principles: How to Get from Where You Are to Where You Want to Be* (New York: HarperCollins, 2005), p. 8.

96. This meme has been bouncing around the Internet for years and is, we think, falsely attributed to Zac Galifianakis (i.e., March 2013 @ZacGalifianakis parody account Twitter post), but we'll thank him anyway for this line. It certainly sounds like something he'd say.

97. Charles Duhigg, *The Power of Habit: Why We Do What We Do in Life and Business* (New York: Random House, 2012), p. xi.

98. Cited in Jack Canfield, *The Success Principles: How to Get from Where You Are to Where You Want to Go* (New York: HarperCollins, 2005), p. 51.

99. Eric Blehm, *Fearless: The Undaunted Courage and Ultimate Sacrifice of Navy SEAL Team Six Operator Adam Brown* (Colorado Springs: Waterbrook Press, 2012), p. 138.

100. Roy F. Baumeister and John Tierney, *Willpower: Rediscovering the Greatest Human Strength* (New York: The Penguin Press, 2011), p. 139-40.

101. Cited in Michael Benson, *Winning Words: Classic Quotes from the World of Sports* (Lanham: Taylor Trade Publishing, 2008), p. 80.

102. Ecclesiastes 3:1-8, NIV.

103. Genesis 1:18, NIV.

104. Stephen B. Oates, *Let the Trumpet Sound: A Life of Martin Luther King Jr.* (New York: HarperCollins, 1982).

105. Adapted from Ibid. and Martin Luther King Jr., *The Autobiography of Martin Luther King Jr.* (New York: Warner Books, 1998), p. 10.

106. Laurie Beth Jones, *The Path* (New York: Hyperion, 1996), p. 49-50.

107. True story, the makers of Japanese sports drink Pocari Sweat, are placing a can of it on the surface of the moon. Patrick Winn, "Get ready for ads on the moon," *USA Today*, August 17, 2015.

108. Matt Kapco, "7 staggering social media use by-the-minute stats," *CIO*, April 28, 2015.

109. Neville L. Johnson, *The John Wooden Pyramid of Success* (Beverly Hills: Cool Titles, 2003), p. 189.

110. Kenley Young, "So just how bad was this Super Bowl rout, historically?" *Fox Sports*, February 2, 2014.

111. My friend, Eric Boles, was there for this meeting between Pete and the players and relayed the story to me.

112. Gio Valiante, *Fearless Golf* (New York: Doubleday, 2005), p. 87.

113. Reported in *Look*, November 16, 1965.

114. Martin Seligman, *Learned Optimism: How to Change Your Mind and Your Life* (New York: Vintage Books, 2006), p. 4.

115. Nick Vujicic, "No Arms, No Legs, No Worries," *YouTube*, uploaded October 20, 2010, accessed October 9, 2015.

116. This quote is frequently attributed to Abraham Lincoln, but didn't likely come from Lincoln, which is why we leave it unattributed.

117. Abraham Maslow, *The Psychology of Science: A Reconnaissance* (New York: Zorba Press, 2002).

118. Martin E.P. Seligman, *Learned Optimism: How to Change Your Mind and Your Life* (New York: Vintage Books, 2006), p. 19-20.

119. Ibid., p. 28.

120. See Joseph Wolpe and David Wolpe, *Our Useless Fears* (Boston: Houghton Mifflin Company, 1981), p. 4.

121. E.J. Gibson and R.D. Walk (1960), "The 'visual cliff'." *Scientific American*, 202, 67-71.

122. Joseph Wolpe and David Wolpe, *Our Useless Fears* (Boston: Houghton Mifflin Company, 1981), p. 7.

123. Brian Palmer, "The Maximum-Gluten Diet," *Slate*, January 25, 2012.

124. Julie Upton, "Think You're Sensitive to Gluten? Think Again," *US News Health*, June 11, 2015.

125. Based on analysis from the Washington State Department of Transportation, "2011 Washington State Collision Data Summary."

126. United States Department of Transportation, Bureau of Transportation Statistics.

127. Michael Reilly, "Shark Attacks: What Are the Odds?", *Discovery News*, August 2, 2010.

128. For the backstory of this quote, and when and where she said it, see http://quoteinvestigator.com/2012/04/30/no-one-inferior/, accessed May 2016.

129. This section is a combination of personal conversation with Tim and citations from his book, Tim Brown, *The Making of a Man: How Men and Boys Honor God and Live with Integrity* (Nashville: W Publishing, 2014), p. 43-46.

130. Daniel Coyle, *The Little Book of Talent: 52 Tips for Improving Your Skills* (New York: Bantam Books, 2012), p. 49.

131. Sheri Ledbetter, "What Americans Fear Most—New Poll from Chapman University," *Chapman University Press Room*, October 20, 2104.

132. Seinfeld, "The Pilot," Season 4, Episode 23.

133. Joseph Wolpe, *Life Without Fear: Anxiety and Its Cure* (Oakland: New Harbinger Publications, Inc., 1988), p. 36.

134. Daniel Coyle, *The Little Book of Talent: 52 Tips for Improving Your Skills* (New York: Bantam Books, 2012), p. 103.

135. For more on this, I suggest the research of Albert Bandura and Joseph Wolpe.

136. Tim Brown, *The Making of a Man* (Nashville: W Publishing, 2014), p. 46-47.

137. Matthew 13:44, NIV.

138. Kerry Patterson et al., *Influencer: The Power to Change Anything* (New York: McGraw-Hill, 2008), p. 51.

139. Daniel Kahneman, *Thinking: Fast and Slow* (New York: Farrar, Straus and Giroux, 2011), p. 86.

140. Ibid, p. 269.

141. National Highway Traffic Safety Administration, Traffic Safety Facts.

142. John Stossel, Kristina Kendall and Patrick McMenamin, "The Surprising Risks of Playing it Safe," *ABC News*, February 22, 2007.

143. Steven Watts, *The People's Tycoon: Henry Ford and the American Century* (New York: Vintage Books, 2005).

144. Ibid., p. 19.

145. Susan Butler, *East to the Dawn: The Life of Amelia Earhart* (Boston: Da Capo Press, 2009), p. 94-95.

146. Proverbs 20:5, New International Version.

147. Viktor Frankl, *Man's Search for Meaning* (New York: Pocket Books, 1984).

148. Barbara L. Fredrickson, "Updated Thinking on Positivity Ratios," *American Psychologist*, July 15, 2013.

149. Marcial Losada, Emily Heaphy, "The Role of Positivity and Connectivity in the Performance of Business Teams: A Nonlinear Dynamics Model," *American Behavioral Scientist*, February 2004, 47: 740-765.

150. R.M. Schwartz, C.F. Reynolds, et al (2002), "Optimal and normal affect balance in psychotherapy of major depression: Evaluation of the balanced states of mind model," *Behavioural and Cognitive Psychotherapy*, 3: 439-450.

151. Loss aversion and its corollary, the "Endowment Effect," come from the research of Daniel Kahneman, Amos Tversky, Jack Knetsch, Dick Thaler, and other behavioral economists. For a striking illustration of loss aversion, see Dan Ariely's story of prices for basketball tickets at Duke University, told in, *Predictably Irrational: The Hidden Forces that Shape Our Decisions* (New York: Harper Perennial, 2008), p. 167-173. See also Daniel Kahneman, *Thinking, Fast and Slow* (New York, Farrar, Straus and Giroux, 2011), p. 292-297.

152. Thomas Gilovich, *How We Know What Isn't So* (New York: Free Press, 1991), p. 62.

153. For more information about happiness, optimism, pessimism, and how it relates to our thought patterns or "explanatory style," see Martin Seligman's books, *Learned Optimism* and *Authentic Happiness*.

154. Martin Seligman, *Learned Optimism* (New York: Vintage Books, 2006), p. 82.

155. Ecclesiastes 12:12, NIV.

156. Proverbs 8:34-36, NIV.

Index